Submarine boats

The beginnings of underwater warfare

Richard Compton-Hall

ARCO PUBLISHING, INC.
New York

(Frontispiece) **C-boats moored off the House of Commons 1909** – presumably an open invitation for the government to buy more submarines!

To Eve

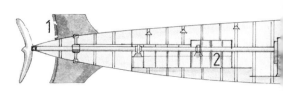

Published 1984 by Arco Publishing, Inc.
215 Park Avenue South, New York, N.Y. 10003

First published in Great Britain 1983 by
Conway Maritime Press Ltd
24 Bride Lane
Fleet Street
London EC4Y 8DR

Library of Congress Cataloging in Publication Data
Compton-Hall, Richard.
    Submarine boats.

    1. Submarine boats – History.   I. Title
V857.C65 1984   359.3'257'09 83-7128
ISBN 0-668-05924-9

Printed in Great Britain

Submarine boats

Contents

Gustave Zédé **1893**

1 vertical rudders	7 air reservoirs
2 accumulators	8 ballast tank
3 conning tower	9 safety weight
4 switchboard	10 air compressor
5 hatches	11 spare torpedo
6 pump	12 torpedo tube

Waddington's *Porpoise* 1886

1 vertical propellers
2 vertical rudders
3 conning tower

4 electric accumulators
5 electric motor
6 water ballast tank

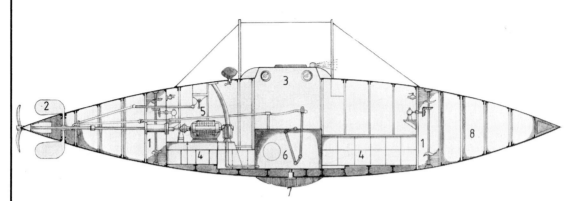

RIGHT **Lt Arnold-Forster, the captain of HM Submarine *No 1*, (on the left) and Diving Coxswain Waller (on the right) on board their newly commissioned boat, Portsmouth harbour 1902.**

8 | Plans of *Holland VI* dated 1 August 1899 after removal of the stern dynamite gun.

HORIZONTAL SECTION.

PLAN of SUPERSTRUCTURE.

LONGITUDINAL SECTION.

Acknowledgements

First and foremost I am deeply grateful to my wife Eve for her patient preparation and expert checking of the manuscript as well as for her constant encouragement.

For research, I thank Gus Britton for his frequent assistance, particularly in uncovering old photographs; Micky Budd for technical comments; and Mrs J R Corcoran for delving into archives.

For illustrations I am much indebted to the excellent drawings made for the Royal Navy Submarine Museum by David Hill whose skill and

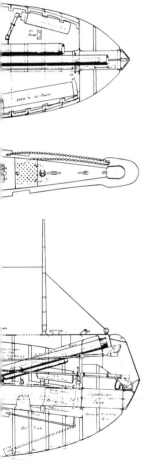

knowledge of submarine details has often been of great assistance. But, above all, I thank the Trustees for permission to use illustrations from the Museum collection. There have been a great many contributors to the collection and it is sometimes not clear where a photograph originated; but in the context of this book my special thanks go to Mr O R Haberlein (Naval Historical Center, Washington), Mr John Albrecht of Toronto (for some very rare pictures), Mr John L Bowers, Mr Stephen Johnson, the Director of the Submarine Library and Museum at the USN Submarine Base, New London and, very particularly, to Professor Richard K Morris whose collection of Holland memorabilia is unrivalled.

Amongst many reference books consulted, *John P Holland* by Richard K Morris was particularly helpful and pointed the way to many original sources. My sincere thanks go to the author for permission to use this excellent book – by far the best in the field – as a basis for reliable research. His subsequent comments and recommendations, as well as his help in securing photographs, have been generous and invaluable.

I am also grateful to the Garrett family in the United States for family photographs and much new information about their distinguished ancestor, the Reverend George William Garrett.

Finally, I thank Captain R W Blacklock (the last Captain of *Holland I*), Mr M Pearn who found the newspaper cutting that put me on the trail of the wreck of *Holland I*, Admiral Sir Edward Ashmore who provided the Museum with his father's Russian memoirs and Mrs G M Barnett who loaned the letters and diaries of her father Rear-Admiral Forster D Arnold-Forster, the first commanding officer of HM Submarine *No 1*, which have greatly helped in bringing the story to life.

I ask forgiveness for not listing the many other contributors who are too numerous to mention. I am, nonetheless, most grateful to them for their interest and I hope they already know how welcome they will be when they come to see HM Submarine *No 1* (*Holland I*) at the Royal Navy Submarine Museum, Gosport.

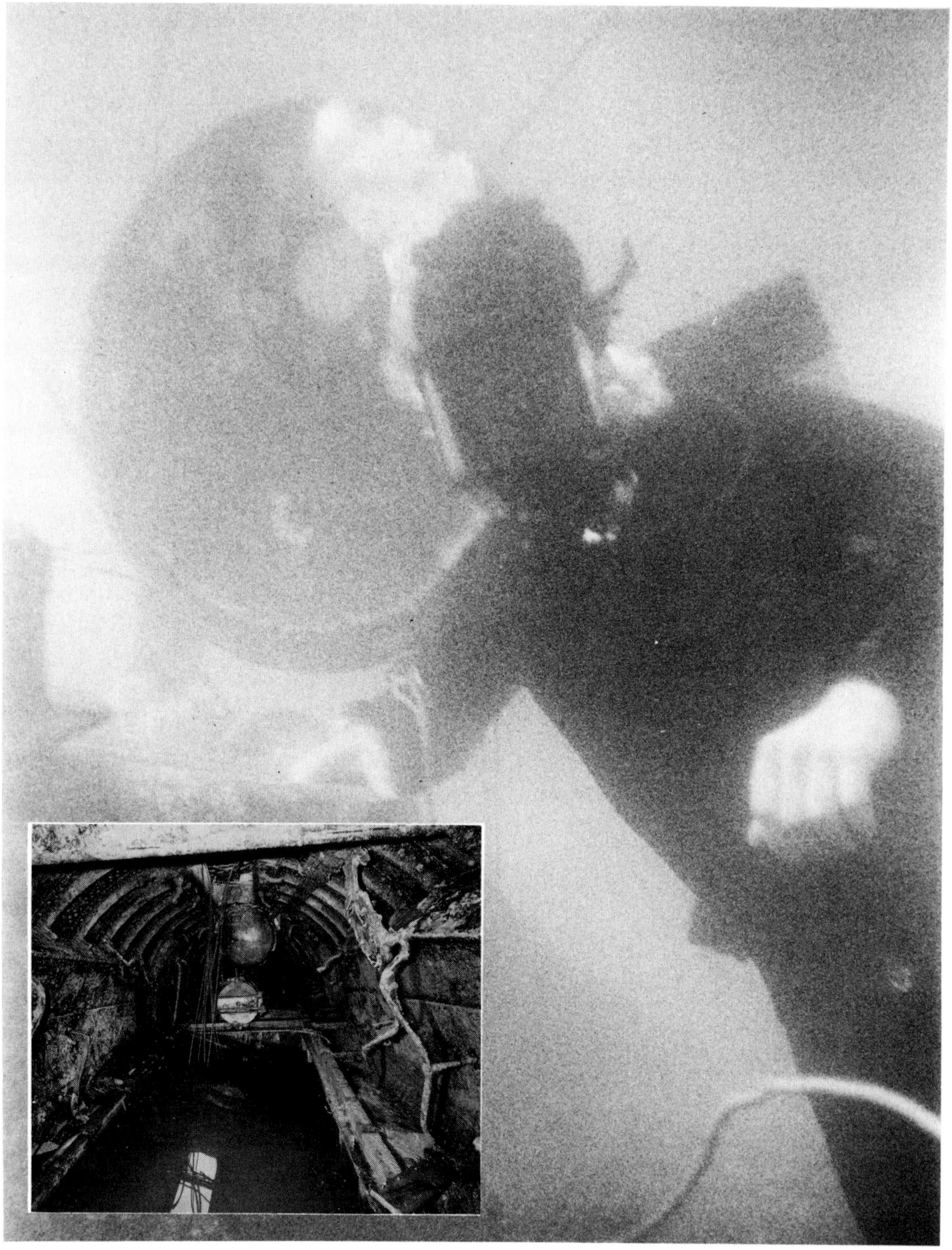

Chapter One
Lost and Found

Diver from Naval Diving Party 1007 having just opened the conning tower hatch of *Holland I* at a depth of 63 metres off Eddystone Lighthouse at 0825, 15 Aug 1982. Two US Navy and two Canadian Armed Forces divers were included in the team working from the expertly handled diving vessel MV *Seaforth Clansman*. Eight divers were kept in saturation and each man worked a daily 4-hour excursion. Three of the teams spent no less than 321 hours in saturation, 9-23 Aug.

INSET **Looking forward to the 18in torpedo tube and air discharge-cylinder (above) immediately after docking at Devonport. The tube rear-door opened easily and the spring catch still snapped firmly when shut. There was remarkably little serious corrosion anywhere except on some of the lighter external fittings. One of the battery cells, removed from the battery tank at the bottom of the picture, delivered 30 ampere-hours after being filled with fresh electrolite and charged by the makers (Chloride). With the help of Vickers, who originally built the submarine in 1901, it is hoped to bring *No 1* back to her service condition.**

On 5 November 1913 the *Naval and Military Record* carried the following report:

Obsolete Submarine Sunk – Accident off the Eddystone

About a mile and a half off the Eddystone Lighthouse there was lost on Thursday submarine *H–1*, but happily the accident was not attended by loss of life. The vessel was one of the first three of the Holland type built for the British Navy, chiefly for experimental purposes, twelve years ago, but in the meantime the progress in the design and construction of submarines has been so rapid that the type has in all essential details become obsolete, so that when *H–1* and her sisterships *H–2* and *H–3* were offered for sale by auction at Portsmouth on the 7th inst, the whole of the equipment was sold with each vessel, and there was no obligation on the part of the purchasers to break them up, except that the torpedo tubes had to be mutilated. Of the three submarines, *H–1* was purchased for £410 by T W Ward (Limited) of Sheffield. She remained at Portsmouth until Wednesday, when she left for the westward in tow of the tug *Enfield*. After the vessels had shaped course down Channel very severe weather was encountered, but the risks were considerably minimized by the fact that there was not a soul on board the submarine. So far as is known, the voyage was continued without mishap until about midday on Thursday, when it was noticed from the *Enfield* that the stern of the submarine was dropping. The conclusion arrived at was that she had sprung a leak in the heavy seas, and was gradually filling. To attempt to board her in the circumstances was out of the question, and preparations were made to slip the towing hauser should the necessity arise. Eventually she sank by the stern and disappeared, and the *Enfield* proceeded to Plymouth.

Late in the evening of Tuesday, 14 April 1981 the mine-hunter HMS *Bossington*, searching an area off the Eddystone Light on behalf of the Royal Navy Submarine Museum, made contact by sonar with a substantial object on the seabed at the depth of 63 metres. By midnight the diving vessel *Seaforth Clansman* had moored accurately over the position and lowered a diving bell with a deep-diving team and an underwater television camera, down to the reported contact. At 2.15 on the morning of 15 April the Diving Officer was able to signal that the wreck was 'confirmed as small

Holland boat, thought to be *No 1*, on the crane at Vickers after launch, probably late 1901. The porpoise-shape with its almost ideal length-to-breadth ratio is the obvious fore-runner of modern nuclear designs. The lifting strops for the salvage were positioned almost as here.

The hand-pumped Doulton No 612 porcelain WC, the 'heads' [in naval terms] on the starboard side, [open to view] by the torpedo tube. This essential, albeit rather public, convenience was omitted in the early all-British designs which followed. The toilet has now been cleaned up and restored.

Holland I soon after arrival, on Army tank transporters, at the RN Submarine Museum, Gosport. Cut into three sections for display and

submarine of correct dimensions for Holland Class'. At noon a further signal was made: 'Submarine in reasonably sound condition. Hull is heavily encrusted but easily identifiable and sits with keel approximately two feet into the seabed with slight list . . . nets and fishing tackle abound . . .'

HM Submarine *No 1*, more often known after her launch in 1901 as *Holland I* (and sometimes incorrectly as *H–1*—a much later submarine), had been found. Apart from a considerably later version, the Swedish *Hajen* at Karlskrona, and a conning tower at Den Helder in the Netherlands, no other relic of this, the very first class of practical, warlike submarines common to the British, United States and several other navies, was known to be in existence anywhere. The discovery was therefore of immense importance to marine archaeologists and naval historians every-

ease of transport, she stands opposite her much larger descendent HMS *Alliance* which was opened to the public in 1981.

where: it immediately excited world-wide interest. If the little boat had not fortuitously foundered with nobody on board, on her way to the breaker's yard, nothing would be left to show of the final triumphant work by the brilliant Irish-American inventor, John Philip Holland, which culminated in the giant nuclear submarines that dominate undersea warfare today.

Holland I was successfully salvaged in September 1982 and now stands proudly outside the Royal Navy Submarine Museum at Gosport in Hampshire close by the submarine base where she first saw service during the reign of King Edward VII at the beginning of the century. Meanwhile, very little is generally known, and still less understood, about Holland or the other intrepid Victorian and Edwardian underwater mariners and their 'submarine boats'. This book tells their story.

BELOW **The first sight of HM Submarine *No 1* after 69 years submerged. The Waterblast and Fertan cleaning-off and preservation processes had not yet been carried out when this photograph was taken.**

RIGHT *Holland I* **in No 12 Dock Devonport Dockyard still listing slightly to port. The dome abaft the conning tower housed the base of the periscope.**

14 | HMS *A6 c.* 1905. No signalman was included in the crew and the captain is here seen making a semaphore message himself. (Fleet instructions said 'send *slowly* to submarines . . .'). Edwardian submarine officers had to learn a number of trades to which ordinary seaman officers in the surface fleet were by no means accustomed.

Chapter Two
Algerians, Pirates and Edwardian Naval Officers

The year was 1904. In Britain Edward VII was King and Emperor. Having waited a very long time to ascend the throne he was settled firmly into power and was clearly dedicated to enjoying all the splendours that the British Empire had to offer. Society in Edwardian England, amidst a swirl of beautiful dresses and a good deal of adultery, was devotedly following his example in the sparkling new century that had opened after the last rather dull and dowdy years of the widowed Queen Victoria's reign.

The King, in his sixties, set a brisk pace which kept courtiers and doctors alike in a constant state of agitation while His Majesty travelled widely to conduct affairs of State and affairs of the heart with equal vigour and success, undaunted by increasing age, obesity and bronchial trouble due to smoking twelve large cigars and twenty cigarettes every day (but only one cigar and a few cigarettes before breakfast). The Royal entourage always included a generous number of beautiful women, amongst them the strange Mrs Lace with 'eye-glass, short skirts and a murky past'[1], and enthusiastic replacements for discarded attendants flung themselves forward at every opportunity. Maude Walker, for example, was invited to dance for the King at Marienbad where her speciality turned out to be a performance clad only in two oyster shells and a 5-franc piece[2]. The King's companions were also proffered a part in these delights. There was, for instance, 'a beautiful lady from the half-world of Vienna who wanted to have the honour of sleeping with the King. His Majesty was otherwise engaged and Sir Frederick Ponsonby, escorting the King, told her it was out of the question: whereupon she said if the worst came to the worst she would sleep with him instead.' For the record, the offer was refused. It must have been an unexpectedly churlish reaction from an Edwardian gentleman of rank.

This was the society which opened its doors to the King's majestic battleships and cruisers as they toured the world and showed the flag. Naval officers, who were very poorly paid, could not possibly afford expensive liaisons: but they mar-

16 ried late, their uniform was attractive and they were not monastic in their habits. At a more modest level than the Court they enjoyed an ample share in the deliciously upholstered pleasures of the era. 'Poodle-faking' was one of the more polite terms for their activities ashore. The Royal Navy was, in fact, an important part of the social scene. Only wardroom officers, of course, were admissible to Society. Officers and men enjoyed, in most of His Majesty's Ships, a high degree of mutual respect and even affection; but the class system, on shore and afloat, was rigid and absolute.

It is true that engineer officers, for long totally unacceptable, were nowadays permitted to mix

The captain, Lt A Quicke (left), Second Capt (First Lt) Lt Adrian Keyes (right) and the Diving Coxwain, Petty Officer Waller, at the wheel of *No 1* c1904. The Diving Coxwain, whose equivalent initially was Boss Diver in the USN, was to become simply 'the Coxswain' controlling the diving rudders (hydroplanes) when at diving stations and the wheel when entering or leaving harbour as well as administering discipline.

with upper-deck society in the wardrooms of the British Fleet, but only very grudgingly because 'they scarcely spoke the same language'[3] as the upper and middle classes. Attitudes were necessarily changing as the industrial revolution at long last caught up with the Royal Navy. Some of the less impoverished officers owned secondhand motor-cars and thereby introduced themselves to engines. But, unlike their American cousins, they were usually incapable of putting them right if they went wrong, as they very often did. Their ignorance was not, however, generally so profound as that of the King who was unable to tell the Kaiser what fuel the royal cars used. The Kaiser, equally at a loss but anxious to appear knowledgeable, said it was probably potato spirit.

Like it or not, better communications and a more common language between engineers and seamen would have to be devised – and quickly – for a navy that found itself being transformed, much against its will, into a modern, technical, fighting service. It was even proposed, under the 'Selborne Scheme', to draw executive and engineering officers from a common entry of young cadets, 'making greasers of us all' as one horrified member of the Establishment predicted. An identical system had been adopted in the United States Navy in 1899 and was working perfectly well. However, in the Royal Navy it is understandable that the demanding professional transition to a mechanical fleet was not altogether welcome, especially to officers who had been used to foreign-going commissions which were 'a sort of yachting cruise with endless entertainment'.[4] As a journalist of the time said about the late Victorian navy, 'For lawn tennis, waltzing, relief of distress or ambulance work after an earthquake it was admirable; for war purposes it was useless . . .'.

However, captains like George Henry Cherry, who commanded HMS *Argonaut* from 1900 to 1904, had their own inflexible opinions about what was useless. Cherry put torpedoes and breech-loading guns into that category and took not the smallest interest in his own ship's capabilities. Cleanliness, smartness and strict obedience to

orders were the principal components of efficiency. On the China Station at Night Quarters the Captain sternly enquired of a newly joined Marine Subaltern where his slow match was and whether it was alight! 'Repel Boarders' was a favourite exercise and, under Cherry's archaic orders, the Maltese bandsmen and Chinese stewards careered about the ship with pikes, while the Marines mustered on the quarterdeck with their rifles. The same Subaltern, loyally entering into the spirit of the thing, gave the order, 'At the cavalry advancing over the stern – Volleys – Fire', but Cherry, a strict Victorian by upbringing, was not amused.

In the more forward-looking ships, the new navy's specialists came in for continual snide wardroom criticism of one kind and another. Gunnery, with all its new-fangled equipment, was a traditional and still reasonably reputable pursuit although it had become rather noisy (especially on the parade ground). Gunnery Officers were, it seemed, apt to be quickly deafened by their own excesses and were not universally popular. Indeed, one young officer, who was known to loathe drill and gaiters, explained to his amazed term-mates that he was joining the Gunnery Branch simply because it was the only way to avoid serving in a ship with others of that ilk. Torpedo experts were also just acceptable so-

HMS *B1* lying alongside HMS *Victory* in Portsmouth Harbour on Trafalgar Day, 1905, supplying electricity to Nelson's old flagship.

Petty Officer Waller, the first Coxswain of HM Submarine *No 1*.

18 cially, although they dealt with technicalities and electrical circuits incomprehensible to sailors used to 'Masts and Yards', and they had a tedious tendency to talk shop at table. But, against the rich and colourful background of Edwardian England, the great majority of seamen officers drew the line at donning overalls and getting their hands dirty: so the early submariners, often filthy and oil-stained in a service that had only come into being three years earlier with the new King's reign, were both literally and figuratively looked down on by their elegant contemporaries striding the spotless, holy-stoned quarterdecks above.

The consequence was that submariners withdrew into their steel shells where they banded together in an elite, unparalleled society of professionals. The Submarine Service became, in effect, a private navy. Its capabilities and limitations were not properly understood either by the surface fleet or by the Government. Although they were rather less inhibited by considerations of what was a gentlemanly occupation and what was not, a lack of understanding prevailed to a similar degree in other navies, and in the United States the navy was said not to like submarines 'because there's no deck to strut on'[5]. Misemployment was bound to follow and, although outside the scope of this book, it became strikingly evident in both World Wars.

Fisher's Reforms

The task of revitalising the Royal Navy needed vital energy. Nowhere was this so abundantly evident as in the forceful personality of Admiral Sir John Arbuthnot Fisher – 'Jackie' Fisher to his friends and far more numerous foes. Jackie, with a Jewish mother who was the daughter of a London tradesman, was socially inferior to most of his enemies, notably Lord Charles Beresford, and it may well be that a chip on his shoulder fired his driving ambition. His declared object was to shake the Navy out of its long lethargy and reform a service which had become stale and out-of-date during a century of almost unbroken peace and some quite exceptionally heavy drinking. To ach-

King Edward VII with his favourite Admiral Jackie Fisher – *Ruthless, Relentless, Remorseless.*

Admiral of the Fleet Sir Arthur Wilson VC (1842–1921) – *Old 'ard 'eart* – urged in 1900 that submariners be hanged in wartime.

An officer and a gentleman *c*1905. Submarine officers were called, amongst other things, 'unwashed chauffeurs' with some justification!

ieve this aim (with his customary underlining) he would be 'Ruthless, Relentless, Remorseless'. For Fisher, all was fair in love and war. A favourite aphorism was 'Favouritism is the secret of Efficiency'[6]: those he favoured ('in the Fish-pond') prospered; those who disagreed with him – the 'blue-funk school' and 'yellow admirals' – were doomed. In 1904 Fisher was favouring submariners. Like a fair number of flirtatious ladies in the past they had taken his fancy.

Although 'very busy hatching plans'[7] to become First Sea Lord, he relished his post as Commander-in-Chief Portsmouth just as King Edward relished the throne and Jackie, now in his 63rd indefatigable year, relished a close relationship with the Monarch. The facilities for entertaining at Portsmouth were excellent and the Admiral was entitled to the highest rate of table money. He could afford to enthuse in every sense and he did not intend that any of his machinations should be thwarted. However there were difficulties to be overcome with the surface-bound admirals. On 5 January 1904 he made a note to himself in a large forceful hand:

> Satan disguised as an Angel of Light wouldn't succeed in persuading the Admiralty or the Navy that in the course of some years Submarines will prevent the Fleet remaining at sea continuously either in the Mediterranean or the English Channel.[7]

Not only admirals afloat, growled Fisher, but politicians ashore dubbed submarines as 'playthings' so 'the money had to be got by subterfuge'. As an important preparatory part of Jackie's persuasive process it was arranged for the King to come and stay for a weekend at Admiralty House. No trouble or expense was spared for the visit (although the Admiralty rather than Jackie bore the brunt of all the costs incurred). According to Lady Fisher, 'a bathroom, WC and lavatory' were hastily installed for the use of the two best bedrooms, there being formerly 'nothing accessible of this sort without going up the back stairs' which only the servants used.

The royal visitor was 'so genial, so kind and pleased with everything'[8] that, later in the year,

20 | Lt Leir, correctly dressed in stand-up collar and
seaboots, on the rudimentary bridge-platform of
his A-boat.

A part of the Royal Navy's growing submarine fleet at Fort Blockhouse, Christmas 1906. Three Hollands and one A-boat.

he appointed Fisher as principal ADC, a position 'giving access to the King at any time'. It was just what Jackie wanted. Meanwhile the sales talk on behalf of submarines must have bored the Monarch stiff, but he took care not to show it. First, Fisher 'explained the principles on which a submarine worked', then Captain Bacon (Inspecting Captain of Submarines) came to dinner and said it all again; and finally, on board a submarine the following day, a 'very keen young officer' gave a beautifully rehearsed repeat performance. The King still managed to ask some interested questions: *noblesse oblige*!

Moreover, the King agreed to the Prince of Wales (the future King George V) taking a trip to sea in HMS *A-1* shortly afterwards. The Prince was greeted by officers formally dressed in wing-collars and seaboots. Three white mice were standing by in the engine-room ready to die for King and Country; but more of them later. Apparently 'everyone was averse from the Prince's going down' (wrote Lord Esher[9]) 'but he *insisted* and I think he was right. It will give a lift to the submarines [crafty Jackie] and, being a sailor, why should he not take risks?' The Princess of

Wales cheerfully remarked that she would 'be very disappointed if George doesn't come up again' and they all had a good laugh, little thinking that disaster was soon to strike. Fisher himself, despite his avowed belief and confidence in 'submarine boats' was 'jolly glad when he saw the heir to the Throne reappear' after the Royal dip in the Solent.

A few days later the same submarine *A-1* became the first British submarine casualty: eleven men went down in her. The Prince of Wales immediately received a full report from the Commander-in-Chief. For sheer political cunning and reassurance it was hard to beat by any standards:

To the Prince of Wales	Admiralty House, Portsmouth. (20 March 1904)

Sir,

This is how the submarine was sunk. About noon on Friday the cruiser *Juno*, of the Home Fleet, was sighted in the offing. Submarine *No 2* was given her direction and went after her, followed by Submarine *No 3*. Submarine *No 2* got in a shot at *Juno* about two o'clock but the torpedo missed her. This probably distracted *Juno's* attention, so *No 3* got unobserved within 400 yards of *Juno* and hit her with a torpedo. The head of the torpedo smashed up and knocked off, and the body of the torpedo came up just as the King saw it when His Majesty witnessed precisely the same shot fired by the same submarine at the battleship *Colossus*. Well! Captain Bacon (not knowing at the distance he was off what his young heroes ,were accomplishing) made a signal to Submarine *A–1* (the big submarine in which the King and Your Royal Highness spent so much time in her internal regions) also to attack the *Juno*, observing that Bacon did rightly what would be done in war – sent a regular hornet's nest of submarines on to one part or one ship of the enemy's fleet, because he gets so distracted and flustered by all these infernal brutes popping up from different directions that he hesitates which way to go, and 'the ship that hesitates is lost' because the only escape from the submarine is 'full speed ahead and helm hard over'.

I hope, Sir, this won't get into the *Daily Mail*, because it's the secret of the manoeuvres! Well, Sir, to resume – the Submarine *A–1* steered for the *Juno* far off in the distance, and, poor fellow, I much fear her gallant Commander was only looking at the enemy and didn't care a damn for anything or anybody else. I am much afraid I might have done the same; so don't wish to throw a stone at him; besides, it's the secret of war to be regardless of the consequences, provided you hit the enemy. At that moment the Castle Line steamer *Berwick Castle*, from Southampton to Hamburg, was steering a course exactly at right angles to

Submarine *A–1* and was about 2 or 3 miles off, but never having seen a submarine in his life (he saw her three quarters of an hour before he struck her), her Captain thought it was a torpedo. His words are: 'He saw something'. Just before he struck Submarine *A–1*, the *Berwick Castle* went full speed astern and put his helm hard a starboard, but, alas, too late! . . . .

Believe me, Sir, in great haste,

Your Royal Highness' obedient servant,

J A Fisher

The tragedy in no way caused Jackie to lessen his submarine campaigning by subterfuge and influence. Exactly a month later, the Angel of Light was writing to 'a High Official'. The letter

was probably addressed to Knollys, Private Secretary to the King and a powerful *eminence grise*. It was almost certainly intended that the King should see it; as Lord Esher assured the rumbustious Admiral, 'the King will always back you'

BELOW **Japanese Holland *No 1* at launch, 1905. Japan, spurred by the Russo-Japanese War, was to press ahead quickly with a substantial building programme based on the Holland design. A second short periscope was added.**

BOTTOM **HM Submarine *No 4* with the periscope partially lowered and sleeved with canvas.**

and the Submarine Service was backed in turn.

Admiralty House,
Portsmouth.
20 April 1904

My Dear Friend,

I will begin with the last thing in your letter, which is far the most important, and that is our paucity of submarines. I consider it the most serious thing at present affecting the British Empire! – That sounds big, but it's true. Had either the Russians or the Japanese had submarines the whole face of their war would have been changed for both sides. It really makes me laugh to read of 'Admiral Togo's eighth attack on Port Arthur!' Why! Had he possessed submarines it would have been one attack and one attack only! It would have been all over with the whole Russian Fleet, caught like rats in a trap! Similarly, the Japanese Admiral Togo outside would never have dared to let his transports full of troops pursue the even tenor of their way to Chemulpo and elsewhere!

It's astounding to me, perfectly astounding, how the very best amongst us absolutely fail to realise the vast impending revolution in naval warfare and naval strategy that the submarine will accomplish! (I have written a paper on this, but it's so violent I am keeping it!) Here, just to take a simple instance, is the battleship *Empress of India*, engaged in manoeuvres and knowing of the proximity of Submarines, the Flagship of the Second Admiral of the Home Fleet

24

nine miles beyond the Nab Light (out in the open sea), so self-confident of safety and so oblivious of the possibilities of modern warfare that the Admiral is smoking his cigarette, the Captain is calmly seeing defaulters down on the half-deck, no-one caring an iota for what is going on, and suddenly they see a Whitehead torpedo miss their stern by a few feet! And how fired? From a submarine of the 'pre-Adamite' period, small, slow, badly fitted, with no periscope at all – it had been carried away by a destroyer lying over her, fishing for her! – and yet this submarine followed that battleship for a solid two hours under water, coming up gingerly about a mile off, every now and then (like a beaver!), just to take a fresh compass bearing of her prey, and then down again!

Remember, that this is done (and I want specially to emphasise the point), with the Lieutenant in command of the boat out in her for the first time in his life on his own account, and half the crew never out before either! Why, it's wonderful! And so what results may we expect with bigger and faster boats and periscopes more powerful than the naked eye (such as the latest pattern one I saw the other day), and with experienced officers and crews, and with nests of these submarines acting together?

I have not disguised my opinion in season and out of season as to the essential, imperative, immediate, vital, pressing, urgent (I can't think of any more adjectives!) necessity for more submarines at once, at the very least 25 in addition to those now ordered and building, and a 100 more as soon as practicable, or we shall be caught with our breeches down just as the Russians have been!

And then, my dear Friend, you have the astounding audacity to say to me, 'I presume you only think they (the submarines) can act on the defensive'! . . . Why, my dear fellow! Not take the offensive? Good Lord! if our Admiral is worth his salt, he will tow his sub-

marines at 18 knots speed and put them into the hostile port (like ferrets after the rabbits!) before war is officially declared, just as the Japanese acted before the Russian naval officers knew that war was declared! [Fisher advocated similar tactics against the growing German fleet and suggested it should be 'Copenhagened', that is destroyed at its moorings by a surprise attack, but the King was horrified; after all, although he disliked him intensely, Kaiser Wilhelm II was a royal relation.]

USS *A4* (SS5 – ex-*Moccasin*) *c*1904, commissioned 17 Jan 1903 with Ensign F L Pinney commanding. The cowl-type ventilator above the engine room contrasts with the standard 5ft mast in similar British Holland boats. A periscope was not initially fitted in the early American Holland-type (it is a mast that appears in the photograph) but one was later installed through the port forward ventilation hull-opening. The formal uniform suggests that this photograph was taken on trials or during a demonstration run – probably the latter.

In all seriousness I don't think it is even *faintly* realised –

The immense impending revolution which the submarines will effect as offensive weapons of war.

When you calmly sit down and work out what will happen in the narrow waters of the Channel and the Mediterranean – how totally the submarines will alter the effect of Gibraltar, Port Said, Lemnos and Malta, it makes one's hair stand on end!

I hope you don't think this letter too personal!

Jackie was referring in part to Japanese attacks on the Russian fleet at Port Arthur in February where submarines, if available, might indeed have proved a deterrent if not a positive barrier to the Japanese forces although for an attacking force, at that stage of the game, the concept of submarines bolting enemy warships out of a harbour like rabbits from their burrow was far-fetched in the extreme. The most significant part of his letter, however, described (with Jackie's not unbiased interpretation) the recent trial of strength demanded by the Admiral commanding the Channel Fleet, Sir Arthur Wilson, a dour character widely known on the lower deck as 'Old 'ard 'eart'. It was, incidentally, the same exercise that had seen the loss of HMS *A–1* but that was not a matter for mention when putting the case for submarines.

Wilson, in common with most of his contemporaries, hated the whole idea of submarines although he was to change that view later when

British 'C' class looking aft from what would now be called the control room; there were no watertight bulkheads (other than those afforded by the various tanks) to separate compartments. The 16-cylinder Wolseley gasoline engine in this class was split and offset on either side.

HM Submarine *No 2* lying alongside HMS *Hazard*.

26

he considered they had demonstrated their ability for he was a just man with no political allegiances. In his previous appointment as Controller of the Navy he had sourly suggested that, in wartime, the crews of all submarines captured should be 'treated as pirates and hanged'[10]. The proposal did not meet with favour in the Admiralty but the gallant Admiral, who had been awarded the Victoria Cross for valour on land in the Sudan, was determined, at least, to prove that the early submarines had no operational value. The whole strength of his powerful force was therefore brought against six 'very feeble submarine boats' which is how Fisher chose, on this occasion, to describe them. Fisher, being senior to Wilson, ensured fair play (on his own terms) during a week's manoeuvres in March off Portsmouth. Two of Sir Arthur's ships were considered to have been sunk and a third narrowly avoided the same fate. These results, pressed home by letters like the one above, at last persuaded the Admiralty to take

Three 'B' class and the ill-fated _A-13_ at Fort Blockhouse 1906. The B-boats were to continue in service well into World War I with _B-11_, seen here, penetrating the Dardanelles to sink the Turkish battleship _Messudieh_ in December 1914. This won Lt N D Holbrook the first submariner's VC.

submarines seriously. Wilson, displaying no particular sadness over the loss of *A–1*, complained that 'the most effective way of dealing with the submarines, namely running into them, was barred by the dangers, both to the destroyers and submarines.'[11]

The Royal Navy Accepts the Submarine

The introduction of submarines had been bitterly opposed at the turn of the century but, due more to Fisher's force and influence than to original thinking (for his ideas were far from new), 1904 can fairly be reckoned as the year when submarines – and submariners – were accepted, however reluctantly, into the Royal Navy as a meaningful addition to the strength. The two letters from Fisher, following so closely one upon the other, also anticipated the rapid ups and downs that submarine development was to follow, switch-back fashion, everywhere for years to come. While great advances were to be made in offensive capabilities, losses due to accidents were all too common.[12]

This totally revised and now favourable opinion of the most powerful Navy in the world quickly spread world-wide although in America, the birth place of the truly effective submarine, no par-

ABOVE CENTRE **The new battleship HMS *Dreadnought* in Portsmouth Harbour, Aug 1907, with C-boats passing on their way up harbour watched by the Prime Minister and other VIPs. King Edward VII came on board soon afterwards for the Fleet Review when Adm Fisher told him 'the submarine will be the battleship of the future'.**

LEFT **HMS *B-9* at Malta 1911, Britain's island fortress in the Mediterranean, the bastion of naval society and the 'fishing fleet' – the flock of girls sent out annually in the hope of marrying naval officers. Straw hats were sensible and smart, but bare feet were dangerous on the metal casing, especially when handling ropes and wires.**

A submarine officer at rest. Lt H C Candy, captain of HMS *A-8*, relaxing after observing successful torpedo trials against HMS *Belleisle*, May 1904. Candy and the coxswain of *A-8*, Petty Officer Waller (ex-coxswain of *Holland I*) were two of the three survivors when *A-8* dived inadvertently with the conning tower hatch open off Plymouth a year later.

ticular reaction was expected or forthcoming.

The United States Navy was, anyway, busy with President Theodore Roosevelt's expansionist policies, the Panama Canal and a big ship fleet; Admiral Mahan, who so strongly advocated the latter (and, with his scholarly approach, gained more lasting world-wide fame and credence than Fisher), was not much interested in submarines. Although small submersibles were very appealing to the mechanically-minded American officers and men (who, incidentally, were socially separated almost as much as their contemporaries in the British Navy) they were clearly not going to contribute prestige to the band-playing, flag-waving Great White Fleet then under construc-

tion. Nonetheless, the United States submarine service was quietly progressing along its own dwarfish, unglamorous lines albeit with little or no encouragement from above.

Despite accidents and setbacks, the summer of 1904 saw submarines from Great Britain and the United States well under way above and below the water. On the continent of Europe, France was exceptionally well supplied with a dozen sea-going submersibles of various kinds and a score of harbour-defence boats; Russia, where spasmodic interest had been shown for many years, was said (wrongly) to be embarking on a massive building programme matched by Japan where, indeed, a modest five Holland boats were being assembled;

Submarine sailors were glad to escape the rigid disciplines of big ship life but they still had to polish brightwork as shown here on board *A-1* soon after completion in July 1903.

When the submarine player was on the surface or awash he made his moves on a huge chessboard with the other players, indicating his position with a small pin. He was allowed to take any reasonable means not to attract the enemy's attention to this pin but he was not allowed to conceal it. When submerged he was obliged to retire from the table and sit with his back to it, with only a tiny board of his own on which the umpire located his position. The submariner was thereafter not permitted to use a pencil for drawing lines on his miniature squares and he was only permitted to look at the play through 'a small fragment of looking-glass, not exceeding half-an-inch in diameter'[13]. Having fired a torpedo, he was not allowed to reload inside half-an-hour and he had to do that either on the surface or on the bottom. A submarine on the surface was to be regarded as defenceless: 'diving time varies, but in no case is there any such thing to be allowed as popping up and down again at once. No submarine in existence can yet do this.'[14]

Algerians and Pirates

Italy was showing signs of emulating France with half-a-dozen not inconsiderable boats; Sweden had the Holland *Hajen* and a frighteningly dangerous-looking *Uroth* steam submarine of 116 tons for which much was claimed but which did not belong to the Navy; Argentina had one small, dubious electric boat; Brazil had two Goubet-designed boats with a radius of only five miles but were bargaining for three Holland boats; Chile was building her first submarine, the *Urzua Curat*, a small electric vessel; and, significantly, the influential editor of *Jane's Fighting Ships* was revising *The Naval War Game* to incorporate submarine boats.

The rules for the *War Game* were revealing.

It had by no means been plain sailing to reach this point in submarine development. Except in the United States, where such matters were treated with pragmatical and sound common sense, submarines had been strenuously opposed by the large navies on purportedly moral grounds. Violent were the epithets in Europe. They echoed and re-echoed words like those of Admiral de Crés of France who had said scornfully to Fulton[15] about his *bateau-poisson* a century before 'your invention is good for Algerians and pirates but learn that France has not yet given up the seas.' The Battle of Trafalgar, five years later, somewhat modified French thinking and slowly the concept of underwater piracy – a variation on the strategy

30

of *guerre de course* so popular in France – gained considerable support. Incidentally, it went unremarked by historians that despite, or perhaps because of, Admiral de Crés and his scorn, one of

the first realistic French submarines, built in 1901, was christened *L'Algérien*. It would be nice to think that a typically dark submarine sense of humour, in this case peculiarly Gallic, was already at work.

In 1900 a writer in the *Journal de la Marine* felt able to promise his readers that French submarines 'will make a most formidable fleet, sporting like porpoises round the English warships in the Channel and along her shores, and holding them at the mercy of France.' British politicians

The crew of four British 'C' class boats (*C-12, 14, 15* and *16*) in Nov 1908. Everybody is in the rig of the day, or a close approximation to it, except for the stoker on the conning tower of *C-16* who seems to have escaped the attention of the officers above.

CHAPTER two

and admirals quickly realised that this forecast could conceivably be correct. They promptly mounted a two-pronged attack. One party volunteered superciliously that the submarine was merely the weapon of the weaker power (meaning France) while another protested that submarines were underwater, underhand, and damned un-English. Moral indignation in England and elsewhere was, of course, almost entirely feigned. The truth was that if submarines were successful Britannia might no longer rule the waves; and then where would England and the British Empire be?

There was some opposition in America as well, but it did not spring from any so-called moralists. It was only the ship-builders who voiced a fear and that was to the effect that a submarine construction programme would cause Congress to assign less money to the continued building of battleships which, for shipyards, were likely to be much more profitable than a fleet of small submersibles.

The loud outcry against submarines in England was as two-faced as society itself. But while the British Admiralty stood aloof for as long as it possibly could, most other countries were ready enough to declare themselves interested in this novel form of warfare at a very early stage. Who had been responsible for what, in Britain's view, was a doom-laden downward surge in naval strategy?

There were several inventors who might have laid claim to such an awesome responsibility. Robert Fulton from America, Isaac Peral of Spain and several skilful French engineers had a share in the ancestry of submarines and are duly credited in later chapters. But if rightful parenthood has to be established, the paternity suit should be served on a comparatively remote and unexpected figure; for the father of submarines as we know them today was born in a country known for imagination, flair and poetry but not usually noted for advanced naval architecture – Ireland.

The story that follows of that remarkable Irish-American, John Philip Holland, and his work on submarines extends from the 1860s to the outbreak of World War I in 1914. This, coincidentally, was also the period of major torpedo development and the time during which Jackie Fisher was so zealously reforming England's navy while, during the latter part, promoting submarines. The span of some forty years, peaking at the beginning of the twentieth century, encompassed the most critical and dramatic changes in naval warfare that the world has ever known, and those changes were very largely due to what was originally an Irish invention.

Chapter Three
An Irish Invention

It was in 1898 that the American cartoonist McAllister drew his famous sketch of a bespectacled, derby-hatted inventor with a walrus moustache emerging through the conning tower hatch of his submarine. 'What?' read the caption 'Me worry?'

Submariners everywhere, then and now, would agree that the sentiments implied were admirable. They gave a lasting and correct impression of the submersible navy's attitude to life and, come to that, the unthinkable possibility of a watery grave. It has never been worthwhile worrying when underwater.

John Philip Holland

John Philip Holland, a steadfastly capricious Irishman behind a shy, inquisitive smile, and the subject of McAllister's cartoon, was born in a single-storied cottage off Castle Street, Liscannor, overlooking the bay on the desolate, windy Atlantic coast of County Clare on 24 February 1841.

Following the curious tendency of submarine inventors over the ages Holland became involved with the Church and, at the age of 17, in 1858, he took the initial vows of the Teaching Order of the Irish Christian Brothers. Coincidentally, a notably less monastic association, the Irish Revolutionary Brotherhood – well known on both sides of the Atlantic as IRB – was founded on St Patrick's Day in the same year. Holland was to be linked financially with the IRB later, and he joined the Christian Brothers now to earn sufficient money to pursue his own studies rather than for reasons of religion. His stipend from the Order rose eventually to a goodly sum, by Irish standards, of £30 a year – about the same salary as that enjoyed by the cook in a well-to-do English household, equivalent to 150 dollars at the time.

Like the most famous of his submarine-designing predecessors, the rather elderly Yale undergraduate David Bushnell, Holland was physically weak and suffered continually from ill-health in youth. Although his parents were reasonably secure (his father was in the Coastguard Service for many years) he saw poverty and

John Philip Holland (1841–1914) at the height of his career, emerging from Holland *No VI* (later USS *Holland*) at Perth Amboy, New Jersey in April 1898. A quarter of a century of hard work, disappointment and frustration had elapsed before this famous photograph was taken.

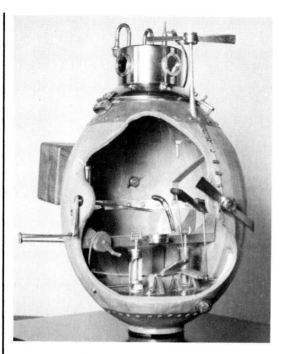

Model of Bushnell's *Turtle*, made by Major M C Gray, in the RN Submarine Museum, Gosport. Although the operator, Sergeant Ezra Lee, could draw in oxygen through the snorkel-like mast, carbon dioxide would quickly have built up around him and this might well account for *Turtle*'s abortive attack on HMS *Eagle* in 1776.

John P Holland's birthplace, now a holiday cottage, in Castle Street, Liscannor, Co Clare, Republic of Ireland.   *Rev E A Pratt MA*

disease all round him: the Hungry Forties were a decade of the Great Famine. One of John's brothers and two uncles died during the cholera epidemic that swept through Ireland in its wake and another brother caught smallpox. Throughout these hard times the wicked landlords twirling their elegant moustaches on the Victorian stage were real enough. They were always ready to evict defaulting tenants from their cottages and strip off the thatch to prevent their coming back: it was a process known as 'levelling' and young John saw plenty of it. Levelling symbolised the effects of British rule and Holland believed, like so many of his countrymen, that England was entirely to blame for Ireland's pitiable condition. All true

Irishmen sought some means of throwing off the intolerable English yoke which, in Holland's view, was largely imposed by the background presence of the all-powerful British fleet. He was, of course, debating exactly the same problem that had so vitally concerned Bushnell before and during the American War of Independence.

The Civil War in America and the rumblings of war in Europe encouraged submarine designs and rumours of several reached Ireland where Holland quietly absorbed them. Most of the accounts were probably exaggerated or garbled but the widespread underwater activity was by itself enough to suggest that submarine warfare would eventually become a practical possibility. So far as Holland was concerned submarines could well be poor Ireland's future answer to England's present might. Unfortunately, there were certainly no facilities for building submarines in Holland's native land which, anyway, was going through another bout of troubles in the 1860s when Holland was employed with the Teaching Order.

Prospects, generally, looked no more hopeful when order was restored. Those who could afford the modest price of a ticket on the transatlantic packet emigrated to America and in 1872 Holland's family was amongst them. A year later, with dispensation to quit the Order on grounds of ill-health, John followed, leaving behind some advanced theories about flying-machines as well as the Tonic-Solfa system of musical instruction which he had introduced into Irish schools when not investigating more scientific and warlike matters. He sailed from Liverpool, as a steerage passenger, with little in his pocket, but amongst the few personal possessions that he carried were the drawings of his first submarine design.

Soon after arriving at Boston in November 1873 he slipped on the ice, broke a leg and was laid up with enforced time to reflect on the design. He concluded it was sound but he was not yet in any position to contemplate building a prototype. He had to make a living and was lucky to resume teaching, in a lay capacity, with the Christian Brothers at Paterson, New Jersey.

America's First Submarine

When Holland was granted citizenship America was the only country where submarines had been carefully considered, North and South, and had actually played a part in real warfare. In the New World they were by no means thought of as mere toys. So exactly what experience was there for the fresh immigrant to build on? Nearly a century before, the 'effort of genius'[1] by Bushnell in launching his rudimentary *Turtle*, albeit abortively, against Lord Howe's flagship HMS *Eagle* in New York on 6 September 1776 had suggested that covert submerged attacks might be a weak nation's challenge to a strong maritime power, and Holland drew his own conclusions from that important, if largely legendary, fragment of submarine history.[2]

Although he seems not to have remarked upon it, he must also have noticed, in his own time, that the concept was revived with some success during the American Civil War where Confederate semi-submersibles, 'Davids', were pitted with biblical imagery against giant Northern men-of-war, 'Goliaths'. Not that the hazardous little Confederate craft could really be called submarines or even submersibles: the most successful of them achieved immortality hand-cranked and awash;

but it would be ungenerous to call the sinking of USS *Housatonic* by the *Hunley* anything but a submarine victory – and, at that, the first. The bald facts are well known. The full story is not well or reliably documented but can be pieced together from contemporary accounts.[3]

By the winter of 1864 the American Civil War had entered its third bitter year and the Confederate States of the South were ready to resort to desperate measures. At Charleston, a port vital to the interests of the weakening South, a Northern Squadron under Admiral Dahlgren was continuing a thoroughly effective blockade. Charleston itself was safe: an attempt in the previous year to take Fort Sumter, guarding the harbour entrance, had failed miserably and the guns of the fort had dealt out severe punishment to the Union ships engaged in the endeavour; but if the Northerners could not gain access to the town from the sea neither could Southern supplies or reinforcements bring relief. Nor had the Confederate Navy any longer anything to match the powerful, heavy vessels of the Northern Fleet – or so the Federal commanders thought.

The moon rose early over Charleston on the evening of 17 February 1864. The skies were clear and a light breeze scarcely ruffled the water. The blockading Federal fleet lay peacefully at anchor in the outer harbour where they were safe from the spitting cannon of Fort Sumter, and they had good reason to believe that there was nothing to fear from seaward. Nonetheless Dahlgren had ordered a special look-out to be kept in light of the worrying attack on the battleship *New Ironsides* in the previous October by something variously called a 'cigar-box' or a 'torpedo-boat' looking, it was said, like a 'plank with a cylindrical pole on it.' *Ironsides* had been damaged, though not fatally, by this mysterious attacker.

Gossip in the crowded coffee-shops[4] indicated that the young Captain, Lieutenant W T Glassell of the Confederate Navy was still alive although the torpedo-boat itself had been damaged and sunk. Then spies began to report that the Southerners had improved this vessel which was some

A Confederate steam-driven 'David', 1863. These boats were not intended to dive but took in water ballast for running on the surface in an awash condition. Lt W T Glassell, commanding one of these craft, damaged the 4120-ton Federal broadside ironclad *New Ironsides* on 5 Oct 1863.

kind of an underwater device. The Minister for the Navy Department warned Dahlgren that the Confederates had indeed launched a new but similar craft capable of destroying his whole fleet.[5] Few officers thought, however, that there was any real danger of attack in the remote outer harbour. They were wrong.

As the light faded on that February evening a curiously shaped contrivance slipped from the inner port. Built of $\frac{3}{8}$-inch boiler plate, it was 40 feet long, 42 inches in diameter and had very little freeboard.[6] A hatch or manhole at either end served for access. The CSS *Hunley*, named after her naval designer and constructed at no cost to the Confederacy by James R McClintock at Mobile, was not a lucky craft. During trials, the *Hunley* had sunk and then been recovered no fewer than three times killing, in all, twenty-three men. In each case the sinkings were caused by the craft being swamped while on the surface and had

nothing to do with attempts to dive. Now she was setting out, on her first operation of war, manned by a fresh crew of eight under the command of Lieutenant George E Dixon of the 21st Regiment of the Alabama Light Infantry. The Navy was entirely content to have the Army in charge after the previous unfortunate experiences. The mystery of how the new crew was recruited in the circumstances is explained by the huge rewards, amounting to several hundred thousand dollars in today's money, offered by firms like the local John Frazier Company for sinking Union warships.

Dixon was undeniably courageous in the extreme. So were the well-paid volunteers who went with him, but they were probably the sweepings of the water-front whilst Dixon was a Southern gentleman. A natural reluctance to shut himself up with them in such a confined space may have played a fatal part in subsequent events.

Previous 'Davids' lacked the ability to seal themselves completely; they were driven by steam and their funnels were dangerously susceptible to swamping in the low awash conditions that were their normal state in action. The *Hunley*'s advantage lay in being hand-propelled so that, for two or three hours she could be independent of the atmosphere with the hatches shut. The trouble was, though, that they seldom were. The *Hunley* could also, in theory, be made to submerge completely with the aid of two side-rudders but it was certainly not controllable submerged, whatever McClintock claimed and historians were led to believe. At best she might have been able to dip momentarily below the water and bob back up. Alternatively, water could be let into tanks until the added weight took the craft vertically down, in shallow water, to the bottom where she could sit for a short while before pumping out the tanks to bring it up again.

With eight men sweating over the hand-crank connected to the propeller in the narrow, claustrophobic, unlit cylinder it must have been tempting to leave the hatches open for as long as possible. The *Hunley*'s Captain therefore navigated and steered the craft by standing up and looking out of the forward hatch. If he had wanted to shut the hatch there were glass scuttles in the coaming which might have sufficed by daylight in open waters but they were hardly adequate for navigating by night in Charleston Harbor. So, for two reasons, the Captain left the hatch open.

Making up to 4 knots, with only a small part of the semi-submersible showing above the surface,

Dixon succeeded in taking his command across the harbour bar. Then, getting his bearings he made straight for the motionless, dimly visible Union Fleet, singling out the new 1264-ton frigate *Housatonic* as his target.

A little before 8.45pm, Acting Master F K Crosby, the *Housatonic*'s Officer of the Deck, glimpsed a low shape in the water a few score yards away. In the moonlight it looked like a piece of driftwood or a tree-trunk; but no stray timber could possibly be coming towards him without the benefit of wind or tide.[7] Crosby did not hesitate. Beating to quarters, he ordered the anchor cables to be slipped and the engines backed. But it was too late. Within two minutes of first being sighted Dixon had manoeuvred the *Hunley* alongside. The deadly 30-foot projecting spar, supporting 143lb

The Confederate *Pioneer* at the Louisiana State Museum, New Orleans. Commanded by James K Scott, this Confederate privateer submarine was built early in 1862 at New Orleans. The hand-cranked boat was scuttled to prevent capture by Federal forces.

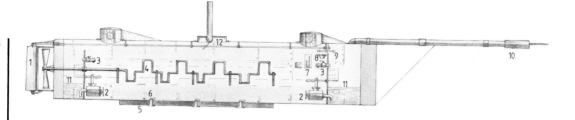

The Confederate *Hunley* 1863

1 rudder
2 pumps
3 sea cocks
4 propeller crank
5 cast iron keel
6 release bolts

7 mercury guage
8 compass
9 steering wheel
10 spar torpedo
11 ballast tanks (open)
12 air box

Holland was against diving rudders amidships. This is HMS *A-7* with primitive experimental planes *c*1905, later discarded.

The Confederate *Hunley*. Although on the first, and last, operational sortie the craft did not submerge *Hunley* was credited with the first submarine kill when the Federal *Housatonic* was sunk off Charleston by her spar torpedo.

of gunpowder in a fuzed copper container on the end, was partially concealed below the surface. Dixon, firing a pistol resolutely, pulled a lanyard with his free hand. A moment later the charge, heavy for those days, was triggered: it exploded just forward of the mainmast on the starboard side of the ship abreast of the magazine. Amidst a deal of panic and confusion USS *Housatonic* lifted bodily into the air and then settled rapidly by the stern, heeling over as she went. As the frigate touched bottom in the shallow water, with her hammock nettings just awash, she gained the doubtful distinction of becoming the first ship to be sunk by submarine action.

The gallant *Hunley*, too, was lost with all her company. She simply disappeared. For a while she was thought to have escaped but in fact she was flooded through the open hatch and sucked into the huge hole she had blown in the *Housatonic*'s side. The little boat was discovered, years later, lying with her victim in a common seabed grave. If the hatch had been shut and if some means had been devised of detonating the spar torpedo from inside the hull, Dixon and his men might have lived to reap rich rewards.

The *Hunley*'s success was such that it eclipsed the Federal government's attempts to enter the submarine business. Union interest resulted very early in the war from the harbour police at Philadelphia stumbling upon a 'submarine monster' at the lower end of Smith's Island in the Delaware River. The circumstances were reported in the *Philadelphia Evening Bulletin* 17 May 1861:

Never since the first flush of the news of the bombard-ment of Fort Sumter, has there been an excitement in the city equal to that which was caused . . . by the capture of a mysterious vessel which was said to be an infernal machine, which was to be used for all sorts of treasonable purposes, including the trifling pastime of scuttling and blowing up government men-of-war. For a few days past the police have had their attention directed to the movements, not of a 'long, low, black schooner', but of an iron submarine boat, to which very extraordinary abilities and infernal propensities were attributed.

Externally it had the appearance of a section of boiler about 20 feet long, with tapered ends, present-ing the shape and appearance of an enormous cigar with a boiler iron wrapper. . . . The after end was furnished with a propeller, which had a contrivance for protecting it from coming in contact with external objects. The forward end was sharkish in appearance . . . as only the ridge of the back was above water, while the tail and snout were submerged. Near the forward end was a hatchway or 'manhole', through which egress and ingress were obtained. This hole was covered with a heavy iron flap, which was made airtight, and which was secured in its place by numerous powerful screws and hooks. Two tiers of glass bull's eyes along each side of the submarine monster completed its external features, afforded light to the inside, and gave it a particularly wideawake appearance.

The police towed the 'mysterious stranger' to the Noble Street Wharf where a large crowd gathered, eager to see inside; but, presumably with some financial advantage to the police, only the *Bulletin*'s[8] capable reporter was permitted to enter:

After dropping from a high wharf into a skiff and then jumping a few feet, we found ourselves upon the back of the iron mystery. . . . The top of the manhole was lifted off, and divesting ourselves of our coat and hat, we squeezed into the machine. . . . We suddenly found ourselves squatting inside of a cigar-shaped iron vessel, about 4 feet in diameter. There was a crank for the purpose of operating upon the propeller already described, apparatus for steering rods, connected with fins outside, which could be moved at pleasure, and which had something to do with steadying and sink-ing the craft. There were . . . pumps, brass faucets, pigs of ballast lead, and numerous other things, which might be intended for infernal or humane purposes for

aught we know. The interior was abundantly lighted by means of the double tier of bull's eyes we have described.

Enquiries determined that the device was the work of a Frenchman, Monsieur Brutus de Vil-leroi, a man well past middle age who had been endeavouring to peddle his underwater wares for thirty years or more. He was now trying to persuade the Federal Government to purchase his latest boat and its apprehension by the police gave him just the publicity he was looking for. Captain Samuel F Du Pont, Commandant of the Phila-delphia Navy Yard, ordered a thorough examina-tion of the craft and the Board of three officers appointed for the task were impressed. A French journal[9] described one of de Villeroi's trial trips:

At 4 o'clock the water was calm. M Villeroi was in his machine and it was pushed off shore. The submarine ran awash for about half an hour, after which it descended into from 5 to 6 metres of water, when it descended to the bottom and gathered some sea shells. [Evidently this feat was accomplished by letting out a drag from its hull.] He cruised in various directions during his submersion to deceive a party of boats which had followed him since the beginning of his experiment, M Villeroi coming to the surface of the water in different directions. After this experiment had lasted an hour and a quarter, he opened his hatch and was received with lively interest.

The inference is that de Villeroi's submersible could not be controlled below water any more than other craft of the time. It could either trim down awash on the surface or settle on the bottom or, an advance on other ideas, it could probably be propelled a few feet off the bottom by dragging a weight along the river bed. It was the problem of how to manoeuvre freely between the surface and the bottom that inventors had not solved at this stage. When their various contrivances were made to submerge they became, at best, no more than mobile diving bells.

Nonetheless de Villeroi had the right idea and on 4 September 1861 he addressed himself by letter[10] to the President of the United States:

40

To His Excellency, Abraham Lincoln, President of the United States.

To the grave circumstances which threaten the union of this glorious country and perhaps its independence, in the end, no means whatever, defensive or offensive, should be neglected; for courage and the holiness of the cause are sometimes in vain to restore order and to make right triumph. Victory too often leans towards force and stratagem. In war the best system, beyond all doubt, is that one which, at the same time that it economizes men and money, can present results the most prompt and decisive; in other words can present great effects with little means. In this train of thought, I wish to propose to you a new *arm of war*, as formidable as it is economical. Submarine navigation which has sometimes been attempted, but as all know without results, owing to a want of suitable opportunities, is now a problematical thing no more. The last experiments which have been made at New Castle and at Marcus Hook in the Delaware River have demonstrated *positively* that with a submarine boat like mine, well constructed and properly equipped, it becomes an easy matter to reconnaissance the enemy's coast, to land men, ammunition, etc at any given point, to enter harbors, to keep up intelligence, and to carry explosive bombs under the very keels of vessels and that without being seen. With a few such boats manoeuvred each one by about a dozen men and the most formidable fleet can be annihilated in a short time. The one that I have experimented with is 32 feet in length. It is built of iron and furnished with a screw propellor. It can be made to go on the surface of the water or at any depth almost below and without any communication whatever with the external atmosphere. When under water the men can go about the boat to perform any work, to remove any object from the bottom, etc and come in again without the least difficulty. (See the relation in the *North American* and *United States Gazette* here inclosed.)

After this communication, Sir, should you judge my services to be profitable to the Union I could place myself at your disposal with my boat and a well practised crew. And should several such boats be deemed necessary I could have them promptly built and their respective crews could be made to practise the original one during the construction of the others.

I have the honor to be with distinguished consideration,

Your Excellency's most obedient servant,

De Villeroy,

Civil Engineer

1325 Pine Street

De Villeroi's proposals were favourably received and the government contracted for a larger 'Submarine Propellor' which, after some contractual delays, was launched on 30 April 1862 at Neafic and Levy's shipyard, Philadelphia. One opinion at the time was that if the *Alligator*, as the new vessel came to be called, had been in service at Fort Monroe (Hampton Roads) the heavily-armed much-feared Confederate ironclad *Virginia*, constructed Phoenix-like from the burned-out wooden Union *Merrimack* and renamed, would have been 'destroyed or at least rendered harmless'[11] at her moorings. There would have been no need to send Ericsson's controversial low-lying *Monitor*, the 'cheesebox on a raft' with her twin 11-inch guns in a revolving armoured turret, into Hampton Roads to engage the powerful enemy vessel on 8 March 1862. The subsequent battle was a draw but the *Monitor*, with her hull protected by being almost totally submerged, remained in possession of the Roads while the *Virginia* (persistently remembered as the *Merrimack*) limped back to Norfolk.

The *Monitor–Merrimack* affair, which had passed into history by the time that Holland landed at Boston, particularly attracted the Irishman's attention. There were two important lessons to be learned. First, ironclads seemed virtually indestructible in a surface-to-surface engagement – and the British were bound to build many such vessels to replace their 'wooden walls': they would have to be attacked where they were still vulnerable, below the waterline. Second, a new type of warship had to prove its worth in a well-publicised fashion; the *Monitor*, criticised on all sides for her ungainliness would probably have been rejected if she had not gone into spectacular action. Then, too, there were the remarks about what a submersible might have been able to do. Holland pondered over these points and formed his own conclusions.

So far as de Villeroi was concerned, Federal procrastination and bad luck prevented the *Alligator* from having any effect on the war, but an account survives of trials with a volunteer crew

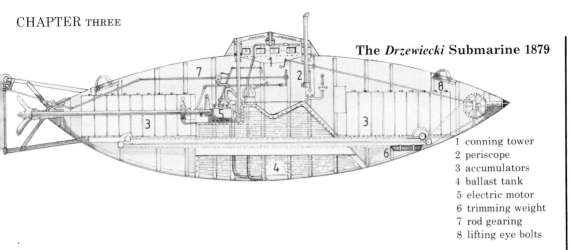

The *Drzewiecki* **Submarine 1879**

1 conning tower
2 periscope
3 accumulators
4 ballast tank
5 electric motor
6 trimming weight
7 rod gearing
8 lifting eye bolts

Drzewiecki's first submarine, analogous to Holland's first boat, was built in 1877. This is his second craft constructed at St Petersburg in 1879. Russian designs were advanced in the early days.

under Lieutenant T O Selfridge when the craft began to founder on the surface. Selfridge wrote, laconically after the incident, that on glancing down the manhole he saw the crew scrambling to climb out when 'a lack of air supply became strikingly evident'[12]. The Captain understandably turned in a discouraging report and little more was heard of the *Alligator* until she finally sank under tow off Cape Hatteras on 2 April 1863.

Another boat, nicknamed the *Intelligent Whale* became better known. Built by Oliver Halstead for the Federal Government the *Whale* caused, according to some reports, the deaths of even more men than the Confederate *Hunley*; thirty-nine men were supposed to have been drowned during various trials in the broad-waisted 26-foot iron boat which was hand-cranked by six muscular seamen.[13] The whale shape was hydrodynamically sensible and the propeller was protected by a skirt. Holland's boats were to look much the same and he knew about Halstead's design although exactly how or how much he knew is uncertain. There was a great deal of industrial and military espionage during the 1860s and 1870s. The Govern-

ments in Europe and America were all anxious to find out what was going on underneath the surface. One senior officer, who should emphatically not have been involved in clandestine activities, was the British Naval Attaché in Washington. A letter from him to the Admiralty, postmarked New York and dated 4 March 1872, is an interesting example of how an English gentleman engaged himself in spying:

PRIVATE

Sir,

Having obtained permission from Sir Edward Thornton to communicate to you privately the information contained in this letter, I beg now to acquaint you that I have had an opportunity afforded me of examining a very ingenious vessel for submarine warfare.

I have heard from officers who had served in the Confederate Services that, what had been thought was a huge fish, had been observed by the people on board their vessels on more than one occasion, crossing the river, just below the surface of the water at nights, but no-one had been able to distinguish more of its nature than that it appeared before and behind in a luminous track – its shape was exactly that of a whale, and it was at first supposed that it might be some monster of the deep.

I afterwards heard accidentally that there existed in one of the Navy Yards a torpedo boat that had been nicknamed the *Intelligent Whale*, that the Gov'mt had faced a large sum for the search of its construction and that it was only known to the Gov'mt officials and

42

the vessel was concealed and secured by a Gov'mt deal. All the enquiries I cautiously made failed to afford any further information.

At my last visit to Brooklyn Yard, I was shown by the Chief Constructor and his assistant all the vessels built or under construction and amongst them the *David* and the new gun-torpedo boat. He and his assistant told one of these that they were all of the sort they had there. When these gentlemen went to their luncheon I found means to get to a remote part of the ordnance wharf which had been avoided during any previous visits, where I had reason to believe the craft might be found.

By a process it is unnecessary to describe I not only found this vessel, but after a while got inside her and noted fully all the peculiarities of her construction, making myself as much master of the secret as those who have paid for it.

I quite believe what I heard rumoured (and which the messenger who assisted me in my examination declared) being that the inventor and his wife and two daughters had remained hours under the water – he occasionally leaving the boat and coming to the surface – and that, since, the Government have purchased the secret and men had remained for 24 hours without inconvenience moving about at pleasure underwater. I fancy the seal must have broken for the purpose of cleansing the machinery and I was fortunate to visit the spot at that moment. [How very fortunate!]

I made ample notes and a sketch on my return to the hotel but these would hardly convey to the whole of the information I acquired I therefore retain them for future service should it be desired.

I proposed proceeding to New London on Friday and then to Philadelphia, on my return to Washington.

I am Sir,
Your obedient servant,
E A Inglefield
Rear Admiral and Naval Attaché

Holland's Early Work

It is impossible to say how much information of this type was available to Holland during his first few years in the United States but the numerous reports in circulation were too vague to be much use to a submarine designer. As Holland himself remarked querulously,[14]

. . . the development of vessels of this type was hindered by the secrecy maintained by everyone who had any knowledge of their design. Governments guarded the particulars of their experiments in order to preserve to themselves the advantage conferred by a successful submarine boat, and the results of individual efforts were just as carefully hidden to prevent the competition of other inventors. As each designer was thus compelled to face the problem without the knowledge of what had been accomplished by his predecessors, he had to discover for himself the main requirements of a submarine vessel, and to foresee and provide against difficulties.

In other words, once he had settled down in his new country Holland was reconciled to starting from scratch. This apparent disadvantage was to work in his favour: if he had closely copied his competitors he would not have achieved the success that ultimately came his way.

Like a number of immigrants from the old country Holland found his sense of patriotism

Halstead's *Intelligent Whale* built in the US in 1862. Hand-cranked by six men out of the crew of 13, it was hoped to achieve a speed of 4 knots. The vessel was designed for anchoring at a given depth so that divers could climb out through hatches in the bottom. Trials were disastrous.

strengthened by distance. There was plenty of Irish revolutionary fervour in America to encourage him. The Fenian Brotherhood, the American counterpart of the IRB at home, was powerful and militant but it was divided and confused within itself about how to take action against the British, whether in Canada or in Ireland, at sea or on land. However the secret societies of the Fenian movement welcomed Holland's submarine proposal. They were just what they were looking for – wild enough for the headiest imagination. The *Irish World* launched an appeal for funds and money from Irish-Americans throughout the country quickly started to roll in.

In 1876 Holland built a 30-inch model submarine and demonstrated it to prospective Fenian supporters at Coney Island. It was enough to convince them that a full size 'wrecking boat' should be built. Considering the degree of thorough-going Irish enthusiasm and through-going alcoholic encouragment which attended the project and the number of enthusiasts involved, the precise nature of the secret was remarkably well kept.

Holland's first submarine was lozenge-shaped, 14 feet 6 inches long and 2 feet 6 inches high with a squat turret-like attachment on the top. She was completed, after being laid down at the Albany

Iron Works, by J C Todd & Co on Van Houton Street, Paterson in the spring of 1878 for a total cost of about 4000 dollars funded by Jacobs, Senior of Jacobs & Company, codename for the leading Fenian Jeremiah O'Donovan Rossa and his Skirmishing Fund. On 22 May the dwarfish boat was winched on to a wagon and drawn, reportedly by eight pairs of stallions, to the water's edge close by the Spruce Street Bridge on the right bank of the Passaic River. Somebody standing on the bridge and looking down cheerfully remarked, 'I see the Professor has built a coffin for himself.' The quotation is believable; the newspaper report of stallions (why stallions?) is less so. The craft weighed two-and-a-quarter tons. When hauled and tipped off the wagon she settled rapidly into the water and, in a moment, sank out of sight. Nobody was on board. The coffin, fortunately, was empty.

Holland had probably calculated the displacement of the boat in relation to salt water. The upper reaches of the Passaic River were fresh and hence the water was significantly less dense; it could well have been insufficient to provide the buoyancy. Doing the arithmetic incorrectly and putting on a heavy trim with respect to density and a hundred or more other factors are mistakes not unknown to successive generations of submariners. Serious trimming errors can, to say the least, be disturbing, and there have, over the years, been plenty of them in all navies. If the trim is hopelessly out it can result, even today, in rising damp, a complaint well known to house-owners, but a euphemistic term for catastrophe in submarines. It is comforting to think that the first and foremost practical submariner got his sums wrong at the beginning.

Holland's prototype was easily hauled up by means of strong lines prudently, if pessimistically, attached before launching. A week later she was floating free and level after various repairs and adjustments had been made. But now Holland found that the two-cylinder engine, intended to run on gasoline, would not work. He put on a good show of being undismayed though he knew full well that a serious defect at this stage would lead

44 not only to bankruptcy but also to dangerous accusations from Rossa and the rest. Spurred by necessity his inventive genius succeeded in adapting the engine to steam power. Surprisingly, it worked. Steam was passed through a rubber hose from a hired steam launch alongside through shaky but sufficient improvised connections. Chugging along under borrowed propulsion on the surface at 3 knots the submarine and her attendant parent launch, together with a quorum of prominent Fenians, soon reached a stretch of water unencumbered by other craft. Holland evidently had complete confidence in his invention and has to be admired for moral and physical courage as well as ingenuity.

Combining the duties of Captain, Navigator and Engineer – all the Chiefs and no Indians – he was compressed into a space 3 feet 8 inches long and only a little more than 2 feet high with his head protruding into a sealed conning tower. Deadlights allowed limited vision ahead and abeam. A larger man could not have forced himself into the tiny compartment which must have been extremely uncomfortable, hot and humid. The steam pipe was not permanently joined to the engine: the female end was brutally forced on to a male connection when Holland was ready to go. There is no record of the joint's efficiency but it can scarcely have been called a sealed unit.

When he was ready to submerge, the inventor flooded the two principal ballast-tanks and pushed forward to the down position the lever which controlled a single pair of diving rudders amidships. Slight positive buoyancy, a feature of all Holland's early designs, was maintained by leaving small tanks forward and aft empty so that if any emergency occurred the craft would automatically come to the surface.

At the very first attempt to submerge the little boat obediently tilted her blunt nose downwards and slid beneath the water to an estimated depth of 12 feet and soon reappeared safely a few yards farther on. A further trial, during which Holland probably remained on the bottom all the while – perhaps for as much as an hour – was equally successful. On that occasion the dive was made 'standing' without forward propulsion and hence without the doubtful assistance of the awkwardly placed horizontal rudders. It was not, in fact, until about 1904 that submarines were customarily dived with way on although there was much controversy about which method was best. Either way, in this prototype Holland demonstrated guiding principles of buoyancy and stability and decided that diving rudders were handicapped by being at the centre of buoyancy; they would be much more effective if placed right aft. That realisation alone put Holland well ahead of his competitors.

The Trustees of the Fenian Skirmishing Fund, on the basis of these efforts, were convinced that financial support for a bigger and better 'wrecking boat' was merited. At thirty-seven years of age Holland looked to a bright engineering future. He ceased teaching in 1878 and, from now on, nothing was heard of his allegiance to the Christian Brothers. The richer and more powerful Fenian Brothers had replaced them.

A cynic might therefore say that Holland was all along intent only on his own ambitious career and that Irish patriotism, let alone the Christian Brothers, never really mattered. To some extent the cynic would be right. But neither politics nor religion – nor even self-interest – really pushed him to the heights or, more accurately, to the depths. The fact was that submarines were fascinating and he was not the only man to find them so. That fascination alone was quite sufficient to sustain his single-minded devotion to 'submarine navigation' for the full twenty-six years that were to elapse before his efforts bore recognisable fruit. For the moment, in the summer of 1878 some five years after his arrival in the United States, Holland had every reason to be encouraged by the progress he had made so far.

Chapter Four

And in the Depth Be Praise

George William Garrett (1852–1902) as a young man.

Nobody knows exactly why submarines had such a peculiar appeal for the clergy throughout the ages but the idea of going underwater captivated a number of churchmen. In 1634, for example, Fathers Mersenne and Fournier wrote a small book proposing a submarine boat with a metallic, pisciform hull and 'two extremities spindle-shaped to make progress equally easy in both directions'[1] which would have been handy; and in 1648 John Wilkins, Oliver Cromwell's brother-in-law and later to become Bishop of Chester, published *An Ark for Submarine Navigation; the Difficulties and Consequences of Such A Contrivance.*

Wilkins allowed his imagination free rein but he made some remarkably accurate observations and prophesies about submarines of the future. Amongst other advantages he cited a submarine as being 'private': 'A man may thus go to any Coast of the World invisibly without being discovered or prevented in his journey.' Further, he said, it would be safe from 'the Uncertainty of Tides' (not quite correct: deep-sea currents and tidal streams tend to be most uncertain and are not yet fully charted); 'the Violence of Tempests, which do never move the sea above Five or Six paces deep' (not quite true either because a submarine can roll quite heavily down to 300 feet or more but the effect of the weather is certainly not comparable with that felt on the surface); 'from Pirates and Robbers which do so infest other voyages' (fair comment: hijackers have yet to board a submarine); and from 'Ice and Great Frosts which do so endanger the Passage towards the Poles' (the submerged passage between the New and Old Worlds via the North Pole is now an established route for nuclear submarines which may well carry cargoes or tow submersible barges below the northern ice-cap in the next decade).

But it was a much more humble, albeit essential aspect of underwater life which the good Bishop Wilkins was the first to recognise: this was the problem of waste disposal. Submariners, including John Philip Holland, have always been keenly interested in the critical matter of plumbing and sanitary devices.

46 Wilkins clearly foresaw the difficulty of ridding a submersible of noisome sewage and refuse noting that

> If it hath not such a convenience these kind of Voyages must needs be very dangerous and uncomfortable both by Reason of many noisome and offensive things that must be thrust out . . . so that anything may be put in or out, and yet the Water doth not rush into it with such violence as it doth usually in the leak of a Ship.

The remedy was to affix

> certain leather bags made of several bignesses, long and open at both ends, and answerable to these let there be divers windows made in open places in the frame of the ship round the sides, to which one end of these bags might be fixed, the other coming within the ship. The bag being thus fastened and tied closely about towards the window, then anything that is to be sent out might safely be put into that end within the ship, this being again close shut, and the other end loosened, the thing may safely be sent out without the admission of any water.

Historians should immortalise the Right Reverend gentleman not as a Founder of the Royal Society nor even as a strategist far in advance of his time, but as the founder of underwater lavatories ('heads' in naval terms) and garbage disposal units.

The Submarine Curate

Now, in the 1870s, while Holland was embarking on the long and difficult road to success in the United States, the Church Militant was again at work in England. It is hard to be sure what prompted the Reverend George William Garrett to desert the duties of his Manchester curacy and enter the submarine business. Unlike Holland he was not inspired or backed financially by rebels or insurgents; on the contrary he believed that a ring of submarines would secure the defences of the British Isles and her island dependencies amidst a mounting fear in England of maritime attack by Russia. The Russian bear afloat was beginning to loom large and, on the other side of the Atlantic,

John Wilkins (1614–72), Bishop of Chester, a Founder of the Royal Society, Oliver Cromwell's brother-in-law and submarine prophet.

the Fenian Brotherhood was watching with keen interest, hoping to exploit any move that Russia might make against Britain. 'If the fight between England and Russia begins,' wrote one of the Fenian leaders[2] in October 1878, 'our time has struck . . .'.

The Irish intention, albeit vague, was to use Holland's submarines in some kind of joint offensive with the Russians, but Garrett, so far as he conceived of them as war machines at all, thought of submarines as purely defensive weapons. It was an important difference and one that was to divide opinion in Europe for many years to come.

Whatever his real motives, Garrett was a fanatic in the field, an astute man of business and a brilliant engineer. From Manchester Grammar School he went to Owens College, where he studied advanced Chemistry and General Science, and thence, at the age of seventeen, to Trinity College, Dublin (the Irish connection again) where, during a single week, he passed all the examinations required of a first year undergraduate. His studies at Dublin enabled him to take up an appointment as an assistant master at the Manchester Mechanics Institute where, in his spare time, he gained certificates in Science, Art, Physical Geography, Geology, Mathematics and

CHAPTER FOUR

Higher Chemistry. Boosted by additional studies at the South Kensington Museum he was given a BA degree and was said to have 'dipped deeply into theology'. The remarkable breadth and worldly nature of his studies was evidently condoned by the Bishop of Manchester who, in 1873, duly ordained George William, after he had passed the Cambridge Theological Examination, and appointed him as curate to the Manchester parish where Garrett's father was vicar. The Bishop can scarcely have foreseen the unclerical course on which the new minister was set.

Garrett obviously had a very tolerant vicar in his father because he was next seen voyaging around the world to learn navigation while studying, from a distance, the Russian Navy and the Tsar's expansionist ambitions. Two events which occurred during the Russo-Turkish War of 1877, just after Garrett's Grand Tour, particularly attracted his attention. On 10 June Lieutenant Zinovi Rozhdestvensky, commanding a spar-torpedo boat, led a concerted attack against the 2266-ton *Idjilalieh* of the Turkish Danube Flotilla. The flotilla was so well defended by steel chains and other obstructions that Rozhdestvensky bent the bows of his boat without being able to make his torpedo penetrate the defences. Two weeks later two more boats were launched against a Turkish monitor up the Danube at Nikopol, and these also failed because of the anti-torpedo nets that had been spread around the gunship. How much better, thought Garrett, if the attacks had somehow been made under the water and below the defences. His thinking was close to Holland's

A Russian torpedo-vessel of 1877 of the type which led Garrett to believe that torpedo-boats should go underwater. *Illustrated London News*

on the other side of the Atlantic, but Garrett favoured explosive charges, suitably positioned on unprotected hulls below the water-line while Holland was looking into the possibilities of an underwater gun; neither, at this stage (1878) was considering free-running 'fish' torpedoes which were (rather expensively) available through the good offices of Robert Whitehead and his Fiume factory. (The engines for these, incidentally, were from 1875 the product of yet another Brotherhood – no relation of the Irish Christian Brothers or the IRB but plain Peter Brotherhood of Peterborough, England.)

Garrett's first interest lay in enabling a man to survive in a coal-mine disaster or in a suit, independent of the atmosphere, below the water. For these purposes he invented a self-contained breathing apparatus, quite unlike the common air-supplied 'hard hat' diving dress. His first public appearance below water in the suit was in the River Seine, possibly in 1877 and certainly in 1880, at the dam near Lavallois. During the latter demonstration, before a committee appointed by the French Minister of Marine, he remained on the bottom, with no air hose, for 37 minutes; and 'when coming to the surface again, he was in perfect health and spirits, although the dress employed, being one bought in Paris for the purpose, did not fit him comfortably.'[3] The French

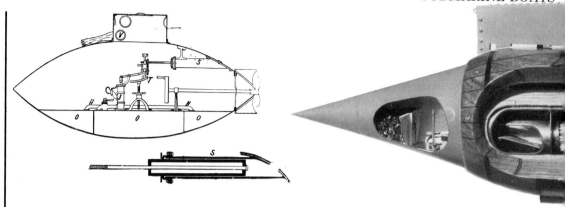

French drawing of Garrett's first *Resurgam*. When submerged, the piston in cylinder S was driven in or out to change the buoyancy and hence the depth.

Government was much more interested in submarine possibilities than the British and Garrett did not permit patriotism to prevent him showing off his inventions abroad. Commercial reward, as well as enthusiasm, was a prime mover behind most early submarine inventors.

By the spring of 1878 the recalcitrant curate felt he had enough experience to take out Letters Patent. One Patent, No 1838 dated 8 May 1878 and sealed on 29 October in the same year, was for 'Improvements in and Appertaining to Submarine or Subaqueous Boats or Vessels for Removing, Destroying, Laying or Placing Torpedoes in Channels and other Situations, and for other Purposes'. The 'torpedoes' were what would now be called mines and the 'other purposes' were underwater surveying and diving tasks. At the same time he founded a new firm, the Garrett Submarine Navigation and Pneumataphore Co Ltd at 56 Deansgate, Manchester with a capital of £10,000 in £1 shares. Five Mancunian businessmen took stock in the enterprise encouraged, no doubt, by the standing of the founder's father, the Reverend Dr John Garrett DD, a much respected Clerk in Holy Orders and a consistently staunch supporter of his son and curate, who bought 2000 shares himself.

Resurgam

Garrett now had sufficient money to build an experimental boat. This first craft was 14 feet long and 5 feet in diameter, and she displaced $4\frac{1}{2}$ tons when dived. For trimming he reverted to a very old device, first suggested in the sixteenth century,[4] of altering the volume of the submarine by means of a piston connecting with the sea: this, of course, had the effect of changing her weight submerged, although from then on most submariners were to use tanks inside their boats which could be partially filled or emptied for the same purpose. Power was provided by a hand-crank and the crew of one – Garrett himself – was kept fully occupied with revolving the screw, steering, regulating the depth and thrusting his hands through greased leather gauntlets in the hull in order to assess the feasibility of attaching explosives to enemy ships. It was a strange occupation for a cleric but a realistic means of underwater warfare which was to be revived during World War II. He confidently christened the prototype *Resurgam* ('I will rise again').

Warlike schemes for *Resurgam* boats included 'placing torpedoes in various situations' for cutting anchor cables and (a singularly ambitious project) using several submarines connected together to tow an enemy vessel away from its moorings by 'connecting powerful cables, first taking the precaution (with a steam vessel) to disable the propeller and rudder'. It was undeniably a new approach to Nelsonian cutting-out

correspondence with the Press. He eventually wrote at length to the editor of the *Manchester Courier* on Monday 15 December 1879 saying, amongst other things, that he fully appreciated 'clergymen ought to have nothing to do with war or its destructive appliances' but that 'clergymen as a class are very much unfitted to take part in the ordinary works of human life.' Presumably submarining was one of the 'ordinary works' to be encouraged in Victorian England where muscular Christianity was the aim of every decent public schoolboy. He went on to say that all would be

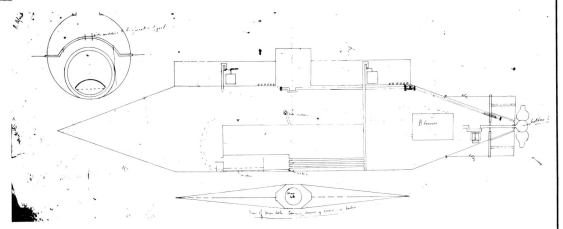

tactics. In light of Russian experience he recommended that a submarine's propeller 'should be protected by guards to preclude the possibility of chains and other obstructions fouling them'. Holland was to take the same precaution.

In his first patent Holland also remarked that 'the boats can easily be carried on the decks of iron-clads and can be lowered into the water when required.' This was to prove a recurring, though theoretical, theme in the early 1900s. Jackie Fisher was very keen on the idea but it was only brought to profitable fruition during the period 1941–1944 when 'chariots' and midget submarines were carried for long distances on board support ships, large submarines and other craft.

While work was getting under way at Birkenhead the Reverend John Garrett Senior tried to justify his son's extra-clerical activities in prolix

TOP **Model of *Resurgam II*, by Lt-Colonel Paul Bowers, in the RN Submarine Museum, Gosport.**

ABOVE **The final construction drawing for *Resurgam*.**

well with 'our National religion' and that 'all the labours of life in our country would derive increased stability and energy if clergymen as a body could earn public confidence in their skill and power to develop a healthy example of all that is good and practicable in the life of Englishmen . . .'.

He went on in the same vein, after passing references to 'our unseen Friend', to a sound explanation of his son's invention for purifying air underwater and concluded with the firm opinion that *Resurgam* and her like would alleviate the need for 'vast fortifications to defend harbours

50 and towns round our coasts' and become 'a means which a few brave coastguard men can easily keep ready to effectively prevent any enemies . . . from attacking our Island home . . .'. Defenders, by means of submersibles, could 'provide defences for their vast extended shores . . . as will enable them all to sleep at rest . . . because no large iron-clad or troopship will dare to approach a coast upon which a few [*Resurgams*] will be maintained.'

Garrett Junior did not rely solely on his father's spiritual support. The prospectus of the Garrett Submarine Company began with the remark, 'As to the inventions being for murdering people – this is all nonsense. Every contribution made by science to improve instruments of war makes war shorter and, in the end, less terrible to human life and to human progress.' This deep feeling was expressed by no less a divine than the Reverend Norman McLeod, Chaplain to Her Majesty and a former editor of *Good Words*. Churchmen, staunchly supporting the submarine as ever, were quick to close ranks in the face of public opposition.

The Second *Resurgam*

The first experiments with the 14-foot boat were encouraging and it was decided, in 1879, to build a larger vessel powered by steam. Garrett, in the best tradition, designed the engine on the back of an envelope bearing a small Victorian halfpenny stamp now on display in the Royal Navy Submarine Museum at Gosport. A letter was despatched to Messrs Cochran & Company, the new and dynamic owners of the Britannia Engine Works and Foundry at Birkenhead, requesting an estimate of building costs 'not wanting the immediate price to be such as will frighten potential backers and perhaps stop the *proper* carrying out of my plans.' The curate was rapidly adding commercial politics to his fund of expertise.

The letter was posted in Manchester on 31 March 1879, arriving in Birkenhead the following day and the estimate of £1538 (about five noughts short of the price of a modern submarine) was ready a week later on 7 April. Business, including

the postal services, moved quickly in Victorian days. The estimate included £53 for the cost of launching but omitted (an afterthought in pencil) £60 for 'centre rudders' (hydroplanes) which were destined to be less than effective in practice positioned where they were amidships (Holland was soon to perceive that they had to be right aft). Mr Cochran was a shrewd far-seeing man and quickly got on with the work of building the second *Resurgam*.

The new boat weighed close on 30 tons. It was cigar-shaped (like all her best successors in the years to come) and had spindle-ends as advocated by Fathers Mersenne and Fournier. The hull's

The *Resurgam* on completion at Britannia Engine Works and Foundry, Birkenhead in late 1879 with Garrett supporting his one-year-old son John William. Capt Jackson is on the right and Mr George Price (Engineer) on the afterpart.

calculated resistance to pressure was 71lb; that is to say it would collapse at a depth of about 150 feet. Propulsion was by steam on the Lamm fireless locomotive principle, used on London's Underground Railway and in the Royal Dockyards. A coal furnace heated water in a large steam boiler at a pressure of 150lb per square inch. The fire-door and the smoke-escape valve leading to a short funnel inside the superstructure were then shut. Latent heat, turning the water into steam when the throttle valve was opened, supplied the return connecting-rod cylinder-engine.

Thus the new boat was independent of the atmosphere for as long as the steam held out – four hours at two or three knots – while the crew could supplement the air for breathing with Garrett's pneumataphore device when necessary. The design was promising and, to ensure the best workmanship, Garrett ended his first letter to Messrs Cochran with the admonition: '. . . it is almost as necessary for yourself as for me that a good article is produced'. He signed himself 'yours very faithfully', the 'very' doubtless showing parsonical intent.

It was intended, in due course, to abandon the idea of 'mine' torpedoes and attach one of Robert Whitehead's free-running types to either side of the central part of the boat which was encased in heavy timber for protection. The torpedoes were to be discharged 'by means of the usual telescope and springs which are used in the Admiralty'[5].

Garrett was clearly not concerned about secrecy because at the beginning of December 1879 'photographic views' were shown of 'The new 30-ton Submarine Torpedo Boat and its Crew' at a sale of work and entertainment held at Christ Church School, Moss Side, Liverpool, for Church and School Expenses and organised by the Reverend Dr J Garrett. The well-informed *Man-*

52 *chester Courier* attended and afterwards took its readers to task for supposing wrong tactics:

> An idea has prevailed that the natural position of the boat is under water and that it comes to the surface at a given time. But the real fact is that its proper position is what the inventor calls on the surface, with the tower just out of water. When the boat has to go under the water, it is made to do so by means of side rudders, which depress the body of the boat under the surface and it remains there as long as the navigator desires. It is meditated that in action such boats should attack an enemy under water, so as to be safe from attack itself and that it should discharge torpedoes when within about 50 yards of its object, afterwards moving invisibly out of the way. Its natural state is to remain submerged to within a buoyancy of about 3 tons. . . .[6]

Presumably this meant that its normal condition was trimmed down and awash when, in modern terms, rigged or opened up for diving.

Resurgam II was launched from a 50-ton crane at Birkenhead into the Great Float on 10 December 1879 ready to go to sea right away. The ship's company consisted of Garrett in command, Captain Jackson (Master Mariner) and Mr George Price, Engineer. On that same dark, misty Wednesday night at about 9pm the little craft shoved off and proceeded cautiously down the Mersey under her own steam-power, reaching the Rock Lighthouse 'without accident of any sort' as Garrett related in a detailed letter to the *Courier*. At the start Captain Jackson, as befitted the only proper seaman in the crew, remained on the upper deck where he must have got very wet because little more than the tiny conning tower protruded above the surface. Garrett took the helm inside the conning tower. The Master Mariner prudently came below while they were passing through the Rock Channel and 'we shut ourselves up and fairly started on our way while the boat answered splendidly in the sea way.' The seas, said Garrett, 'passed easily over her and caused hardly any motion.'

The intrepid crew was greeted with thick fog on Thursday morning which 'necessitated our proceeding very carefully'. They carried out various trials on the surface and remained at sea until Friday morning 'when the sun rose beautiful and clear'. They had by then been at sea for thirty-six hours, much of which had been spent virtually underwater with the hatch shut; one report says they spent the night on the bottom but this is uncertain. They were understandably 'desirous of making some port, as sleeping on board is not attended with as much comfort as we wished.' This understatement was amplified by a letter written by Garrett's son many years later. As a small boy he had in a later boat been taken as an extra crew

The final estimate for *Resurgam* which, apart from the additional cost of launching at £53, was below the initial estimate.

CHAPTER FOUR

The rich Swedish inventor Thorsten Nordenfelt (1842–1920) who 'head-hunted' Garrett.

member because he was small enough to crawl from forward to aft and back, across the 12-inch gap above the boiler tubes, to hand his father spanners and other essentials for careful submarine navigation. The temperature owing to the Lamm boiler, he recalled, varied between 100° and 150°F and there was apparently a considerable leakage of compressed air from the pneumataphore because the crew all complained of pressure on their ear-drums.

None of the surviving accounts states clearly whether or not *Resurgam* ever ran fully submerged. It seems most likely that she steamed for most of the time in the low-buoyancy condition, possibly dip-chicking with the aid of her clumsy hydroplanes against the permanent 100lbs of positive buoyancy built in as a safety factor.

Like all submariners *Resurgam*'s crew endured both trials and tribulations. They were particularly humiliated when Captain Jackson, the expert, lost his bearings in Liverpool Bay and Garrett had to open the conning tower hatch to enquire of a passing ship which way to go. The Captain told him but also confided that they were the three biggest fools he had ever met.

Garrett aimed to make for Portsmouth where he planed to show off his craft to the rich and famous

Mr Nordenfelt, the Swedish inventor, but further trials were necessary before proceeding south. *Resurgam* accordingly adopted Rhyl, on the coast of Flintshire, as a temporary submarine base while certain modifications were made and tested. Mr Cochran had long advised the voyage to be made by rail (a method of getting about which was much favoured by the crews of X-craft in World War II) but Garrett himself was determined to go by sea. However, experience in Liverpool Bay had taught him caution and he now used his firm's remaining capital to purchase a small steam yacht, the *Elfin*, to escort and tow his command.

Elfin towed *Resurgam* out of Rhyl Harbour at 10pm in pitch darkness on 24 February 1880. She then headed west along the Welsh coast but the glass was falling and the seas were rising. By the following day a gale was forecast and was soon blowing from the West-North-West. The sea quickly became so rough that the *Elfin* was unable to keep her boilers going. The only competent engineer was in *Resurgam* herself so a boat was sent across for the submarine's crew, all of whom, fortunately, went over to the yacht to help. At the same time the little yacht resumed the tow.

At 10am on 26 February the towing hawser parted under the strain of wind and waves. It was all over in moments. Probably the hatch was cracked open by the sea. Sadly, Garrett and his ship's company watched *Resurgam* founder and sink, never to rise again despite her name. *Elfin* had to run for shelter but was rammed and wrecked by another boat that tried to come to her assistance.

Britain's first practical submarine still lies off the Welsh coast today. She should be relatively easy to find and recover with modern sonar and lifting equipment and a search and salvage operation has been planned. There is no record of *Resurgam* being insured and it has to be presumed that the Company bore the loss. At any rate, Garrett was in no way discouraged. He now set about establishing a formal relationship with Nordenfelt which was to result in some notorious new submarines, far larger and much clumsier.

54

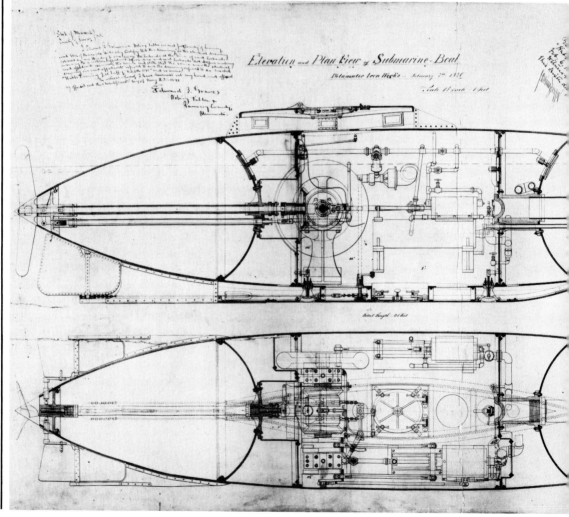

Chapter Five
Salt Water Enterprise

The Fenian factions in America were supposedly united in the Clan-na-Gael (or United Brotherhood) but rivalries, loose talk and liquor were, by the beginning of 1878, starting to split the association and threaten the success of the Irish submarine project, the 'Salt Water Enterprise' as it was called to preserve some measure of secrecy. Codewords, however, were not enough. On 6 February a leading Fenian, John Devoy, wrote to a colleague[1] 'I do not propose to fritter away my life in endless squabbles, nor do I think it safe to go into serious revolutionary work with men who cannot keep a secret.' Secrecy was vital because the Brotherhood's Skirmishing Fund now proposed to provide money for a new craft which was to be used entirely for war against the British as soon as the opportunity offered. Holland's brother Michael was largely responsible for persuading the Clan-na-Gael to provide the backing. Holland himself proceeded with great caution to avoid jeopardising security. Indeed, he was so reticent in his approach to managers of the Delamater Ironworks on West 13th Street, New York City, that they were at first reluctant to consider undertaking the project, at least until they knew who the backers were. However, they were eventually persuaded and they produced an estimate guaranteeing that the cost would not exceed 20,000 dollars.

The *Fenian Ram*

Work began on 3 May 1879 but progress was slow. Simon Lake, the other principal submarine pioneer in the States (who appears later in this story) quotes Holland as complaining that the Delamater engineers were continually raising

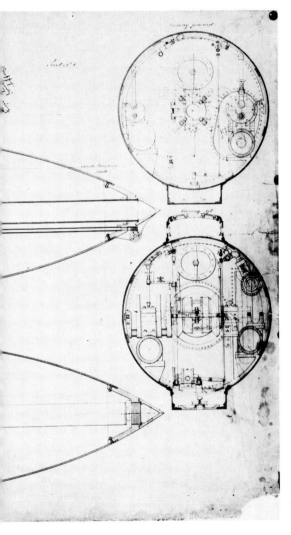

LEFT **Plans, authenticated by the Notary Public, of the *Fenian Ram*.**

ABOVE LEFT **The *Fenian Ram* launched in May 1881. The boat cost about 20,000 dollars (£4000 in those days) and was built with $\frac{11}{16}$ inch charcoal flange iron. There was joystick control for the rudder and diving planes.**

unnecessary objections which resulted in the building programme taking a whole two years to complete. As submariners have since discovered there are always plenty of critics who, for every solution, are ready to find a problem. The trouble, said the unremittingly Irish Holland, was the same as he later encountered amongst staff officers of the United States Navy, that is, 'they were, almost without exception, of English, Welsh or Scotch descent....'[2] Holland went on to remark that these people appeared 'to know by intuition that the project was absurd': modern submariners are familiar with that obstacle, too.

There were many foreign visitors to the Ironworks while Holland's second submarine was under construction. Mostly Swedes, Russians, Italians and Germans, they included two representatives from the Sultan of Turkey who displayed an artless disregard for diplomatic confidences and were apparently sent to discover whether the poor English opinion of Holland's project was correct or whether the inventor should be asked to build a boat for the Ottoman Navy. The meeting confirmed Holland's suspicion that the world, including America, was distrustful of any naval proposal that did not originate in England. He was not in the least deterred.

The construction contract was completed for 18,000 dollars, well below the estimate, but this figure did not include some auxiliary machinery. The submarine was launched in May 1881 and towed across the Hudson River to the Morris Dredging Company's Dock, Jersey City. The three-man 19-ton boat was 31 feet long, 6 feet broad and was propelled by a Brayton twin-cylinder, double-acting petroleum engine. George Brayton, said Holland sourly, asked more for his engine than it was worth. It gave a lot of trouble. The numerous visitors and much bar-chatter dispelled any hope of real secrecy. The notorious British spy Major Henri Le Caron, alias Thomas Beach from Illinois, circled like a jackal around Holland and the Clan-na-Gael hoping to pick up saleable titbits and cause dissension amongst the Fenians and other Irish patriots. His efforts in the

latter direction were scarcely necessary: the Irish factions were constantly warring and the United Brotherhood was for ever disuniting without any encouragement from outside. He also endeavoured, by passing information to the British Consul General at New York, to make the American Government put a stop to the *Ram*. Washington refused on the rightful grounds that the invention was a private concern.

Holland denied access to strangers so far as he could and refused to let the Press examine the interior. Nonetheless, the *New York Sun* through its determined reporter Blakely Hall, was able to make some intelligently speculative comments. The craft was described as a 'Fenian Ram': the description caught the public imagination and *Fenian Ram* became the name thereafter. Holland was not displeased. It is possible that the inventor did indeed consider ramming as one method of attack. The potential effectiveness of this tactic was demonstrated one day, inadvertently, on trials when the *Ram* ran into the end of a pier at 6 knots 'owing to my bad steering or forgetfulness at the time'[3]. It was the first of a long, long line of submarine ship-handling incidents in all navies. The effect, on this occasion, was quite dramatic: a 12-inch pile was split and a solid horizontal tie-bar, with 4 feet of stone ballast lying on it, was forced upwards. The *Ram* was tough. So far as the submarine was concerned, no damage was done and 'nothing but the engineer's respect for good English' was hurt[4].

The *Ram*'s crew consisted of the pilot (Holland), the engineer (George M Richards of Erie, Pennsylvania) and a Gunner who seems not, in fact, to have been appointed because the records speak only of Holland and Richards being embarked together except for one disastrous occasion when the engineer took the craft out by himself. There was plenty to keep two men occupied.

The little boat was powered only by its petrol engine which developed 15hp – quite sufficient when it spluttered into action. There was no alternative means of propulsion and the submarine was unique in using an internal combus-

The *Fenian Ram* 1881

1 air tanks
2 water ballast tanks
3 high pressure air tank

4 hatch in conning tower
5 gasoline engine
6 levers for vertical and horizontal rudders
7 pneumatic gun

tion engine both on the surface and submerged. The streamlining was near perfect with the porpoise shape typical of all Holland's designs. The hydroplanes and rudder were just forward of the single propeller which, at maximum revolutions, drove the boat at eight or nine knots on the surface and could probably, judging by experience today with similar hull-shapes, give about the same speed submerged although that could not be measured at the time.

There was, of course, no difficulty in running the engine on the surface. Below water it was another matter: back pressure through the exhaust, which was expelled through a non-return flap-valve, was obviously liable to stop the engine just as the old trick of plugging a motor-car's exhaust pipe with a potato prevents it from starting. It was a problem that did not recur in submarines until the *Schnorchel* was introduced half a century or more later.[5] The engine exhaust pressure was sufficient, on trials, to overcome external sea pressure down to 10 feet and, when he was more sure of the engine's performance, Holland said he dived under way down to about 45 feet but probably only for a few moments. When he took the boat down to the maximum known depth of 60 feet and bottomed, the engine was stopped. For longer periods under way at depth he intended to overcome the difficulty of back pressure by

opening up valves on the compressed air reservoirs. A depth of 40 feet, and possibly more, should then be achievable if a pressure of one and a half atmospheres could be built up internally; but it would have to be held by bleeding air continuously from the reservoirs as the engine used it up. He admitted blandly that the pressure might be uncomfortable for the crew but was quite prepared to tolerate it himself. It would have needed nice judgement and careful balancing between the depth and air-pressure gauges to run at differing depths for any length of time in this way: submariners today would shy away in alarm from the whole idea. Nonetheless in theory the proposed system, within strict limitations, satisfied Holland's aim of enabling the *Ram* to operate as a true submarine independent of the surface atmosphere.

The *Ram's* Sea Trials

The first dive in the summer of 1883 was entirely satisfactory. In Holland's words: 'I drew back the little iron levers on either side of my head.' These operated Kingston valves in the bottom through which water was admitted to the two internal ballast tanks forward and aft and

... almost immediately the boat began to settle, giving us the suggestion of slowly descending in an elevator. I looked through the ports in the superstructure and

58

observed that the bow had entirely disappeared and the water was within a few inches of the glass. A second or two later everything grew dark and we were entirely submerged, and nothing could be seen through the ports except a dark green blur.

The boat obviously dived with no way on because

Our next sensation was a slight jar, when the vessel struck the bottom. It might also be mentioned here that we had no light except the glow that came through the conning tower. This just about sufficed to read the gauges but was too poor to be of much interest to the engineer.

The depth was a little over two fathoms, perhaps twelve or fifteen feet. Richards made the rounds in the dark (they resolved to carry a lantern for the next dive) and discovered no leaks. It was enough for the day. Holland opened the blowing valve to the ballast tanks and heard the reassuring hiss telling him that compressed air was driving out the water.

The green blur of the ports in the conning tower grew lighter as I gazed through them until suddenly the light of full day burst through, almost dazzling me. After blinking my eyes I looked out again and saw the familiar surroundings . . .
I now opened the hatch and stood on the seat, thus causing my head and shoulders to protrude from the tower. As soon as I was observed doing this a cheer burst from the crowd of observers on the dock, among whom opinion was equally divided as to whether we would ever emerge alive from our dive or not. We had now demonstrated the fact that our ballasting system was perfect.

The ballasting and flooding arrangements were much better than others of the time although quite different from the external main ballast tanks introduced in double-hulled boats later. The latter had, and still do have, holes in the bottom (which are always open) and vents at the top to release the cushion of air supporting the submarine on the surface. It is not clear where the tank vents in the *Ram* were but they must have been internal. They may not to have been opened on diving during the

first trials so air would have remained at the top of the tanks when the Kingston valves were opened at the bottom but normal working called for the tanks to be filled completely except when compensating for the discharge of a missile and it may be assumed that the *Ram* was not plagued by free-surface problems causing the longitudinal instability that for long dogged other inventors. (The danger of free-surface can be seen by half-filling a sealed tin box and tilting it.)

The next trial was to show that the *Ram* could dive with the engine running.

For this occasion Richards and I entered the boat, I taking my place in the conning tower, while he went forward to start the engine. After a little kicking and muttering [Richards was the archetypal submarine engineer] he succeeded in getting it started. We then let in the clutch and the boat started forward. When we reached the far side of the basin I turned her around and threw out the clutch, causing the boat to slow down and stop. Closing the hatch, we then made sure that everything was tight and opened the Kingston valves. When the water reached the observer's ports in the conning tower, I closed them again.

The tanks were so nearly full that the free-surface effect would be negligible on diving completely and he reasoned that it was sensible, at this stage of the game, to maintain extra positive buoyancy over and above that built into the boat by means of the compressed air reservoirs at the bow and stern.

We then proceeded along awash; that is, with only the little tower showing above the surface. I found that from this position I could observe objects quite a distance ahead, and my vision was obscured only occasionally when a wave washed against the glass. I next threw forward the lever on the right side of my seat (controlling the diving rudders aft). Immediately the nose of the boat went down and before I realised it our gauge showed a depth of about 10 feet. I now drew the lever back to centre, and the boat straightened out on an even keel. There was very little or no tendency to buck or be cranky; in a word, I had no difficulty in preventing her nose from rising or dipping down. After running about one hundred yards submerged I steered the boat up, and in a few seconds the superstructure of the boat was again above water. I then opened the air valve and expelled my ballast, causing the boat to rise and assume her normal position.

The boat could also be used as a diving bell and had a hatch in the bottom for this purpose. The pressurising system already provided for the engine enabled the hatch to be opened without taking in water and George Richards wanted to see if the concept was practicable. All alone he settled the boat down on the bottom while alongside the dock at high water to find out what happened when the hatch was opened, having first built up the pressure internally. He was not wearing a diving suit and contented himself with dropping his feet on the bottom and passing his

hands under the boat on either side whereupon he 'lifted the boat slowly and with little exertion about one foot from the bottom'. The unauthorised experiment was successful but Richards was incurably inquisitive and liked to do things by himself. His next solo effort was expensive. He decided, one morning early, to take the boat out for a run. Holland arrived a few minutes after he had slipped and found a gaggle of onlookers excitedly pointing to a huge uprush of foam and bubbles on the surface about 200 yards off the pier. There was no sign of the *Ram*. One of the spectators said that a barge and a tug had just passed very close to the submarine, washing water over and down the conning tower; it was the story of the Confederate 'Davids' all over again. For-

The *Fenian Ram* looking aft towards the gearing driven by a 15–17 hp Brayton petroleum engine with a large flywheel.

The heavy iron-cast breach of the 9in diameter, 11ft pneumatic gun which accommodated a 6ft projectile – the *Fenian Ram*'s weapon system. A 400lb per square inch air charge fired the weapon.
Christian Grube, Photographer
Paterson Museum

60

tunately, it transpired that Richards was only just below the hatch when the water started pouring down. He was able to get out with the escaping air and reappeared on the surface almost immediately 'still a bit pale' but the accident cost the Skirmishing Fund some 3000 dollars to raise the *Ram* and dry her out.

The more advanced submerged trials were conducted across the Narrows below Stapleton. Before diving Holland made certain that there was no ship in the vicinity drawing more than 25 or 30 feet. Excursion steamers, fishing boats and small yachts could be ignored because he intended running at a depth of not less than 20 feet when close to them. The paddles of the excursion steamers could be heard underwater quite a long way off and Holland found he had no difficulty in avoiding other vessels by changing course or going to a greater depth until they had passed. On one occasion he 'frightened the devil' out of the *St Johns* (a Long Branch steamer) by porpoising across its bows. There is enough supporting evidence of this kind to confirm beyond doubt that the *Fenian Ram* was perfectly able to operate, under control, several feet below the surface with the engine running and change depth by using the diving rudders for steering up or down at a slight angle. The submarine was already, in 1883, ten or fifteen years ahead of her rivals.

However, the particular problem which bothered Holland was his inability to see under water. The *Ram* had no compass and presumably, with a single propeller turning clockwise, she had a tendency to veer continually to port. Holland may not have appreciated this. It would have been simple enough to correct the tendency when the conning tower viewing ports were above the surface but it must have been very easy to get lost when submerged and the *Ram* had no periscope. Midget submarine captains in World War II were to find it quite impossible to know where they were when their compasses went 'off the board' in the narrow confines of a harbour, and they enjoyed better facilities for navigation than Holland ever had.

J P Holland in 1900, age 59. By now his designs were fully accepted and the problems with his Fenian backers were long past and done with; but those early difficulties were nothing compared with the worries that confronted him in the turn of the century business world.

One excursion, on 3 July 1883, was made even more difficult by Holland finding that his view of Staten Island ahead and Bay Ridge to port was 'obscured by what seemed to be a pair of brown rags hanging on either side of the turret'. It turned out that the brown rags were trousers and they belonged to a small coloured boy who had managed to drop down on to the conning tower when the craft was leaving the dock. Holland opened the hatch and kindly invited the stowaway inside to avoid him being swept off by the sea. The boy politely refused the invitation and said he was 'puffecly safe' where he was and that he would 'hold on like grim death'. Holland was not going to risk drowning the lad and he resignedly headed back to the shore. But a good deal of time had been wasted and the sun soon set. It was too dark to make for the usual moorings but as the craft headed up towards the Bay Ridge Ferry landing-place two well-spoken boys in a rowing boat came alongside. Holland, always the schoolmaster at heart, showed the astonished youngsters around his own invention. As he so often found, his natural kindness bore dividends: one of the boys announced he was the young brother of Mr Vanderbilt Bergen, a noted shipyard owner, and he arranged for the *Fenian Ram* to berth at Bergen's very convenient dock at Bay Ridge. It became the submarine's base for the next two months.

It was now time to test the *Ram*'s extraordinary armament. Robert Whitehead's torpedoes were quite well proven but there was as yet no way of discharging them underwater. In England, Garrett was planning to hang torpedoes on a type of release-gear externally and the French had the same idea but these arrangements would have spoilt the *Ram*'s streamline and upset her handling qualities. Holland's weapon was quite different and was, in effect, an underwater gun although it closely resembled a torpedo tube of the future. The gun was 9 inches in diameter with a breech (rear door) and a muzzle (bow cap). It was large enough to hold a 6-foot projectile and this was fired pneumatically by high-pressure air. Holland had long admired Captain John Ericsson for his *Monitor* of Civil War fame and, by chance, found that the Captain was building a new *Destroyer* in Delamater's Works. If Ericsson's missiles fitted Holland's gun a great deal of trouble and expense would be saved. Fortuitously, they did. Ericsson generously agreed that Holland could use copies of his experimental models and discharge trials were quickly arranged.

The *Ram* was partially submerged with the tube horizontal and about $3\frac{1}{2}$ feet below the surface. There was a floating dock lying in the water about 150 yards right ahead of the bows so a reduced firing pressure of 300lb per square inch was used.

When the firing valve was opened the projectile passed out and travelled about six or eight feet beyond the muzzle of the gun. Then it turned upward and climbed into the air to a height of 60 or 70 feet before falling point-foremost into the water where it buried itself so deeply in the mud that we could never find it again.

For the second shot the boat was depressed a few degrees and the *Ram* was swung to port to avoid hitting the floating dock. The firing pressure was doubled to 600lb per square inch and the shell travelled about twice as far as its predecessor underwater, 'then rose 15 feet in the air and passed over the wall limiting the Basin, striking a pile that projected above it, and frightening a fisherman who was dozing thereon'. Holland, wary of claims against him and adverse publicity, was quick to point out that 'the fisherman was in no danger as the pile and the stringer – a piece of heavy pine – afforded him protection.' In short, the new weapon system looked promising. In fact it had exceeded expectations to the point of being dangerous.

The Fenians seize the *Ram*

Unfortunately, the Irish faction had by now become impatient. John J Breslin, one of the leading Fenians, and a few colleagues resolved to take matters into their own hands. They wanted action and were not willing to wait. Forging Holland's name on a pass, they manoeuvred a tug alongside the *Ram* and, with a new 16-foot model which Holland had constructed for further experiments on a line astern, towed the craft away up Long Island Sound towards New Haven. The flimsy tow-rope on the small model quickly parted and it sank, never to be seen again. On arrival at New Haven the Fenian Group, who knew nothing whatever about ship-handling, made such a hash of operating the submarine on the surface that the harbourmaster declared her a menace to navigation. Realising that they were quite incapable of becoming submariners without Holland's help, the Fenians beached the boat and endeavoured, but failed, to sell her to Russia.

Holland's reaction was predictable: 'I'll let her rot on their hands.'[6] In the event, the *Ram* did not rot although she never entered the water again. She was exhibited at Madison Square Gardens in

1916 to help raise money at the time of the Irish Uprising, then she was moved to the New York State Marine School. She was then placed on a plinth in West Side Park at Holland's own Paterson, New Jersey. The boat has now been opened up and is being renovated.

Holland had no more commercial dealings with his fellow Irishmen. As an American citizen he now directed his efforts towards designing submarines for the United States although, so far as the Navy Department was concerned, he became 'totally sick and disgusted with its actions, and was seriously tempted to abandon all further attempts to convince and awake it from its lethargy'. He noted, correctly, that submarine designs in Europe were markedly inferior to his own, but, for the time being, he had no funds with which to build another craft. However, there were straws in the wind.

Holland had made some useful friends outside the IRB during the *Fenian Ram*'s brief career and one young naval officer, Lieutenant William W Kimball, was to prove a prominent supporter for the future. Kimball, junior as he was, promised to prod the Navy Department into taking a more active interest in submarines and endeavoured to secure Holland a job as a naval draughtsman. Kimball underestimated the resistance of bureaucracy: as Captain Edward Simpson had remarked a few years earlier, 'to put anything through in Washington was uphill work'.

The *Zalinski Boat*

Holland could not wait for Washington. With very little capital left and no income he was obliged to accept a position as a draughtsman with the Pneumatic Gun Company where he encountered the quite well known and ambitious ordnance expert Captain Edmund L Zalinski of the US Army. Zalinski was anxious to promote a new 'dynamite gun' and believed that one of Holland's submarine boats, for which the inventor quickly sketched a new design, was the best vehicle in which to mount it. The gun was not to be fired submerged as in the *Fenian Ram*, but the bow of

the submarine would be made to break surface, just before firing, at an angle appropriate to the range of the target which could, Zalinski reckoned, be up to half-a-mile distant. In other words the submarine would serve as a very flexible gun-carriage able to train and elevate the gun barrel to any required degree. In fact, it would certainly have been all *too* flexible: a precise trim angle is hard enough to achieve in any kind of sea even in a modern submarine when half awash. The interesting concept, which foreshadowed the giant British Monitor *M-1* of 1917 and submarines armed with cruise missiles in the 1950s, was never put into practice. Although the craft was duly built to carry two dynamite guns she was a total failure. The most she did was to provide Holland with meat for a provocative article entitled 'Can New York be bombarded?'

Surprisingly, for it must have been against his better judgement, Holland allowed the boat to be constructed of wood. She was an elongated vessel, 50 feet overall and quite unlike the stubby *Ram*. Holland had no heart in her. An absurdly high launching platform was built out over the sea wall of Fort Hamilton on an island off the Brooklyn shore. The launch on 4 September 1885, under the supervision of a young engineer for whom Holland had scant respect, was disastrous. The heavy boat careered at ever increasing speed down the steep slipway which collapsed at the seaward end, precipitating the submarine into some piles at the water's edge. Salvaged and repaired, the *Zalinski Boat* made a few desultory trial runs in New York Harbor but Holland's fourth submarine and the Nautilus Submarine Boat Company which had promoted the venture were soon forgotten.

Holland ruefully remarked, towards the end of his career, that the misguided *Zalinski Boat* project held him back for at least ten years. It was not until 1893 that he was able to secure backing for his next submarine. Meanwhile, powerless to build a boat himself, he had to read galling and voluminous newspaper reports about well supported but less competent submarine inventors in America, France and England.

Chapter Six
The Sultan and the Tsar

While Holland was looking for a new backer and filling in time by reviving his old ideas about flying machines (*The Practicality of Mechanical Flight* was published in April 1891) the Reverend George William Garrett and his rich Swedish associate Thorsten Nordenfelt were busying themselves with ambitious international submarine projects on the opposite side of the Atlantic. Nordenfelt saw that the sales potential was enormous, especially for those navies which could not match the maritime might of England. The inventions which he had already perfected, a reliable machine-gun amongst them, had made him independent and he now perceived that submarines and torpedoes (referred to in their modern Whitehead sense) were natural allies. Furthermore, the fragile and intricate torpedo mechanisms could best be safeguarded if they were maintained inside a submarine, or at least a tube, until the moment of firing. Garrett had proved himself as a sound, level-headed engineer with a flair. Today it would be said that he was head-hunted by Nordenfelt. As a result their joint efforts were to be categorised as Nordenfelt boats but their machinery owed much to the curate from Manchester. When the partnership was established Garrett abandoned parochial allegiances altogether. His ideas about a ring of small submersibles for the defence of the realm were forgotten. Big business was beckoning.

The Swedish *Nordenfelt I* on the slipway at Ekensberg, near Stockholm, in 1883 about a year after construction had begun.

The First Nordenfelt Boats

Unhappily the two inventors overstepped themselves. They did not stick by Garrett's practical, well-proportioned plans which had been reasonably well demonstrated. Instead, all but the first of the Nordenfelt–Garrett boats were long, thin and narrow, more like foreshortened eels than the porpoises which Holland used as his models and which present-day designers usually try to copy. *Nordenfelt I*, laid down in Stockholm in 1882 but not launched until 1885, was reasonably proportioned with an elliptical hull 64 feet long and a maximum pressure-hull breadth of 9 feet – a good seven-to-one ratio – but other features were against her. The torpedo was held in an external tube, which protected it to some extent although it hazarded the crew, which only totalled three men, when firing the weapon. In anything other than glassy water they would have been washed overboard. There is, in fact, no record of a firing taking place from this first boat. It was, from a submariner's point of view, the handling characteristics below water that were so dubious.

The maximum safe depth was 50 feet, presumably measured at the surface water-line. The internal frames were circular and spaced two feet apart and the hull varied in thickness from five-eighths of an inch to three-eighths at the tapering extremities. It must have been the valves and hull-glands which restricted the diving depth because these thicknesses (assuming that the rivetted construction was sound enough) would have resisted considerably greater pressures than 22lb per square inch at 50 feet.

The steam plant was similar to that in the second *Resurgam* but drove a propeller that was 5 feet in diameter – much too large for the plant.

BELOW **The main engine of *Nordenfelt I*. The steam plant was arranged on the fireless Locomotive principle.**

BOTTOM *Nordenfelt I* at Landskrona, with a rowing boat temporarily suspended on the casing, during trials, probably in early Sept 1885 before the surface and submerged demonstrations given later in the month.

Subsequent Nordenfelt engines were more elaborate, being based on the Franq principle. Most of the interior was taken up by the propelling machinery with a large marine boiler, a steam accumulator and a compound main engine driving the propeller through an inclined shaft with universal couplings.

The accumulator had a heat exchanger in the bottom, live steam from the boiler being conveyed through the coils of the heater, giving up its latent heat to the water in the accumulator and being returned to the boiler via a feed pump. By this means a large store of superheated water was stored in the pear-shaped tank which, when released into the main boiler at a lower pressure, flashed into steam. The main engine had exceptionally large-bore cylinders to accommodate low-pressure steam as the pressure dropped. Pumps and ancillary units on the engine worked on a vacuum produced by a powerful air pump: vacuum was as important as pressure for the engine's efficiency. The boiler had to be fired, in harbour, for a full three days to heat up the reservoir fully so an extended operation on latent heat alone,

Turkish Nordenfelt at Constantinople in 1888. The lin gun, a Nordenfelt of course, was perhaps the only reliable piece of equipment on board: the Swedish inventor knew a great deal more about arms than submarines.
National Maritime Museum

replenishing at sea, was out of the question. This considerable disadvantage was not explained to potential purchasers.

At least one of Garrett's designs included a rudimentary 'schnorchel' which would have enabled a craft to steam safely in an awash condition, requiring the boiler to be banked only when carrying out a proper dive. The Nordenfelt boats did not incorporate this device but, with the conning tower, albeit small, and 3 feet of hull above the water when surfaced, they were able to steam by drawing air in through the conning tower hatch in the same way that later submersibles depended on air sucked down for their gasoline and diesel engines. However, unlike a modern boat, the Nordenfelt was equipped with a centrifugal fan. This gave a forced supply to the furnace.

Nordenfelt differed diametrically from Holland in his concept of submerging and he did not believe in achieving Archimedian neutral buoyancy submerged:

I feel confident that previous attempts have proved unsuccessful mainly because either they depend upon varying the displacement of the boat by taking in water to submerge her, and to regulate the depth at which they desire to operate, or they descend by steering downwards. My objection . . . is that, practically, there is no difference of the specific gravity of water on the surface and at 50 feet depth – thus, when

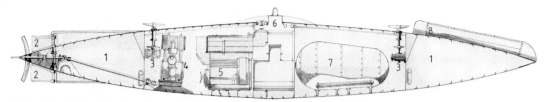

The Turkish Nordenfelt 1887

1 ballast tanks	4 steam engine	7 hot water tank
2 rudders	5 boiler	8 torpedo tubes (Whitehead)
3 descending engines	6 conning tower	

the boat has lost its buoyancy at the surface, it has also no buoyancy at any given depth, and the risk is thus very great of suddenly descending beyond a safe depth. Further, by this method they relied upon some mechanical means for ascending by ejecting water. In case such mechanical means failed the boat would be lost . . .[1]

It is easy enough, now, to see how wrong Nordenfelt was, but taking a very large steel cylinder under water in those days, when the public mind was still accustoming itself to steel ships floating on the surface, was a daunting prospect. Nordenfelt's timidity, amounting to more than justifiable prudence, contrasts sharply with Holland's more courageous and pragmatic approach.

Submergence was therefore achieved by two downhaul propellers which overcame a constant buoyancy of between 600 and 800lb. The downhaul screws were driven by separate 6hp three-cylinder steam-engines with the cylinders in star formation around the crank and able to start from any position. A counterpoise weight worked against sea pressure to regulate the position of the steam valve on these engines to shut it off if the safe depth was exceeded. The boat would then rise by natural buoyancy until the sea pressure decreased to a point where the valves reopened to admit more steam to the downhaul propellers.

There were diving rudders at the bows of *Nordenfelt I* but no stern planes. Again, in this, the boat was radically different to Holland's designs. The bow diving rudders could be worked by yet another engine and they, too, were automatic. By the action of a plumb weight, according to the inventor, 'they were always held in the horizontal position, and therefore, should the boat for any cause tend to take a direction other than the horizontal, these rudders will immediately bring the boat back to the horizontal position.' Basically this system resembled Whitehead's 'secret' for controlling the depth of his torpedoes but he would not have been flattered by Nordenfelt's complicated and ineffective imitation. Anyway, it is certain that this gear would never have worked in the submarine which, at best, could only make two knots submerged – quite insufficient for the planes right forward to take effect.

The boat was surfaced either by shutting off steam to the downhaul screws or pumping water from the main ballast tank or by using steam pressure (if enough was left) to blow out the main ballast. Secondary armament was provided by a one-inch Nordenfelt gun on the deck just forward of the conning tower: it was to be fired by the captain who was a busy man in *Nordenfelt I*.

Sea trials at Landskrona in 1885 attracted thirty-nine distinguished spectators from the major European naval powers, Japan and, surprisingly, Mexico. Nordenfelt's contacts were worldwide. The best that can be said was that the boat was not lost during the demonstration. It succeeded in passing underneath the *Edda* which had the observers on board but the longest period dived was only five minutes and then the boat hit the bottom. Nobody was impressed. Nor did the ability of the three-man crew to remain shut up in the cylinder for six hours persuade the assembled company that this was a war-worthy vessel. Lord Sydenham of Combe was moved to write in *The Times*[2]:

> It is certain that the Nordenfelt boat, as at present existing, will effect no revolution: but it seems equally clear that we shall shortly have to face possibilities which we have hitherto been able to neglect. Scientific experiment, in other words money judiciously employed, will enable us to hold our own in any future development of submarine warfare.

So far as conservative England was concerned Lord Sydenham was being unduly optimistic.

What living conditions were like underway can only be imagined. The *Nordenfelt*s became bigger but by no means better as time went on. Giant three-inch diameter candles provided a glimmer of light but the heat and humidity were almost unbearable, and the briquette coal-fired boiler, with carbon monoxide escaping in significant quantities through the furnace door to mix with coal-dust in the heavy atmosphere, together with an ever-increasing carbon dioxide level must quickly have made conditions thoroughly unpleasant by any standards. Garrett himself was once put out of action for three weeks after being gassed and if, as seems likely, carbon monoxide was principally to blame it may well have contributed towards his premature death later. The long-term effects of carbon monoxide on submariners have only recently been understood; precautions against poisoning have to be taken even in modern diesel-electric submarines which have comparatively few internal exhaust leaks.

However, the operation of these boats submerged was so exciting that mere breathing difficulties were scarcely noticeable. The principle method of diving a Nordenfelt boat was ingenious. To submerge, the furnace was shut down, the telescopic funnel lowered and the funnel flap-valve was sealed (a foretaste of the notorious 'K' boats built towards the end of World War I). The ballast tank, a four-ton affair amidships, was

The Lamm engine of a Turkish Nordenfelt before the sections, shipped out from England, were reassembled at Constantinople in 1888.

flooded and the boat now settled into the water at rest with the crew fervently hoping she would do so on an even keel. With only the conning tower still showing above water and with a positive buoyancy of about one quarter of a ton remaining the craft was then clawed fully under by the 'descending' propellers which, on *Nordenfelt I*, were on either side of the hull amidships but on later models were positioned at either end in faired recesses.

Whatever its shortcomings *Nordenfelt I* was bought by the Royal Hellenic Navy in 1886 for no readily apparent reason but the shady figure of Mr (later Sir) Basil Zaharoff, the 'Mystery man of Europe', was in the background as agent for the sale. He was a most persuasive personality. The submarine reached Piraeus safely whither the

68 | Duke of Edinburgh, flying his flag in HMS *Temeraire*, sent a young officer, Sydney Eardley-Wilmot, to investigate. He had little to report other than 'she had some ingenious qualities, one being a greater difficulty to submerge than to come to the surface, reversing the procedure in early submarine boats.'[3] The ultimate fate of *Nordenfelt I* is not known but the £9000 which Greece paid for her was undoubtedly wasted. This, though, was not the view taken by Lieutenant-General Sir Andrew Clarke in England: he strongly recommended, well out of his military depth, that the British Government should purchase one of Nordenfelt's boats at the same price 'for the protection of important strategic ports abroad, and in preference to a large expenditure on land fortifications and a corresponding increase of military personnel'.[4] Strategists today may care to note this extraordinary and, at the time, unremarked example of the Army favouring naval schemes in the interests of economy. Despite Sir Andrew the Greek Government was thereafter very cautious about submarines. It did not attempt to acquire another until 1911.

Nordenfelt Boats for Turkey

While Garrett and Nordenfelt were pursuing their plans with international ambitions it was widely rumoured that Russia was acquiring a huge fleet of fifty midget submarines. The purpose of this large flock of tiny boats was by no means clear. Anyway the Tsarevitch changed his mind after witnessing some trials and the craft were ignominiously converted into pontoons and buoys. However, Turkey was alarmed by the supposed threat and, following the unprofitable visit to Holland in America, the Turkish Admiralty hastily decided to order two Nordenfelt submarines which were to be built in England. They were constructed at Chertsey on the peaceful River Thames populated by swans and ducks disturbed, normally, by no more than peaceful sculls and punts.

The two boats, *Abdul Medjid* and *Abdul Hamid*, were shipped in sections to Constantinople for reassembly under the now commissioned Com-

The Russian Nordenfelt 1887

1 descending engine	9 funnels
2 beds	10 stokehold
3 stove	11 passageway
4 ballast tanks	12 compressor
5 conning tower	13 spare torpedo
6 main engine	14 torpedo tubes
7 coal shoot	15 torpedo door
8 boilers	16 vertical propellers

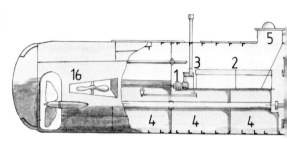

mander Garrett's expert supervision. Only the *Abdul Medjid*, nicknamed the 'Whale Ship', was put together and completed. The Turkish boat was half as long again as *Nordenfelt I* and the steam engine was a good deal more powerful, offering theoretical speeds of ten knots on the surface and five knots submerged. The armament consisted of two internal torpedo tubes vertically mounted, and two one-inch guns. Such a vessel must have seemed to the Turkish Government an attractive and powerful addition to its forces. Certainly it was better (on paper) than anything that the Greeks or Russians had so far recruited to their fleets.

The 'Whale Ship' was, to say the least, a vessel fraught with interest at sea. Captain P W D'Alton, representing Nordenfelt and at one time Chief Engineer to the Central London Railway (the Lamm Fireless Locomotive connection), witnessed the trials:

She had the fault of all submarine boats, viz, a total lack of longitudinal stability . . . the moment she left the horizontal position the water in her boiler and tanks surged forward and backwards and increased the angle of inclination. She was perpetually working up and down like a scale beam, and no human

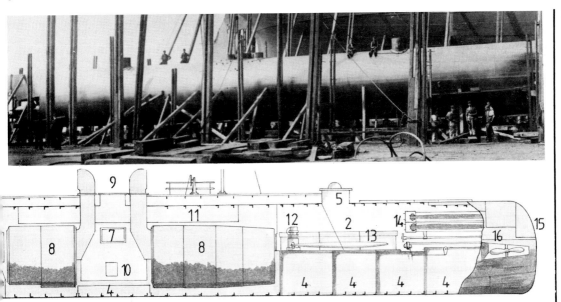

TOP *Nordenfelt IV*, destined for Russia, under construction at the Barrow Shipbuilding Company (later Vickers) in 1887. This boat underwent trials at Southampton, mostly over the Mother-bank Shoal in the presence of numerous British and foreign officers. In light trim she made 14 knots and was compared favourably with torpedo-boats. *Vickers*

vigilance could keep her on an even keel for half a minute at a time. Once, and we believe only once, she fired a torpedo, with the result that she as nearly as possible stood up vertically on her tail and proceeded to plunge to the bottom stern first.

It was a fair description of a Nordenfelt boat's faults but obstinacy, pique, politics and crafty finance militated against lessons learned in bringing about any radical changes in the notorious Nordenfelt design.

Shortly afterwards, all hands were nearly lost. 'Mr Garrett', according to D'Alton, 'was in the little conning tower. The boat was being slowly submerged, an operation of the utmost delicacy, before a committee of Ottoman officers when a boat came alongside without warning. Her wash let a considerable quantity of water down the conning tower, the lid of which was not closed, and the submarine boat instantly began to sink like a stone. Fortunately Mr Garrett got the lid closed just in time and the Engineer, without waiting for orders, blew some ballast out. It was an exceedingly narrow escape.'

Not surprisingly the Turkish Navy was unable to find volunteers to form a crew for the unpredictable vessel. All the trials were carried out with Commander Garrett wearing a red fez as was proper for an officer appointed to the Ottoman Navy – even if he had an English crew.

The Greeks had paid up without a murmur for their own valueless submarine but it was only with the greatest difficulty that money was wrested from the Sultan's Treasury for the 'Whale Ship' and her sister which absolutely refused to perform as promised. In the end the cash was handed over but, reading between the lines of various accounts, it looks very much as if the infidel Reverend Commander George William Garrett, BA, Pasha fled westwards to Christian sanctuary just in time to avoid retribution: the Turkish police were perhaps feeling at his clerical collar.

Years afterwards, in July 1909, a sad little article appeared in the English Press[5]:

70 | A Turkish Submarine

Amongst other oddities to be disposed of shortly by the Turkish Government is one of the oldest submarines in existence. It has been reposing in a weather-beaten shed in the Golden Horn for more than a quarter of a century. It is literally dropping to pieces from rust and neglect, whilst the grass is growing knee-deep around it. It never really saw active service, as it made but one trip after its purchase by the Government. On that occasion, it distinguished itself by making a premature dive not far from the spot where it is now resting, remaining under water with its crew for many hours. The Turkish Admiralty were never able to get together another crew to face the dangers of the new submarine.

Even the attempts to sell the relic failed. The rusty remains of *Abdul Medjid* and *Abdul Hamid* were still there when the German Military Mission went to Constantinople in 1914.

Nordenfelt IV

Undismayed by increasingly obvious failures Garrett and Nordenfelt put their heads together for yet another boat, this time even larger with a length of 125 feet. The designed diving depth was doubled at 100 feet. *Nordenfelt IV* displaced 245 tons submerged, latent steam was again used and the engine power, with a four-crank double compound unit developing 1200hp at 15 knots, was quadrupled. Nine separate diving tanks held the 35 tons of water required to submerge: the inventors had at last realised that divided tanks were the answer to the surging water that had made the first boats so unstable. The obvious market for the improved design was Russia where the Minister for Coast Defence had been interested in submarine boats for several years and had latterly come close to adopting the plans of an engineer remembered chiefly for the impossible English spelling of his name – Drzewiecki. The Russians

Commander the Reverend George William Garrett Pasha, holding only to his scholastic credentials, became a visiting tutor when he finally abandoned submarines.

had very little idea of what they wanted so the last and largest Nordenfelt boat was built 'on spec' at the Barrow Shipbuilding Company's Works (later Vickers) and launched in March 1887, some thirteen years before the Royal Navy elected to risk going underwater.

The boat got off to a bad start. As soon as she slid into the water it was obvious that somebody had made a serious error in calculating the trim: she settled heavily by the stern, drawing 9 feet aft and only 4 feet 6 inches forward. Garrett suffered a kind of seizure and was laid up for six months with 'brain-fever'. The mistake was rectified by adding ballast forward but the extra weight robbed the boat of speed. The upper part of the turtle-back and the two conning towers were plated with one-inch steel, the implication being that the boat was not expected to go into action fully submerged.

The new Nordenfelt had a range of 1000 miles, at the most economical speed, for which she carried eight tons of coal. The conning towers had heavy glass domes for all-round vision and the forward tower contained a depth gauge, inclinometer and a compass which was not compensated for deviation due to the vessel's inherent changeable magnetism. There were nine men in the crew and speaking tubes were provided for internal communication to avoid any movement which might upset the delicate trim. There was a bunk for each man and a primitive galley. Illumination was afforded, through a glass darkly, by candles and oil lanterns which did nothing to improve the atmosphere when the hatches were screwed down.

The craft was demonstrated on the surface at the Spithead Review a few months after the launch and the Tsar was much taken with her. More or less on a whim he made up his mind to buy. For some reason he did not demand proof of her capabilities submerged. Presumably the Russian Navy would be content to contemplate her as a semi-submersible torpedo-boat. The low silhouette certainly made the boat practically invisible and when underway at full speed the minimal superstructure, painted a dull grey, was actually below the bow-wave. As a target Nordenfelt calculated she offered only one-thirteenth the visible area of a first-class torpedo-boat.

It took some time to complete negotiations for the sale and it was not until November 1888 that Nordenfelt IV set off for Kronstadt escorted by the yawl Lodestar. Unhappily, navigation, despite the escort's name, was not the crew's strong point. They either mistook the lights they saw or their bearings were hopelessly wrong. En route to the Baltic the boat ran aground off Jutland on an ebb tide. Judging by the recollections of John W Garrett, the inventor's son, the ill-fated voyage may have taken a turn for the worse after calling in at the Dutch port of Amsterdam where two of the crew members, Jim Arm and 'Bosun George' made young John walk the plank 'after sampling the sweet champagne of that town'.[6] Although the submarine was refloated two weeks later the Russians refused to pay for the wreck. The insurance company settled with the owners, the Naval Construction and Armament Company, but that was no comfort to Garrett.

At this point Garrett and Nordenfelt parted. Nordenfelt produced two more designs for Germany in 1891 but these also failed: he continued his career in warlike machinery of one kind and another but he lost interest in submarines. The adaptable Garrett, too, had had enough. His money was gone, the Swedish entrepreneur was gone, and the Church showed no signs of receiving him back into the fold. He emigrated to America where he served with the United States Army Engineers during the Spanish–American War. He died, practically destitute, in New York City on 26 February 1902 at the early age of fifty. It was a sad and unjustly obscure end to the career of the brilliant, erratic curate who built Britain's first workable submarine.[7]

For Garrett and for all those priestly submarine inventors who turned their eyes down into the sea rather than lifting them up unto the hills with the Psalmist, a fitting epitaph can surely be found in the favourite old hymn:

Praise to the holiest in the height
And in the depth be praise . . .

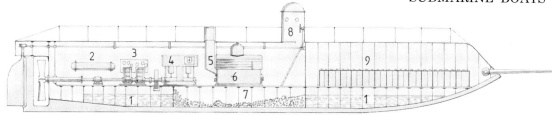

Alstitt's Submarine

1 ballast tanks
2 air flask
3 electric motor
4 steam engine
5 funnel
6 boiler
7 coal bunkers
8 conning tower
9 storage batteries

Chapter Seven
Weird and Wonderful

Besides the principal submarine inventors in the latter part of the nineteenth century there were numerous others, whose work – weird and wonderful as it was – has been entirely forgotten. Some bordered undoubtedly on the lunatic fringe but others deserved more serious consideration than they received. Some of the ideas put forward were rejected out of hand but, especially in the light of twentieth century developments, they were by no means entirely absurd even if they make light reading today.

A Dual Propulsion System

One particular inventor, the American engineer Alstitt, has never been given due acknowledgement for a design which in 1863, many years before anybody else thought of it, had two means of propulsion – steam on the surface and electricity under the water. Holland's *Plunger* (1897) and Monsieur Laubeuf's *Narval* (1899) unfairly took joint credit for the first mixed propulsion systems. In 1863 the Civil War was raging; Abraham Lincoln proclaimed the Abolition of Slavery in January, Stonewall Jackson was mortally wounded by his own troops by mistake in May and history books had little space to spare for lesser known innovations. In any case the Alstitt boat's diving rudders were at the bows rather than abaft the propeller (a recurring fault) and they rendered the invention unmanageable. The creature became extinct almost as soon as it was born at the city of Mobile where McClintock was testing his Confederate boats with more success and subsequent fame.[1]

Free-running torpedoes were not conceived when Alstitt built the craft and his armament

Dr J Lacomme's 1869 proposal, encouraged by the Emperor Napoleon III, for a submarine cross-Channel railway. The submarine, which was to have a powerful searchlight to light the way, could detach from the truck and surface if required. The motive power was to be compressed air and a telephone wire was to maintain contact with either side of the Channel.

consisted of large watertight cases of gunpowder arranged along each side of the craft. They were secured by iron chains connected to the interior. The cases were buoyant and, when released, they rose to the surface, hopefully underneath the ship being attacked, at which moment they were detonated electrically. For attacking a ship underway it was intended to scatter contact mines in its path: the economical Alstitt assured his backers that if the mines failed to explode they could be recovered and used again.

Victorian Oddities

Disregarding the strenuous and realistic efforts in France from 1862 onwards, which have Chapter 8 to themselves, the next odd submersible was Winan's 250-foot semi-submarine launched on the Thames in 1864. She never went beyond the trial stage but had one memorable feature: she was equipped with a propeller forward to cut a way ahead so that the normal propeller at the stern 'would drive the vessel into the vacuum created by the one in the bows'[2]. The same principle was to be employed on the Russian ice-breaker *Ermack* in 1898.

The well-known Isaac Peral, with his excellent battery-driven boat (extinguished by government bureaucracy in 1886) was not the first Spanish submarine inventor. He was preceded, by some twenty years, by Narcisco Monturiol and Cosmo Garcia. These two engineers built *El Ictineo* at Barcelona in 1862. The weapon system was claimed as novel but it really went back to Bushnell's *Turtle* nearly a century before. Besides a cannon (with which the crew displayed 'excellent marksmanship . . . as would be on land or another ship'[3]) she carried a steam-powered auger at the bow for drilling holes underwater in enemy hulls. The gigantic swordfish made sixty dives without mishap but the project petered out, probably through lack of government interest, although it was 'worthy of the notice of both sailors and soldiers'[4].

In England Garrett may have been inspired by a certain Mr Jos Jones, a shipbuilder of Liverpool, who was 'known for his advanced and practical views upon certain questions connected with naval warfare'[5]. In 1877 Mr Jones built a small model and claimed it could 'move forwards or backwards in a straight line at any level and, starting out of sight of the enemy, lodge a torpedo [mine] under the bottom of an enemy ship'[6]. These practical proposals went no further than the model and nothing more was heard from Mr Jones. In the same year Mr A A Olivier patented plans for a fish-shaped boat with a glass conning tower. It had wings instead of diving rudders and they folded back into the hull when not in use but, far more revolutionary, the craft was to be jet-propelled by means of gases generated from the ignition of high explosives, which blasted out through a tube at the stern. Happily, Olivier's design never left the drawing board. . . . In 1879 a Mr Leggo suggested an equally inventive but less hazardous method of propulsion. Leggo's submarine was to move through the water on the principle of a switch-back. Looking like a large kite it was tilted by means of a moveable weight. The idea was for it to slide gracefully down an inclined curve to a predetermined depth at which point gases produced by heating liquid ammonia with hydrocarbon were to be admitted into a large airtight mattress. The machine would then ascend, the gas would be released at the top of the trajectory and another downward glide would commence.[7] The proposal was, incidentally, entirely serious.

Not everybody felt it necessary to design boats which could manoeuvre below the surface. There was still a good deal to be said for a semi-submersible whose vulnerable body could be submerged or partially submerged to avoid retribution from gunfire. Messrs Berkley and Hotchkiss (who later invented the famous quick-firing gun) had a particularly ingenious and simple notion for attaching two long cork floats on either side of a steam-driven craft. The floats were on adjustable arms. In the fully surfaced position they were depressed so that the vessel rode high in the water but they could very easily be elevated

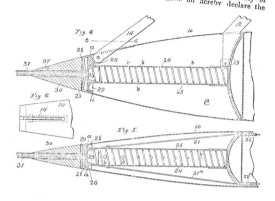

Nº 12,398

A.D. 1891

Date of Application, 21st July, 1891—Accepted, 30th Jan., 1892

COMPLETE SPECIFICATION.

[Communicated from abroad by THOMAS HAMPTON THOMAS, of No. 23, Beaver Street, New York, in the United States of America.]

Improvements in Submerged Boats for Carrying and Discharging Torpedoes.

I, OLIVER IMRAY of No. 28 Southampton Buildings in the County of Middlesex, Fellow of the Institute of Patent Agents do hereby declare the

One of many submarine patents taken out in the latter part of the nineteenth century. The majority were sensible but few came to fruition.

allowing all but the funnel, conning tower and air intakes to drop down below the surface.

Plans for the next submarine proper were patented in July 1881 by Monsieur Génoud. It was to have a gas engine worked by hydrogen and obtained from combining iron filings with sulphuric acid. A top speed of five knots was claimed for this method of propulsion and the inventor explained patiently that high speed was undesirable because it would be dangerous in the vicinity of rocks which would not be visible owing to the impenetrability of water to the human sight. Nothing came of the machine. Another fantasy was conceived by the respected French engineer, Monsieur Boucher: he provided no fewer than three means of propulsion: a screw beneath the keel amidships, automatically feathered oars and a tail fin à la poisson at the stern. Gloomily realising that collisions were all too likely he provided four underwater telescopes, one fitted in the bows, one astern, one for looking upwards and the last for examining the bottom of the sea. If despite these all-round look-out arrangements a collision did occur powerful spring buffers were fitted at the bows and beneath the keel – a boon to careless submariners. There was a large cannon at the stern; and above the rudder 'at the discretion of the constructor' torpedo tubes or other weapons could be placed in or around the hull. Boucher was a little vague but he had the attractive idea of extracting air from sea water by 'energetic pulverisation' through perforated metal plates: in other words he seems to have conceived the principle of osmosis which is used in submarines today not for creating fresh air but as an alternative to the distillation of fresh water.[8]

Professor J H L Tuck came next with his *Peacemaker*. The suggestive name underlined the insistence of many submarine innovators that their vessels would prevent war. It was to be the theme of Holland's own pronouncements (when he had parted company with the Fenians) and he took careful note of the *Peacemaker* which was constructed by the Submarine Motor Company of New York in 1885. The boat looked, in fact, very like Holland's own designs: she was porpoise-shaped and had diving rudders forward and aft but they were unable to keep depth accurately because the gearing made their operation too slow. Nor did the pilot, standing with his head in a little dome with glass windows a foot above the superstructure, have an inclinometer or depth gauge to help him judge the depth and amount of horizontal rudder angle required. Because of these limitations the *Peacemaker* was intended to keep a constant level keel. Holland remarked contemptuously that this was the only way of changing depth considered safe at the time by those who should have known better. Tuck and his contemporaries can scarcely be blamed: it needed a lot of courage to tilt the bows downwards to gain depth. The engine in this not insignificant vessel was fireless and based on the discovery that caustic soda could be used to produce heat for generating steam. It certainly worked and the 30-foot craft was capable of six knots on the surface and five knots submerged. Despite dramatically uncertain depth-keeping the *Peacemaker* passed beneath the keels of two steamers during trials and approached within ten feet of a tug without being seen. However, the Army and Navy officers who witnessed the demonstrations from Fort Monroe were not convinced either by her handling qualities or by the electrically detonated charges which she carried instead of torpedoes.

Soon afterwards (the patent was dated 13 April 1886) Messrs Rundle and Allen devised a human torpedo which allowed practically any fearless diver to propel it either by using his legs, as if he were swimming, or by rotating a paddle wheel. While supplied with air from two canisters attached to a frame he was supposed to dive under the hull of a ship, attach a time-fused mine and make his escape as best he could.

Another water-jet craft, the *Hyponeon* (from the Greek for 'swimming under') was devised by Monsieur Toureau in the same year. Depth-keeping was automatic and propulsion in either direction was obtained by passing water from one end of the vessel to the other through a rotary pump which was, of course, reversible. It did not work.

A Harrowing Experience

One submarine almost succeeded in stirring the stolid British Admiralty's imagination in 1888. This was the *Nautilus*, christened in honour of Fulton's boat of 1800[9] by Messrs Ash and Campbell. It was unusual in having two screws driven by Edison–Hopkinson 13hp electric motors supplied at 104 volts from two sets of 52 storage cells. The cigar-shaped 60-foot hull was strongly made of steel rivetted to circular frames 1 foot 9 inches apart giving a maximum safe depth of 50 feet. Its weakness lay in relying upon four cylinders on either side which could be extended or retracted to alter the boat's volume and hence its buoyancy. This was a similar scheme to the idea patented by Garrett in October 1878 but for this large boat, displacing 50 tons submerged, the cylinders were much too clumsy to catch or keep a perfect trim

despite Mr Campbell's assurance that his boat 'might be kept for hours or days in any position without using a fraction of the stored propelling power'.[10]

A number of important people were invited to witness a trial in the deep-water dock at Tilbury: they included Lord Charles Beresford and Sir William White, Chief Constructor of the Navy. Fortunately there was no room for all the visitors on board as well as the six-man crew. Two of those who prudently elected to remain on the jetty were able to tell what happened with more coherence than those who had been on board.

The boat was all ready to dive and as soon as the hatch had been shut and clipped the mechanism for withdrawing the cylinders was set in motion. Only ten inches of the upperworks were visible above the surface at full buoyancy and now the whole boat rapidly disappeared down into the basin where she thudded onto the bottom at a depth of 25 feet. So far, so good. One of the spectators ashore began to get anxious after an hour or so 'knowing that the supply of air in the boat was not great'. What had happened? After inspecting the interior the order went to 'out cylinders'. They would not move. 'More hands to the winches'. Still no result.[11] The boat was firmly stuck in the thick gluey mud which was also covering the cylinder faces and making them very stiff to operate. Then somebody, probably the Chief Constructor himself, had an inspiration. All hands, including the distinguished passengers, were ordered to take off their coats and rush backwards and forwards as a body. The ruse succeeded, as it has done on many occasions since in similar circumstances. Suddenly the mud released its grip, the cylinders slid out, and the *Nautilus* sprang to the surface. The boat's engineer, entirely unconcerned by the white faces below, flung open the hatch and announced excitedly to his friends ashore that they were going to submerge again. He was forcibly pulled down by his legs to make way for those, including the Director of Naval Construction, who had no wish to repeat the experiment.

The minor accident was enough to doom the submarine. Thirteen years later Sir William White earnestly advised the Inspecting Captain of Submarine Boats, Captain Reginald Bacon, 'never to go below water'[12] as a result of his harrowing experience in a craft that Ash and Campbell had warranted 'extra special safe'.

The general feeling was nicely summed up by Rear-Admiral Sir Sydney Eardley-Wilmot in a masterpiece of understatement: 'As submarine boats have so often to lie on the bottom, any liability to remain there unwillingly must be avoided.'[13] A considerable amount of prejudice was set up within the Royal Navy's Constructive Department which, combined with strong opposition from the surface admirals, served to frustrate any further investigation into the submarine field by the Royal Navy on its own account.

Hence, Waddington's *Porpoise* built soon after the *Nautilus* found no favour although she was a sound and serviceable vessel throughout with the sole exception of her dependence upon vertical propellers in upright shafts forward and aft for diving and keeping depth. Two men were sufficient to navigate the craft and operate the

It is unfair to include the Spanish Navy's Lt Isaac Peral (1851-95) in this 'Weird and Wonderful' chapter because his boat, (built 1886-9) showed great promise. The principal weapon was a single torpedo-tube for Schwartzkopf torpedoes.

machinery which was almost entirely electric. A 500 ampere-hour battery was capable of driving the boat at six knots for ten hours but there was no way of recharging the battery on board. In this respect she was significantly astern of Mr George Baker's designs at Chicago which threatened at one time to compete seriously with Holland's proposals. In Baker's boat the steam engine could be clutched to drive the electric motor as a dynamo. Another feature of this boat has been revived today in commercial 'mini-subs' which have very similar arrangements for tilting the propellers amidships to drive the craft in any required direction. The Editor of the *Western Electrician* accompanied the inventor and his foreman, Mr Goddard, on trials on 20 May 1892. He reported[14] as follows:

Having closed the conning tower Mr Goddard examined all the machinery with great care. A few

78

moments after, the inventor said briefly: 'Let in some water, Goddard – there – now she begins – wait a minute and we shall sink.' All of which orders were accompanied by rapid clangs on a bell and the flapping of the waves on the outside; all these things made one forget the personal danger . . .

The reporter was plunged in reflection at the wonders around him and the novelty of his experience when Baker touched him on the shoulder to point out that he had flooded in more water and that the boat was now slowly sinking. Putting his head and shoulders into the conning tower the guest noted that the water was level with the centre of the look-out glass and quickly rising. He took a last glimpse of the outside world as Baker ordered, 'A little more water ballast, Goddard.' It is clear from the newspaper account that the dive was made standing for 'the last instruction to Goddard was the final order and the propellers being started the vessel commenced her voyage beneath the waves at full speed'.

Some Wild Ideas

Yet another novel feature was introduced in a submarine boat proposed by Mirissimo Barbazo de Souza of Pernambuco. It was constructed in three sections, each entirely independent of the others, so that in the event of accidental flooding the damaged portion could be jettisoned like a frightened lizard leaving its tail behind. As the century drew to its close inventors from all over the world flourished a plethora of designs, some wild, some outrageous and some that were no more than paper plagiarisms, for patents afforded little real protection. Amongst the contributors was Dr Sebastien Lacavalerie, a dentist from Caracas, Venezuela, with a long revolving-worm-screw wrapped spirally around the entire hull. Then there was Mr F W Poole of England on whose boat the ballast tank doubled as a balloon for aerial flight when required; and Mr H Middleton, also British, who envisaged flying through the water on bird-like wings. Amongst sundry hazardous inventions Middleton was well up in front with a gunpowder engine. However, like so many of the early submarine inventors Middleton had the germ of at least one futurism amongst his crackpot notions: if a boat were to dive too deep the ballast tanks would automatically be blown out by gunpowder gas. High pressure air is no use for this purpose at any depth and much research has recently been devoted to devising a means of blowing main ballast tanks chemically in a very similar way.

One of the most interesting, and currently topical, suggestions at the turn of the century was for submarine passenger conveyances across the English Channel. They might, it was thought, be preferable and certainly cheaper than a bridge or tunnel. A writer in the magazine *Truth*[15] had this to say about the scheme:

. . . such a vessel might have her propulsive power outside her, and be worked like an electric tram. Some years ago, when the idea of a railway bridge across the Channel was first mooted, I remember asking an engineering friend of mine why the train should not run on the bed of the Channel instead of on a bridge over it. He laughed at the idea, and raised various difficulties which seemed to me unworthy of his profession. However, if engineers now see nothing impossible in a submarine boat for the Channel service 'worked like an electric tram', my idea may be realised yet, in a slightly improved shape. This submarine conveyance, I take it, would be attached to a

The Venezuelan dentist Lacavalerie's 1894 submarine design. An outer hull revolved round an inner one with crew and machinery.

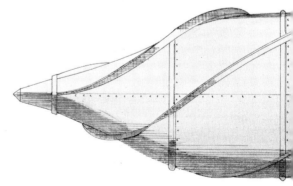

cable, which would serve both to direct its course and to supply it with motive power. Seeing that a very high power could be applied under these conditions, and that we already hear of submarines doing their eight or ten knots, there seems no reason why the boat I have in mind should not, in time, equal the average speed of a Channel steamer. I look forward, therefore, to being able at an early date to cross the Channel in an hour or so, even in the worst weather, without any more discomfort than is experienced in the 'Twopenny Tube'. Neither do I see why there should be any more risk. There are possibilities of nasty accidents in tube railways from which the submarine car would be exempt, and it would be easy to provide for bringing the car to the surface in the event of a breakdown. Moreover, there are considerable risks attached to the navigation of the surface of the sea in all weathers, and from these the submarine 'worked like an electric tram' would be entirely free. We may even get across the Atlantic in this way – in time.

It is easy to laugh at the quaint proposals and dead-end designs of a century ago and it is difficult to think that all of them were entirely serious: but the cranks of yesterday would clearly recognise a good many developments in submarine technology today.

After 134 fruitless (and often ill-starred) submarine trials in Russia, the German lathe turner Wilhelm Bauer ran out of money and wearily left the submarine world in 1858. His efforts to raise 100,000 thalers (£15,000) for this coast defence submarine failed. The idea was to manoeuvre so as to place the cup containing explosive material under the ship to be attacked and then ignite the charge.

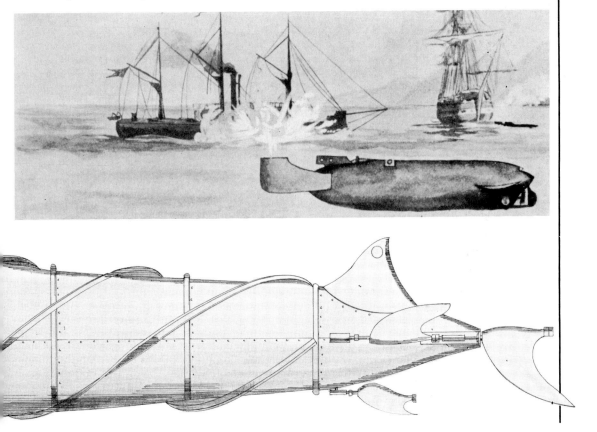

80

Le Phoque, one of 20 *Alose* class ordered in a crash building programme and completed in 1903. Displacing 68 tons, with a crew of one officer and four men, submarines of this class were much cheaper than the larger boats and cost only 365,000 francs (£14,616). One of the two drop-collar torpedoes can be seen on the starboard bow.

Chapter Eight

France and Fulton take the Plunge

Robert Fulton was a man of many parts. Born on a farm in Pennsylvania on 14 November 1765, he started his working life as a jeweller's apprentice and then turned his hand to portrait and landscape painting which earned him enough money, by the time he was twenty-two, to make the crossing to England where he intended studying art. He should have studied the English language first: his spelling ('realy', 'minuets' for 'minutes', 'infalibility', 'extriordinary') was appalling. But by the time of the French Revolutionary War, Fulton, who had earlier shown a strong bent for engineering and invention, was involved in more aggressive matters stemming, strangely enough, from his frequently expressed views on international disarmament.

His intensely warlike activities with 'plunging boats', mines and other infernal devices contrast oddly with his professed concern for universal peace, freedom of the seas and free trade. But Fulton, to his own way of thinking, was being entirely logical. He argued that the world's troubles, which were not so different from those of today, were caused by armies and navies, especially the latter. These were the evil means by which the Old World exercised its power and held the New World in subjection. Further, Fleets of War, whether designed for dominance or defence, demanded heavy taxation and enforced recruitment, both of which were anathema to Fulton. The thing to do, he argued, was to get rid of navies altogether. The great attraction of this policy was, of course, that it would save America, which was decidedly short of ships, from having to build and pay for a proper navy of her own. To achieve these desirable ends Fulton promised anybody who would listen that he would 'devote his whole attention to find out a means of destroying such engines of oppression'.

Gnôme **built at Cherbourg at a cost of 800,000 francs (£32,000) and launched 24 July 1902. The 185-ton boat carried four drop-collar torpedoes and had a design speed submerged of 9 knots. Her surface speed was 12.25 knots.**

The First *Nautilus*

Looking around for backers Fulton decided that France was the best bet. Niceties such as nationality did not at that time unduly hinder private citizens from passing to and fro for commerce or any other reason between countries at war with one another: during the next few years he was to travel unhindered between France and England. He arrived in Paris in 1797, staying at the home of Joel Barlow, the American Minister, to commence experiments with floating mines on the River Seine. The trials were not a great success but they were enough to persuade him that 'submarine bombs' carried by a suitable vehicle, which could only be a submersible, were the answer to the world's problems, providing there was enough money to develop such a machine. There can be little doubt that he had examined David Bushnell's work on the *Turtle* with care before leaving America and this gave him a head start with his designs which culminated in the *Nautilus*. The name was taken from the ocean mollusc with a shell of air-filled chambers which at that time was thought, wrongly, to use its webbed dorsal arms as sails.

On 13 December 1797 he wrote to the French Directory:

> Citizen Director,
>   Having taken great interest in all that would diminish the English Fleet, I have planned the construction of a mechanical engine, in which I have the greatest confidence, for the annihilation of this Navy. Some practise is, however, necessary to perfect the apparatus. The grandeur of this project has excited in me an ardour to share in a demonstration of this engine. To this end in order to save you all trouble, I have formed a company which will undertake the expense and carry out the work . . .

His terms were steep. 'The French Government', he demanded, must guarantee 'to pay the company of the *Nautilus* 4000 francs a gun for every English ship above forty guns which the inventor destroys, and 2000 francs a gun for every ship below forty guns, these sums to be paid within six months of

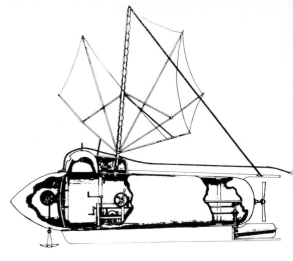

Robert Fulton's *Nautilus* from which so many subsequent submarines took their name.

the destruction of each ship.' A substantial success rate was implied.

Fulton was to retain the monopoly of the *Nautilus* design but the Government was at liberty to construct as many replicas of *Nautilus* as it pleased provided that 10,000 francs was paid for each. As a sop to patriotism Fulton went on to stipulate that the craft 'will not be used by the French Government against the United States, or at least the Americans must use them first against France before this stipulation is annulled'.

Certain important clauses in the letter were refused outright by the French Government and the money demanded was cut substantially. Moreover, the Minister of the Marine refused to recognise and commission a naval crew for the *Nautilus* as he and other French officers of the day agreed that such a method of waging war was unworthy of French honour. These high principles were not going to get in the way when it came to sending *Nautilus* into action, but the admirals did not themselves want to sully their hands.

The British *Naval Chronicle*, whose Editor appears to have had access to an efficient intelligence service, was fully *en accord* with the French admirals: 'it was revolting to every naval principle' and Fulton was a 'crafty, murderous ruffian'. His patrons were 'openly stooping from their lofty stations to superintend the construction of such detestable machines that promised destruction to maritime establishments.'[1] Submariners had to become accustomed to remarks like this in succeeding years and were to pay no more regard to them than Fulton did now. He pressed ahead as quickly as he could with his plans and *Nautilus* soon began to take shape in Rouen Dockyard.

The small submarine had little to commend itself as a weapon of war. One French admiral drawing on good French logic rather than expressing any moral preference said, 'Thank God, France still fights her battles on the surface, not beneath it.' Admiral le Pleville Pelly declared that his conscience would not allow him to have recourse to so terrible a weapon. The facts were, however, that although the little submarine marked a milestone, *Nautilus* was not a practical warship and was certainly not up to the standard of the surface vessels for which, later, Fulton became so justly famous. There was not much reason for anybody to suffer a bad conscience.

Launched in May 1800, *Nautilus* was 21 feet 4 inches long and 7 feet in diameter. She was built of copper on iron frames and, the first metal sub-

mersible, she had an estimated collapse depth of about 30 feet; Fulton wisely restricted dives to 25 feet. A folding mast with a collapsible curiously-shaped sail was hoisted on the surface and a two-bladed propeller, rotated by a handwheel, was capable of driving her at one or two knots submerged so long as the muscles of the crew held out. A bell-shaped conning tower with thick glass scuttles enabled the navigator to see where he was going when the craft was awash and a magnetic compass proved reasonably reliable under water. There were three ballast tanks. So far, apart from adopting a shape that is more familiar to modern submariners, Fulton had not done much to improve upon the barrel-like *Turtle*. His major contribution to the history of submarine design was to fit two 'inclined plane diving rudders' at the stern which could be elevated or depressed by thirty degrees from the horizontal: these were the first hydroplanes and they were placed to the best advantage.

The weapon which Fulton first proposed was very similar to Bushnell's. A spike was to be

Goubet's first submarine of 1885.

Goubet I 1885

1 trimming tank mechanism
2 conning tower
3 compressed air reservoirs
4 pumps
5 water ballast
6 wheel for moving propeller
   to port or starboard
7 motor
8 ballast control valve
9 mine and detonator
10 safety weight
11 accumulators
12 submerging batten
13 net cutter

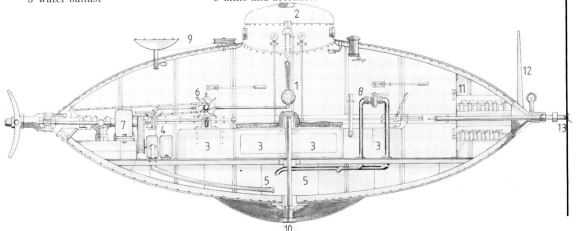

driven upwards into the target's hull and this in turn was attached to a delayed-action explosive charge. It was also possible to tow a 'torpedo' to foul an enemy's cables, drift up against the ship's side and detonate.

It did not take long to build the boat. The first trial took place on the Seine off the *Hôtel des Invalides* and Fulton cunningly used the current to advantage so that in running submerged and awash he was able to make it appear that *Nautilus* could cover a considerable distance very quickly. The onlookers crowding the banks cheered wildly. It seems probable that *Nautilus* scarcely submerged at all; it is more likely that Fulton managed to dip intermittently just beneath the surface. He cannot have remained blind for long or, with the substantial current adding to his speed, he would have risked hitting the bank and other vessels despite the compass. This part of the Seine was probably chosen not only because it afforded a good viewpoint in the heart of Paris but because, conveniently, the depth of water at the greatest was a safe 25 feet.

The American inventor was encouraged by the reception he received in France and it was arranged that *Nautilus* should be taken to Brest where the craft made a fully submerged run lasting between seven and eight minutes. Again Fulton took her only just below the surface, probably with slight positive buoyancy overcome by the planes aft. A few days later, increasing his intrepid ship's company from one to three, Fulton took the boat down by means of ballast and diving rudders to the bottom at maximum diving depth. The crew remained in total darkness (candles would have burned too much oxygen) for one hour. Later, a compressed air cylinder was installed to increase the endurance to one hour and forty minutes. But it was the extremely low speed and very limited range of *Nautilus* that finally dissuaded the French from following the venture any further. Napoleon did not believe the craft was any use and called Fulton a senseless fool.

Fulton Changes Sides

However on the other side of the Channel the British Government appreciated the dangers of an effective submarine, if one should ever be developed. It might well put the mighty Royal Navy out of business. Fulton, disgusted with the French, came to England unabashed at changing sides and still proclaiming lofty principles. Some nervous overtures were made to him and a deal may have been proposed to persuade the inventor to scrap his plans. The English need not, in fact, have worried despite the effective demonstration of a 'torpedo' against the brig *Dorothea* off Deal on 15 October 1805, six days before the Battle of Trafalgar. *Nautilus*, despite an honoured place in history, would never seriously have endangered

Goubet's second submarine launched at Cherbourg in 1889. Supposed to be very stable and carrying a 1.5-ton drop-weight for safety, the submarine had a hull thickness of 1in amidships which, absurdly, was claimed to allow the boat a safe diving depth of 1500 metres.

the British Fleet and, in any case, Fulton was soon too occupied with other matters to concern himself any longer with unprofitable underwater experiments.

Not that he admitted any interest in profit. Writing to Lord Grenville in 1804 he remarked, '. . . it had never been my intention to hide these inventions (torpedoes meaning mines) from the world on any consideration. For myself, I have ever considered the interest of America, free commerce . . . superior to all calculation of a pecuniary nature.' It sounds like sour grapes. Failing to find support in Europe Fulton returned disillusioned to his home country in 1806 where he devoted most of his considerable talents to the development of steam propulsion.

The Legacy of Fulton

Fulton's efforts in Europe were soon forgotten but the seeds were sown. They were carefully cultivated in France throughout the latter part of the nineteenth century. Until the early 1900s, when most people began to realise that submarines were an essential part of a balanced fleet, France was the only nation which was absolutely clear about their *raison d'être*. She was able to call upon some unusually brilliant inventors to serve the *Jeune Ecole* which was led, in the submarine world, by Admiral Aube and supported in print by the far-sighted journalist Gabriel Charmes. *Guerre de course*, the destruction, piecemeal, of merchant ships on the high seas, was the policy of the young French school. The British mercantile marine was, of course, the target: the Royal Navy itself could never be matched by conventional forces. While Aube wrote[2] in 1879 that armoured ships had had their day and a new navy was needed to fight a running battle and wage war against commerce, Charmes declared that giant battleships no longer reigned supreme but would be replaced by myriads of tiny craft, *la poussière navale*, mere specks of dust as others saw torpedo boats. It was a short step to deciding that submarines were the best possible vessels for a torpedo war. Admiral Aube, rightly revered by his contemporaries and by historians, was largely

Gymnote **in about 1899 after reconstruction.**

responsible, as Minister of the Navy, for founding the French Submarine Service which was so far advanced so early by comparison with other navies. It was not an easy course for the French to adopt and they had more than their fair share of oddities made even more odd by the notorious and lasting French predilection for complexity. Nothing that the French did equalled Holland's efforts but, if underwater war had come, France was for many years far better supplied with submarines than America or Britain. How effective the French submarines would have been is another matter but from the surface they appeared a formidable force.

Political jealousies were everywhere at work around the turn of the century. No views were objective then and it is not easy to be objective now; but today we can at least make a more educated guess about the real value of those first French submarines. The important thing is to realise that the French, by now, were embarked upon a policy that depended upon torpedoes of one kind or another as the principal weapons. The craft that carried them needed protection from the huge numbers of guns, large and small, that battleships and cruisers carried. Surprise was a significant factor in both offensive and defensive operations and speed was also essential to reach point-blank range where enemy guns could not depress and from which torpedoes were sure to hit. There was obviously no way of armouring small, fast craft although light protection might be afforded on vital parts. The sea itself was the best cloak and if a torpedo-boat could be at least partially submerged it stood a good chance of survival. There was no real need to submerge completely although the ability to do so would be useful in contributing to surprise. Semi-submersibles or more tactically flexible submersibles, operating primarily on the surface with a wide radius of action, were the best vessels for offensive strikes or for breaking a blockade. On the other hand, in coastal and harbour defence situations, true submarines, never surfacing to expose themselves at all (and sacrificing range

thereby), were preferable because an incoming enemy would be fully alert with only a small sea area to scan.

Looking back into the minds of Admiral Aube and his contemporaries these were the factors which led to France building three quite distinct types of underwater vessel: semi-submersibles, submersibles and submarines. Historians have been understandably confused ever since. The issues in France, too, were far from clear. There was much controversy about which type was best because, unfortunately, the aggressive submersibles were not good sea-boats although French submariners tried their best to prove their seaworthiness by making, for the day, quite long

The unfortunate *Farfadet*, launched 1901 and shown here after being salvaged following her sinking on 6 July 1905 (with the loss of 14 lives) due to the conning tower hatch being left open.

voyages in the relatively calm Mediterranean. Typically a French submersible had a buoyancy margin of only seven per cent on the surface and that was not enough to prevent their being washed over. In America, Holland's designs had a margin around seventeen per cent because he believed that submarines (by which, in French terms, he meant submersibles) should be major vessels of war capable of operating independently for extended periods with full freedom of action on the surface and submerged. In other words, Holland had in mind a much more formidable submarine boat than the French felt was necessary for their particular tasks.

Thus the French line of development led to steam and steam-electric propulsion for semi-submersibles and submersibles and to all-electric propulsion for submarines, the latter not (for a limited period) being dependent on the atmosphere. Strictly speaking the only submarines

today that qualify for the name are nuclear-propelled.

While an anonymous French officer vowed in the early 1900s that submarines would be ruthlessly used as commerce destroyers,[3] Lord Sydenham of Combe was convinced that 'the sentiment of the world in the twentieth century would not tolerate for a moment proceedings which had hitherto been associated with piracy in its blackest form. Considerations of humanity apart, there are strong reasons for believing that this relapse into savagery would not serve the purpose of the navy which had so far degraded itself.'[4] Whether tolerated by the world or not, German U-boats were to play havoc with commerce in both World Wars; but France never did engage in the sort of warfare which the *Jeune Ecole* envisaged. Nonetheless, from 1890 and for a quarter of a century France was numerically in the lead and she had laid the foundations for her underwater fleet well before that.

The French Submarine Pioneers

The first French submarines and their inventors have had so much written about them that they need only a brief reintroduction. The well-known French engineer Dupuy de Lôme conceived the first significant French submersible in the 1880s, the *Gymnote*. He was, like Fulton, a man of many parts although his design for an airship and his important work on the Panama Canal have been forgotten. He died before the submarine project could be executed but his good friend Gustave Zédé continued the work and, with sundry modifications, completed the 59-foot *Gymnote*. No fewer than 564 accumulators drove a 55hp electric motor which, at the full speed of 6 knots, rotated the propeller at the extraordinarily high rate of 2000 revolutions per minute.

Gymnote made her bow on 4 September 1888. A Paris newspaper[5] enthused:

She steered like a fish both as regards direction and depth: she mastered the desired depth with ease and exactness; at full power she attained the anticipated speed of from 9 to 10 knots [sic]; the lighting was excellent and there was no difficulty about heating. It was a strange sight to see the vessel skimming along the top of the water, suddenly giving a downward plunge with its snout to disappear with a shark-like wriggle of its stern, only to come up again at a distance and in an unlooked for direction. A few small matters connected with the accumulator had to be seen to, but they did not take a month.

Gymnote, reconstructed in 1898 with drop-collars, casing and a raised conning tower, was purely experimental; the 'unlooked for direction' noted by the Press was not a *ruse de guerre*; the boat was simply uncontrollable! However, enough was learned for Monsieur Barbey, now Minister of Marine, to order Monsieur Ramazzotti to draw up plans for a larger vessel to be named the *Gustave Zédé* after the inventor who, like de Lôme, had died prematurely. The *Zédé* was launched at Toulon on 1 June 1893. She was 159 feet in length and displaced 266 tons with a pressure hull of 'Roma' bronze, a non-magnetic metal which was thought to be an advantage in light of a superstition that torpedoes could be attracted to steel. More practically, bronze would not be attacked by sea water. Like *Gymnote* she was dependent on a large battery of cells for all-electric propulsion and she proved her range by journeying from Toulon to Marseilles, a distance of 41 miles, unaided. A single torpedo tube was installed with space for two reload Whitehead torpedoes.

The *Zédé* was quirky. She normally dived at an angle of about 5 degrees (with stern diving rudders) but was very liable to get out of control (probably due to free surface in the tanks). It was unfortunate that she proved to be especially capricious when the Committee of Experts was on board to judge her qualities. She plunged up and down at an angle of 30 to 35 degrees 'often throwing the poor gentlemen onto the floor'[6]. No less than six hydroplanes, three on each side, were subsequently added for better control but the *Zédé*'s behaviour was still alarming. Despite opposing claims from other countries, the *Zédé* was

probably the first submarine to have an effective periscope and an elevated conning tower with a light 'flying bridge' extension for surface watch-keepers to stand on.

Before the *Zédé* had finished her trials, which lasted for six long years, another boat was launched on 5 July 1899. This was the *Morse* and, at 118 feet with a displacement of 146 tons, she embodied the best points in *Gymnote* and *Zédé*. Monsieur Calmette, writing for the Paris *Figaro*,[7] described the trials:

. . . I entered the submarine boat *Morse* through the narrow opening in the upper surface of the boat. Our excursion was to begin immediately . . . turning to the crew, every man of which was at his post, the Commandant gave his orders, dwelling with emphasis on each word. A sailor repeated his orders one by one [a rather prosy but necessary procedure adopted by all sensible submariners] and all was silent. The *Morse* had already started on its mysterious voyage but was skimming along the surface until outside the port in order to avoid the numerous craft in the Arsenal. To say that at this moment, which I had so keenly anticipated, I did not have the tremor which comes from contact with the unknown would be beside the truth. On the other hand, calm and imperturbable, but keenly curious as to this novel form of navigation, General André [the French Minister of War] had already taken his place near the Commandant on a folding seat. There were no chairs in this long tube in which we were imprisoned. Everything was arranged for the crew alone, with an eye to serious action. Moreover, the Minister for War was too tall to stand upright beneath the iron ceiling, and in any case it would be impossible to walk about.

The only free space was a narrow passage, 60 centimetres broad, less than 2 metres high and 30 metres long, divided into 3 equal sections. In the first, in the forefront of the tube, reposed the torpedoes with the machine for launching them, which, at a distance from 500 to 600 metres, were bound to sink, with the present secret processes, the largest of ironclads. In the second section were the electric accumulators which gave the light and power. In the third, near the screw, was the electric motor which transformed into movement the current of the accumulator. Under all this, beneath the floor from end to end, were immense water ballasts which were capable of being emptied or filled in a few seconds by electric machines in order to carry the vessel up or down. Finally, in the centre of the tube, dominating these three sections, which the electric light inundated and which no partition divided, the navigating lieutenant stood on the look-out giving his orders.

There was but one thing which could destroy in a second all the sources of authority, initiative and responsibility in this officer – that of failure of the accumulators. Were the electricity to fail everything would come to a stop. Darkness would overtake the boat and imprison it forever in the water. To avoid any such disaster there have been arranged, it is true, outside the tube low down, a series of lead weights which are capable of being released from within to lighten the vessel . . .

The *Morse* after skimming along the water until outside the port was now about to dive. The Commandant's place was no longer in the helmet or kiosque whence he could direct the route along the surface of the sea. His place was henceforth in the very centre of the tube, in the midst of all sorts of electric manipulators, his eyes continually fixed on a mysterious optical apparatus, the periscope. The other extremity of this instrument floated on the surface of the water and, whatever the depth of the plunge, it gave him a perfectly faithful and clear representation, as in a camera, of everything occurring on the water.

The most interesting moment of all now came. I hastened to the little opening to get the impression of total immersion. The lieutenant by the marine chart verified the depth. The casks of water were filled [main ballast tanks with internal vents] and our supply of air was thereby renewed from their stores of surplus air. In our tiny observatory, where General André stationed himself above me, a most unexpected spectacle presented itself as the boat was immersed.

The plunge was so gentle that in the perfect silence of the water one did not see the process of descent and there was only one instrument capable of indicating, by a needle, the depth to which the *Morse* was penetrating. The vessel was advancing while at the same time it descended, but there was no sensation of either advance or roll. As to respiration, it was as perfect as in any room . . . The crew were able to remain underwater sixteen hours without the slightest strain. Our excursion on this occasion lasted scarcely two hours.

Although the *Morse* showed great promise she was overshadowed by Maxime Laubeuf's *Narval*, the winner of an open competition (similar to that in the United States) offered by the new Minister of Marine Monsieur Lockroy in 1896. The Minister asked for a 200-ton submarine with a range of 100 miles on the surface and ten miles submerged. Twenty-nine designs were submitted from all over the world and Laubeuf won with a dual propulsion system (steam and electricity) and the first of the double hulls with main ballast tanks and fuel tanks accommodated between the pressure hull and a light outer skin.

***Anguille* in about 1904 with double her normal complement on board – presumably for training. The drop-collar apparatus can clearly be seen.**

90   *Narval* was the first submersible, being able to recharge her batteries (unlike her sister *sous-marins*) when on the surface. She was very slow to dive because it took at least fifteen minutes to shut down the boiler; but that was not a matter which the French regarded as important. Steam submarines, with all their disadvantages, were regarded as being much safer (with reason) than petrol boats and were less costly.

Sadly, after much initial enthusiasm, France relaxed her submarine efforts as time went on. By 1912 the Royal Navy's submarine service had overtaken the French both in quantity and quality. Lagging more and more behind Holland's guidelines, the French persisted in steam propulsion, to which they were much addicted, for many years.

When war came in 1914 steam proved by no means suitable for North Sea weather. The conditions there were described by Lieutenant Déville, the Commandant of *Archimède*, who found

the steep seas were a startling revelation after the coastal service he had been used to. The *Archimède*, laid down in 1907, was a large boat displacing 577 tons on the surface with a healthy 273 tons of reserve buoyancy. She was supposedly an exceptionally seaworthy submersible of the type that the retired Engineer-in-Chief of the French Navy and the most renowned architect in the submarine field, Laubeuf, was constantly advocating in the press as being vastly better than all-electric defensive submarines. Close on 600 tons was all right but Laubeuf regarded as 'purely Utopian' the idea that a submarine of 650 to 800 tons and of a speed of 15 knots could cruise on the high seas:

> What could such a vessel do against battleships and armoured cruisers with a speed of from 19 to 25 knots and destroyers of 28 to 35 knots? Furthermore . . . the great length of the larger submarine . . . seriously hampers the fulfilment of its most important task – that of coast defence and deprives the Commander of the possibility of seeing personally what is being done at both ends of his vessel . . .[8]

Laubeuf, who had such great influence on design, must be held at least partly responsible for the fact that boats like *Archimède* were simply not up to the strains and stresses of real war at sea. On 17 December 1914 *Archimède* was patrolling off Heligoland when a gale blew up. Déville reluct-

Dupuy de Lôme of 1915, one of the 830-ton ocean-going submarines, steam propelled on the surface with a designed speed of 18 knots and – a very dubious claim – the supposed capability of 11 knots submerged on electric motors. The advertised endurance of 5 knots submerged for 150 miles is impossible to believe. Still she was formidable, with two 14pdr guns and 8 torpedoes.

antly decided he would have to return to harbour but hardly had he altered course to the west when a heavy sea struck the funnel – always the most vulnerable part of a steam-powered submarine. The funnel could not be lowered sufficiently to shut the watertight hull valve and Déville was unable to dive. Even on the surface water poured down the aperture and had to be baled out by the crew who passed buckets from hand to hand. Lieutenant Godfrey Herbert, the British Liaison Officer, was much admired by the French crew for taking his turn with the bucket-chain. He displayed a degree of cheerfulness not expected from an English officer. When one of the crew helpfully remarked *'il fait très mauvais temps, Monsieur'* Herbert replied, in execrable French, *'Oui, mais après le mauvais temps vienne le beau temps.'* This immensely encouraged the hitherto thoroughly depressed crew who shouted the catch-words in chorus whenever a particularly heavy deluge of water threatened to defeat the efforts of the bucket brigade.[9] Submarines with funnels were altogether too vulnerable but the Royal Navy failed to learn the lesson and forged ahead with the disastrous *Swordfish* and 'K' class boats soon afterwards.

The young German U-boat service had, in sharp contrast, no intention of building boats that were susceptible to damage on the high seas: 'we are building big submarines, the only ones which can

carry out the work we want them to do; they will be capable of acting on the offensive in the North and Baltic seas.'[10] The tiny 240-ton *U-9*, launched in 1906, made what the British Press described as a remarkable run of 600 miles from Heligoland to Kiel without any mishap in October 1907 and, as will be seen in Chapter 15, the U-boat fleet, unlike the French, was capable of aggressive operations anywhere.

It was not only funnels that denied the French an operational ability in the open seas. The drop-collars, which carried the torpedoes externally on several boats were too easily damaged by the weather while the cooking arrangements in the galleys could not withstand heavy rolling.[11] Nor were the more robust coal stoves installed in the superstructure protected against the spray; they could only be used on the surface in a lee. Nevertheless when cooking was possible, and somehow or other it usually was, French menus were magnificent.

In short, the French fixation on coastal and harbour defences robbed the Navy of practical sea-going boats; and long arguments about the relative values of submarines and submersibles militated against good general-purpose designs. Although both types and some semi-submersibles were built in huge numbers between 1901 and 1914 (76 boats were listed at the beginning of World War I) French interest in underwater warfare waned over the years and there were few significant technical or tactical advances from 1905 onwards. Professionalism was lacking, not least because of the habit of confining exercises to small, shallow areas inside, or just outside, a harbour breakwater.[13] Even during these stereotype drills Gallic *élan* and an evident contempt for taking precautions which submariners elsewhere thought necessary for the good of their health, French submarines were notoriously accident-prone. Thus, in spite of his inventive mind and undoubted gallantry, the French submariner was ill-equipped and poorly prepared for war when it came, and the results were disappointingly apparent.

Chapter Nine

Success in the States

John Philip Holland was convinced that the emerging French boats, which he admitted 'had attained some slight degree of success' were based on fundamental principles demonstrated in his *Fenian Ram* design. The foreign observers who had visited Delamater's Yard between 1879 and 1881 could hardly 'have failed to take notes'. However, the United States Navy Department showed scant interest in all that was happening in France during the late 1880s. How, asked Holland, could the American Navy remain unconvinced by the success of the *Fenian Ram* 'which was far more interesting and wonderful than anything the French had done?'[1] He was, in fact, 'totally sick and disgusted' with the Navy's lethargy.

Holland Renews his Efforts

In an endeavour to awake the torpid Department, Holland wrote a long article in 1886 about naval vessels, concentrating on 'The Submarine or Diving Boat'. The article was entitled 'Can New York be Bombarded?'[2] and Holland's intention was to alert the public to 'the pitiable condition of our fleet and coast defences, and showing how a few submarines would place us in a position to ward off an enemy's attack from mostly any point on our coast as effectively as if we had an adequate shore defence and a fleet equal to Great Britain's.' Holland had by this time firmly determined in his mind that submarines were primarily defensive weapons but the best means of defence was attack. He did not advocate that the United States should embark upon a *guerre de course*. Indeed, his thinking was developing along the lines of a submarine fleet which could act, in today's language, as a deterrent and he consistently proclaimed that submarines would actually prevent war. He was to be proved correct in modern times but he seems to have disregarded the more aggressive policies that were developing in Europe from which the United States was so widely separated geographically and politically. However, the tactics which he recommended in this provocative article could equally well be applied to offensive operations. The type of 'diving boat'

The inventor in the conning tower of *Holland VI* at Perth Amboy, New Jersey, April 1898.

he proposed was very similar to the design which eventually came to be adopted in the United States and Great Britain although Holland, in 1887, evidently had little faith in the possibilities of Robert Whitehead's torpedoes. He preferred his own version at this stage.

> This boat has a speed of eight miles per hour; she can remain underwater for two days, or longer, without having any connection with the surface. She can be steered by compass when underwater, and her course may be laid and corrected without obliging her to remain more than a few moments on the surface. This can be done without ever appearing over water. She can move at any required depth, and is more thoroughly under control completely submerged than when on the surface. Her horizontal and vertical motions are controlled automatically or by the pilot.
>
> The torpedo, carrying a 100lb charge, can be projected in a straight line to a distance of 80 or 90 feet according to the power employed in expelling it. The method of attack will probably be as follows: the diving boat, with only her turret above water, moves towards the ship. When she gets so close that her presence may be discovered, say half a mile, she descends a few feet under the surface. Once or twice, after the bearing of the ship is observed by means of a telescope projected for a few minutes over the water, corrections are made in the course for deviations owing to currents.
>
> When near the vessel she goes deeper, so as to bring her stem 10 or 15 feet beneath the surface. Netting can thus be avoided. She can now discharge her torpedo to explode on contact. As soon as this strikes, the explosion occurs and a large hole is torn in the ship's side. The ship will now become unmanageable, and with assistance may be captured. Experience has shown that in a seaway she rolls or pitches very little, apparently following the wave slope in large waves, in short sharp ones, she seems to ride and fall bodily with very little tendency to pitching.
>
> A notion seems to prevail that the proper duty of a diving boat would be to carry a diver who would come out and fasten a torpedo to a ship at anchor, then retire into his boat and move away; also, that it would be useful in placing and removing stationary mines. It is very evident that if a diving boat can attain a speed of 10 or 12 miles per hour, fire torpedoes at ships moving at full speed, and keep to sea for days together, her sphere of usefulness would be greatly extended. In fact, there is no insuperable objection to the employment of such vessels for coast defence and operations against ships. Submarine mines are not so effective

against them as vessels on the surface, because they can pass them unobserved. They can enter a harbor that may be fully defended, should it be necessary to destroy vessels inside the defences. If those in the fleet become aware of their presence it is more than probable, judging from the action of the French Fleet of 1877 to 1878, that the moral effect of the discovery will be that they will be convinced of the foolishness of awaiting an attack when the time so employed may be more wisely expended in moving to a safe distance, and in getting there at full speed. Thus, in 1886, did I try to show by comparison the superiority of the submarine over the torpedo boats and gunboats, the two arms of defence on which the Navy placed all its confidence at the time.

The article struck a chord somewhere deep inside the United States Navy Department which, in 1888, announced an open competition for a submarine torpedo-boat. It had to be capable of 15 knots on the surface and 8 knots submerged with sufficient battery capacity to maintain the latter speed for two hours – something not achieved until the German Type VII U-boat put to sea shortly before World War II. Contesting against Thorsten Nordenfelt, George Baker and Professor Tuck[3], Holland won the competition.

The competitors had to submit their plans through the Cramps Ship Building Company of Philadelphia who had been selected to build the craft chosen with the appropriation of two million dollars assured by Secretary of the Navy, William C Whitney. Unhappily, Cramps, after due consideration, were unable to promise that the stringent and, for the time, unrealistic requirements laid down by the Government would be fulfilled. Holland cannot have been surprised, particularly with regard to the underwater performance demanded, but he was bitterly disappointed. A fresh competition was announced in the following year and again Holland's design was selected. But then the administration changed and the appropriation was reassigned to surface craft.

Holland now faced considerable personal difficulties. His own money was running out and, with the Irish 'Salt Water Enterprise' at an end, he desperately sought another backer. He was for-

1890 employment was found for Holland in the dredging company at the modest wage of four dollars a day. Meanwhile Morris and Holland, because inventors have to invent *something*, turned their attention to a remarkable flying machine which foreshadowed vertical take-off. Two variable-pitch four-bladed propellers, automatically regulated by springs, were mounted horizontally on a spar which could be tilted to the vertical position, after lift-off, for level flight. With typical attention to commercial considerations, Holland claimed that the petroleum-fired steam boiler driving the piston engines (with petroleum at four cents a gallon) would propel the two-man aircraft at 63 miles per hour for four and a half hours at a total cost of 34 dollars 12 cents. Nobody wanted to know about the flying machine but it kept Holland in circulation: whenever his name was mentioned the conversation always came round to submarines.

USS *Plunger*

At long last, with President S Grover Cleveland re-elected (he had approved Secretary Whitney's submarine proposals when last in office), the US Navy firmly decided to adopt the submarine as a weapon of defence. Europe, where there were continual rumblings of war, no longer seemed so distant in 1893. It was time for America to open her windows on the world: much was happening. Captain Mahan, recently appointed in command of USS *Chicago*, was generating a forceful current of American imperialism through his books. Kaiser Wilhelm II misread Mahan's *The Influence of Sea Power on History* and concluded that Germany's destiny lay on the ocean; Latin America and the Far East, with Hawaii as the bridge thereto, were being eyed covetously from the White House; relations with Great Britain over the Venezuelan boundaries were strained; and the French submarine building programme looked ominous. While capital ships would be needed for outward expansion, submarines appeared to be the answer for inner defences. On 3 March Congress passed an appropriation of

TOP **The original *Plunger*. The government contract for her was cancelled on 19 Nov 1900 soon after this photograph was taken.**

ABOVE **The control room of USS *Adder* or possibly *Moccasin*.**

tunate to find that his old friend Charles A Morris of the Morris and Cummings Dredging Company at New York was enthusiastic and prepared to help if he could. Morris himself was not able to put up the money and there were no prospective employers for a submarine inventor, but in May

96 200,000 dollars for yet another submarine competition and a third invitation to inventors, with the same requirements as before, was circulated on 1 April. On 4 June Holland completed the drawings for his fifth boat and simultaneously set up the John P Holland Torpedo Boat Company. There was much governmental delay and arguing while interested political and business parties battled on all sides in Washington; but, eventually, on 13 March 1895 the 200,000-dollar contract for Holland's patented design was duly signed. Success was finally in sight but there were plenty of obstacles still to be overcome. William T Malster at Baltimore contracted to build Holland's new boat which the government elected to call the *Plunger*. Malster was already building Simon Lake's *Argonaut* and the keel for the new craft was laid alongside on 23 June 1896.

From the start, Holland was uneasy about the steam plant which was essential to meet the specific and ambitious requirements for speed and endurance. The two 1625hp triple-expansion engines, turning the outboard propellers at 400rpm for the maximum 15-knot surface speed, demanded a large hull; and the 70hp electric motor, charged by an independent steam engine and connected to the centre propeller, was not small. A huge Mosher boiler amidships, supplying steam at 2000lb per square inch, took up a great deal of space and the boat had to be much larger than Holland thought desirable. *Plunger* was 85 feet long and $11\frac{1}{2}$ feet broad; she displaced 154 tons on the surface and 168 tons submerged. Lake's 36-foot *Argonaut* lying alongside was dwarfed. To Holland's mind, the *Plunger*'s 7.4:1 length-to-breadth ratio (although considered close to the ideal today) was too great. Government and financial pressures had forced him to embark on the *Plunger* against his own better judgement but at least he now controlled a soundly based company and enjoyed, for the first time, some freedom of manoeuvre.

He had suddenly become famous, not least due to the extraordinary loyalty and enthusiasm of a young naval officer, William W Kimball, who had long boosted his ideas. In the year that the *Plunger* started growing on the stocks Lieutenant Commander Kimball boasted before the Senate Committee on Naval Affairs: 'Give me six Holland boats, the officers and crew to be selected by me, and I will pledge my life to stand off the entire British Squadron ten miles off Sandy Hook without any aid from a fleet.'[4] It was a bold proclamation from such a junior officer. Amidst mounting public interest Holland was sufficiently confident to persuade his board and backers to finance another submarine built entirely to his own specifications. It was to be independent and it need not necessarily be sold only to the United States Government. Holland recognised at this early stage that the sales potential abroad was promising. Still more astutely, Elihu B Frost, the company's secretary-treasurer, secured an Amendment to the Act granting the *Plunger* appropriation, allowing for two boats to be built 'similar to the submarine boat *Holland*'. The Amendment was very carefully phrased with Frost's gentle guidance. Thus, Holland's much preferred design, *Holland VI*, could be substituted for *Plunger* if, as Holland predicted to himself, *Plunger* were to fail. In the event, although USS *Plunger* was launched in 1897, the trials were never completed. Holland was glad to be rid of the clumsy monster whose boiler made conditions for the crew intolerable. He thankfully turned his full attention to the epoch-making *Holland VI*.

Holland's Sixth Boat

Holland VI, the forerunner of all modern submarines, was built at Nixon's Crescent Shipyard, Elizabethport, New Jersey between 1896 and 1897.[5] As Lieutenant-Colonel Alan H Burgoyne MP remarked in his classical history[6]: 'Of this vessel perhaps more has been heard than of any other ship or boat in the world. She is the prototype of the latest submarine ordered by Great Britain and the American Government and is also, without doubt, the commencement of the "really successful" submarine.'

The sixth of Holland's boats was 53 feet 10

inches long with a diameter of 10 feet 3 inches amidships (a 5.25:1 ratio). The displacement was 63.3 tons on the surface and 74 tons submerged. The design and the construction were entirely along the lines of submarines today with frames, plating and general arrangements which scarcely need listing: they would not be out of place in any submarine drawing-office today. Propulsion on the surface and power for re-charging the batteries was provided by an Otto gasoline 45hp

engine, giving a maximum speed on the surface of about 8 knots at 340rpm, and a 50hp electric motor offering the same designed speed submerged but it is more likely to have been less than 5 knots in reality. A tail clutch and an engine clutch permitted the engine to drive the propeller direct or to recharge the battery by using the motor as a generator, with or without the propeller being turned: that is, a running or standing charge could be applied. The principle was to be used in future submarines for half a century and more.

The diving rudders on either side of the propeller could, in theory, be controlled automatically by a pendulum and pressure-diaphragm system but in practice they were worked by mechanical-linkage gearing from a position at the bottom of the curtailed conning tower which, in this the first really successful submarine, contained the controls, gauges and other instruments now found in a submarine control room.

The main armament was a single 18-inch torpedo tube and two reload torpedoes could be carried. Incidentally, there is considerable confu-

The second *Plunger* (SS2) launched by name on 1 Feb 1902 but subsequently designated *A1*. Commissioned on 19 Sept 1903 under Lt C P Nelson, she was a Holland boat, similar to the six *Adder* class which came into service at the same time or a little earlier. *Plunger* was used mainly for trials and training during her short career. Put in reserve in April 1910, her name was changed to *A1* 18 months later and stricken from the Navy List on 24 Feb 1913. She was then used as a target (when this photograph was taken in 1914) and finally sold for scrap in 1922.

98 sion about the size of the torpedoes in *Holland VI* and in the first American and British submarines which followed. A diameter of 14 inches is often quoted but research shows without doubt that the tubes were 18 inches (45 centimetres) from the beginning: the discrepancy probably arose due to the assumption that 14-inch Whitehead torpedoes, more common at that time, were supplied. If 14-inch tubes were included in the original designs for any of the early submarines they were certainly changed to 18 inches very early in the building programmes although purists would say, correctly, that the torpedoes themselves were only 17.72 inches (450 millimetres) in diameter.

Excellent and effective compensating arrangements were made for maintaining the trim automatically on firing a torpedo while the bow cap, lifted upwards by worm gearing, was made watertight with a rubber gasket as was the rear door. *Holland VI* was also equipped with an inclined dynamite or pneumatic gun, above the torpedo tube forward (and initially one aft as well) on the lines of the weapon fitted in the abortive *Zalinski Boat*.

Holland had every reason to believe that his new boat was all right in practically every detail but he should have realised that every Irishman has to play against Murphy's law, all too well known to all submariners. On the night of Wednesday 13 October 1897 one of Nixon's workmen left open a hull valve while the boat was still on the slip. At high tide water flooded the machinery and, when the boat was pumped out, full earths remained on the electrical systems. The accident might well have put paid to the project but, fortuitously, it brought on to the stage a clever young electrician who was destined to put the British and American Holland boats through their trials in a methodical fashion[7], unencumbered by rules or red tape, that has never since been equalled. Frank T Cable, the electrical expert who saved the day, records[8]:

> I became the skipper of the *Holland* owing to being the accidental means of reconditioning her electrical

equipment after she had sunk. . . . She had remained submerged for about 18 hours during which her electrical equipment and machinery were at the mercy of salt water. The insulation was ruined and some means had to be found to restore it. To remove the electrical equipment and rebuild the boat meant a large outlay; the entire upper part of the hull would have to be cut open in order to take out the machinery. The Holland Company vainly tried every known method of drying out the motors and generators by applying heat externally.

Cable, with nothing to lose, simply reversed the current in the field circuits, abusing all principles

Holland VI on trials in Raritan Bay, New Jersey, 20 April 1898. The trials' Capt Frank T Cable is between C A Morris (Supt Eng) and Holland himself. *Richard K Morris Collection*

of recognised electrical motor management, and soon the wiring generated ample heat to dry out the circuit system. It was a drastic remedy but it worked.

Cable was a modest man but he did not hesitate to state his mind even though he was only on loan from the Electro-Dynamic Company of Philadelphia who had supplied the motor and dynamo. He never claimed the right to call himself the first

'The Cage' for loading torpedoes on board *Holland VI*, summer 1898 Atlantic Yacht Basin. The pragmatic Frank Cable is smoking a pipe on right. Loading torpedoes has always been a tedious and unpopular business and the early boats had no hydraulic power to assist.

Richard K Morris Collection

real submarine captain but he deserves the title and, as will be seen later, he readily took charge in difficult situations. Calm, thoroughly practical and unflustered at any time he was the ideal submariner. Unfairly, although Bushnell, Ezra Lee, Fulton and Holland himself are well remembered and even revered, Cable is seldom given credit by historians for his invaluable services. At this time, however, in the winter of 1897, he was by

no means anxious to submerge himself in a submarine. 'Not for anything,' he said, 'would I attempt to do so.' Putting things right on the surface was enough.

Holland VI showed the inventor's understanding of submarining to be thorough and far in advance of his contemporaries, especially with regard to the diving arrangements and main ballast tanks. The latter were constructed so that when entirely filled the boat would be brought to an awash condition; a final adjustment was then made by means of a small tank which was partially filled so as to enable the boat to dive fully when she went ahead while still retaining a small reserve of buoyancy. There was no instability due to surging water. The main ballast tanks were either entirely empty or completely full as they are in submarines today.

There were no more than twelve openings to

100 sea, and of these only the three main Kingston valves that admitted water to the main ballast tanks were significantly large. The remainder were small and admitted water to instruments such as the Manometer (depth-gauge). The dozen deadlights in the conning tower were made of heavy glass and were thoroughly tested against external water pressure. The maximum safe diving depth was calculated as 100 feet but the boat never went down so far.

In nearly all respects the craft was thoroughly practical although Captain Cable, enthusing about his command, was rather over-optimistic about the boat's capabilities. She could never, as he claimed in the Press, have gone 1500 miles on the surface without refuelling with gasoline, nor could she make 40 knots (he meant miles) underwater without coming up; and there was certainly not enough compressed air in the tanks, as Cable confidently asserted, to 'supply a crew with fresh air for 30 days if the air was not used for any other purpose such as emptying the submerging tanks'.[9] Neither was *Holland VI* able to dive to a depth of 20 feet in 8 seconds from a fully surfaced condition although this might possibly have been achievable when going ahead from a very low-awash state after starting to dive. Nonetheless *Holland VI* was undeniably a sound, obedient boat. She could be kept under control below the surface at all speeds.

The backers, like all stockholders, were sceptical and anxious to see a demonstration. The first surface run on 25 February 1898 went well and Cable, not yet formally attached to Holland's company, wrote in congratulatory terms when he read the reports in the Philadelphia press. But Holland was not yet ready to seek publicity and he made the first static dive to the bottom of Nixon's Yard, where it was only 20 feet on 11 March, with his four crew members without fuss. The submarine surfaced after 30 minutes and Holland modestly announced that he would 'take her for a little dip' on the following Monday. The 'Monday Dip' failed because an insufficient weight of pig-iron ballast was loaded into the keel. Holland had

The inventor standing by the conning tower of *Holland VI*, probably in the late spring of 1898.

Part of Holland's 4-page standing orders for *Holland VI*. It was the gunner's duty to stop any dangerous leak 'with pieces of canvas (carried for the purpose) as quickly as possible'.
Electric Boat Division, General Dynamics

also probably made, again, a wrong allowance for salinity. This time it was on the safe side, unlike the error which caused his submarine to sink in the Passaic River twenty years earlier. It was only a temporary setback. On St Patrick's Day, Thursday 17 March 1898 *Holland VI* made her first successful dive underway off Staten Island. Holland now felt he was ready to demonstrate his craft to even the most critical onlookers and his resolve was strengthened by having on board the 32-year-old Frank T Cable as the permanent electrician.

Official observers were sent by the Navy Department to witness the formal trials on Sunday 27 March. They were entirely satisfactory. On 10 April 1898 Assistant Secretary of the Navy Theodore Roosevelt wrote[10] to Secretary of the Navy John D Long:

My Dear Mr Secretary,
    I think that the Holland submarine boat should be purchased. Evidently she has great possibilities in her for harbor defence. Sometimes she doesn't work perfectly, but often she does, and I don't think in the present emergency we can afford to let her slip. . . .

Roosevelt was, of course, referring to the fact that Spain had declared war on the United States over Cuba four days after the trial run of *Holland VI*. Holland declared himself willing to take his boat to Santiago and sink the Spanish fleet if it was still there adding that, if he was successful, he would expect the Government to buy his boat. It was an honest offer because Holland was neither flamboyant nor boastful but it was not taken up. Worse, the Navy Department sought to criticise everything they could; the naval officers who replaced Holland and his principal crewman for subsequent trials were slow and inept. It is difficult to understand how the Navy expected untrained men, however skilled in their profession, to put the submarine through her paces and arrive at sensible conclusions. As a result of these dubious further trials by naval personnel extensive modifications were demanded. To be fair, some of them were sound. The after dynamite gun

was removed; the propeller was shifted forward a little with some rearrangement of the rudders and hydroplanes; extra, and very handy, small trimming tanks were added; the engine exhaust system was led to a higher point; and a new type of antifouling paint was applied to the hull.

Meanwhile the Electric Boat Company absorbed the Holland Torpedo Boat Company and Isaac Rice became President. John Philip Holland was retained as manager. Rice soon swallowed other companies, including the Electro-Dynamic Company of Philadelphia, and his empire rapidly expanded at the expense of Holland's personal influence. Soon after the takeover and its attendant mergers Holland embarked on a trip around Europe, doubtless encouraged by Rice to keep him out of the way while all the changes were taking place. On 17 May 1899, when Holland returned to his office, he found that he had lost extensive foreign patent rights to the composite company and that his status in the new firm was considerably diminished. Frank Cable was now not only the appointed captain of *Holland VI* but was in practice the arbiter of what was done with the little boat. Rice endeavoured not to offend the inventor's susceptibilities unduly but Holland was slowly and steadily eased out of what was becoming a very powerful concern. His name was still important and highly respected in Washington where politicians recognised its value in securing the Irish vote; but his salary never rose above 90 dollars a week and he reckoned, by the time he left the Company in 1904 at the age of 63, that he held no more than one half of one per cent of the company's share value, stock worth about 50,000 dollars. An Irishman, even after more than 30 years in the United States, was no match for the acumen of American businessmen like Isaac Rice.

Although there was little doubt that *Holland VI* would win the day it took a long time to complete the acceptance trials satisfactorily and there were some worrying moments. On one occasion, when Holland himself was observing from the yacht *Josephine* along with some distinguished guests, the crew were overcome by carbon monoxide from

102 the exhaust gases and were unable to stop the engine when Cable on deck ordered propulsion to be shifted to the reversible electric motor when coming alongside. It was this dangerous accident that led to the introduction of white mice in the engine rooms of petrol-driven submarines to give early warning of the danger. On 23 July 1899 Holland suffered quite a different kind of setback when the 78-year-old Clara Barton, first President of the American Red Cross, went out for a trip which the inventor thought would give her pleasure. It did not. At the end of the day, which was cold and rainy, she turned to Holland and sharply reprimanded him for developing a dreadful weapon of war. He reiterated that he saw the submarine as a deterrent to war but failed to persuade the indignant lady.

The final trial took place in Little Peconic Bay off New Suffolk, Long Island on 6 November. Holland himself was not on board but two senior naval observers were crowded into the little boat

BELOW **Simon Lake** (1866–1945).
BOTTOM **Lake's** *Argonaut First* in 1897.

with seven crew members and three torpedoes embarked. It was a tight fit. Captain John Lowe USN was the senior officer present and his subsequent report[11] included an impassioned argument for submarines in a style, including some capital letters, which Admiral Jackie Fisher on the other side of the Atlantic would have approved. 'We need right off and right now 50 Submarine Torpedo Vessels in Long Island Sound to preserve the peace and give potency to our diplomacy. The French in this matter are much more alive to their needs than we are. What we have left to a private company the French have taken up as a National affair . . .'

Lowe's opinion carried weight. On 11 April 1900 *Holland VI* was bought for the United States Navy amidst headlines describing her as 'the Monster War Fish', 'Uncle Sam's Devil of the Deep' and 'The Naval "Hell Diver"'. She took her place in the United States Navy as the USS *Holland* (SS–1). The other navies of the world paid close attention to these proceedings and their press.

Simon Lake

Meanwhile Holland's principle new competitor, Simon Lake, was having considerable success with his own designs. By the time that USS *Holland* was at sea, his first boat, *Argonaut Jr*, was an obsolete hulk but she had only been built as a prototype for a submarine which Lake intended to employ solely for commercial purposes. He saw a great future in submarines for salvage, underwater mining and diving operations of various kinds. Lake had a head of fiery red hair with a temper and high humour to match. In character and in aim he could scarcely have been more different from John Philip Holland and his accounts[12] make lighter reading than the records left by his Irish-American rival despite the latter's flashes of subtle wit. He had a demoniacal sense of the absurd and a recognition of good theatre which would make him memorable even if he had never invented anything worthwhile.

The young Simon was only a schoolboy when he started experimenting underwater. He constructed a canvas canoe with the help of a description he found in the magazine *Golden Days* and deliberately turned it upside down in the stream running through his village of Toms River. As a drifting diving bell it worked well although it worried spectators on the bank who thought the boy was drowned. The canoe led Lake to sketch a proper submersible at the age of fourteen and this design was a basis for the boats that followed. In Lake's own words *Argonaut Jr* was built of

> yellow pine planking, double thick, lined with canvas laid between the double layers of planking the outer seams caulked and payed. She was a flat-sided affair and would not stand great external pressure. She was propelled on wheels when on the bottom by a man turning a crank on the inside. Our compressed air reservoir was a soda-water fountain tank. The compressed-air pump was a plumber's hand-pump, by which means we were able to compress the air in the tanks to a pressure of about 100lb per square inch.
>
> My diving suit I built myself by shaping iron in the form of an open helmet which extended down as far as my breast; this I covered with painted canvas, I used the deadlight from a yacht's cabin as my eye glass in front of the helmet. I tied sash weights to my legs to hold me down on the bottom when walking in the vicinity of my boat.

Lake had barely fifteen dollars in his pocket when he built the experimental craft and he was necessarily doing things on the cheap. However, the little *Argonaut* functioned adequately, and, with an air lock and a diver's compartment, the two-man crew 'had a lot of fun running around the bottom of New York Bay picking up clams and oysters'. The Press made sport of the craft – 'Fun for Merry Mermen' said the *New York Herald* on 8 January 1895 – but any publicity is good publicity, thought Lake, and he was right. A number of wealthy citizens – Vanderbilts, Astors, Goulds – bought stock in a company promoted on Lake's behalf by a certain Mr H who did very well for himself but very little for the inventor. After a good deal of legal wrangling the unscrupulous promoter was ousted and Lake was relieved to find that sufficient remained to build a full-size bottom-crawler. *Argonaut First*[13] was launched from the cradles alongside the *Plunger* on 17 August 1897.

The new *Argonaut* was 36 feet long and 9 feet broad. She displaced 59 tons submerged and was built of three-eighths inch steel plate. A 30hp gasoline engine drove the single propeller and it could also be connected to two toothed driving wheels forward for running on the bottom: a third wheel, directed from inside or out, steered. Air for the engine was initially sucked in through a canvas hose connected to a floating buoy above but this dangerous contrivance was later replaced by two long intake and exhaust masts: if these extended for 50 feet as Lake claimed, they were a good deal longer than a modern snorkel mast and, unsupported, were a potential menace. The vessel was remodelled and enlarged at the Robbins Dry Dock Company, Brooklyn in 1899 and was finally completed with a length of 66 feet in July 1900.

The *Argonaut* was not a warlike submarine and does not directly compare with Holland's boats but the curious commercial craft led to other designs by Lake which had a marked influence on naval designs and much valuable information was gathered. Some of it was negative, particularly with regard to the lack of visibility below water which demanded instruments for navigation. The compass was satisfactory when mounted in a bronze binnacle above the hull but it was apparent that future boats would need a viewing device projecting above the water.

Lake was very happy with *Argonaut*. One day in the log he recorded: 'the spirits of the crew appeared to improve the longer we remain below; the time was spent in catching clams, singing, trying to valse, playing cards and writing letters to wives and sweethearts.' The British Naval Attaché to the United States was certainly impressed when he accepted an invitation for a short voyage in 1900 during which Lake, reading between the lines of the various surviving reports[14], was determined to discomfort the Limey officer.

The Attaché enquired, after the boat had dived, whether the submarine (which was vibrating heavily at the time) was actually proceeding along

the bottom of the harbour. It was too dark to see anything through the glass scuttles and the electric searchlight in the bows was little help. Lake said that they were indeed on the bottom. He took his visitor through the air-lock into a chamber at the bottom of the craft with a large hatch, secured with butterfly nuts, where he equalised

PROTECTOR.

the pressure by means of bottled high-pressure air until it was the same as the water pressure outside. The inventor then opened the test-cock and regulated the internal pressure until water ceased to flow. Satisfied, he dropped open the hatch with sublime confidence.

In effect Lake had made this part of the submarine into a diving bell. Shells and starfish could be seen lying on the bottom as the intruder passed over them and the British officer no longer had any doubts about where he was. 'Mr Lake,' said the Attaché, 'you can close the door as soon as you like; I have seen quite enough . . .'

Unfortunately at that moment the submarine took a sharp down-angle. Mr Lake turned very pale (according to the Attaché) and announced that they had dropped into a hole in the seabed and that they might be held down with some doubt about whether they would ever get out. The guest responded with gratifying concern. However, after some thought, Lake announced that he could release a 10,000lb weight (it actually weighed

4000lb) as well as blowing water from the tanks; if everybody rocked the boat at the same time the *Argonaut* would come to the surface. Everybody on board participated in this performance, which was almost certainly invented and quite unnecessary, and the submarine duly bobbed up above the waves. The impressionable British officer was

safely and politely put ashore where he penned a full report to the Admiralty about his grim experience concluding with the remark 'we were all very thankful to land.' Lake, meanwhile, was no doubt laughing with his crew. The unimportant incident deserves its place in history as the first recorded instance of the peculiar and rather cruel sense of humour which submariners, from now on, were to develop as their trade mark.

The Attaché was either too nervous or too ignorant to understand some important points which, quite apart from the wheels, made the *Argonaut* so different from the rest. The craft was the first to have a double hull; that is to say a light external structure, flooded on diving, was doubled around the pressure hull to give a high surface

Lake was a first-class showman but his habit of running *Protector* partially submerged with the conning tower hatch open was rather reckless.

Lake's *Protector* 1902

1 horizontal rudders	9 conning tower
2 ballast tanks	10 crew space
3 dynamo	11 batteries
4 engine exhaust	12 release gear
5 petrol engine	13 drop keels
6 hatches	14 wheels (retractable)
7 omniscope	15 diving chamber
8 gun cupola	16 torpedo tubes

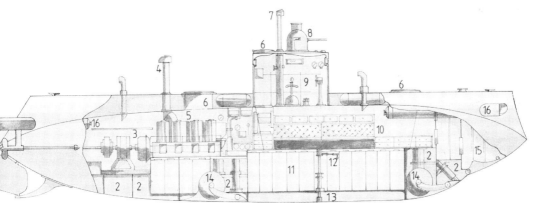

buoyancy of 40 per cent. When submerged the four 'levelling valves' did exactly what their name implies: they kept the boat on a substantially level keel rather than being used to steer vertically up and down.

The most usual method of diving was to lower two anchor-weights to the bottom and flood in water until buoyancy was less than their weight. The anchor cables were then wound in until *Argonaut* was on the bottom when more water was let in to the ballast tanks and the weights were drawn up into their pockets. It was an ingenious system and enabled *Argonaut* to make a prolonged operation, lasting two months, during which she covered more than 1000 miles under her own power on the surface and on the bottom with five men on board. From Lake's log-book dated 28 July 1898:

> We spent some days with Hampton Roads as headquarters, and made several descents in the waters adjacent thereto; we were desirous of making a search for the cables which connected with the mines guarding the entrance to the harbour, but could not obtain permission from the authorities, who were afraid we might accidentally sever them, which would, of course, make their entire system of defence useless.
>
> It was, therefore, necessary for us, in order to demonstrate the practicability of vessels of this type for this purpose, to lay a cable ourselves, which we did, across the channel leading into the Patuxent River. We then submerged, and taking our bearings by the compass, ran over the bottom, with the door in our diving compartment open, until we came across the cable, which we hauled up into the compartment with a hook only about four-and-a-half feet long, and we could not avoid the impression that it would be a very easy thing to destroy the efficiency of the present mine system. And how many lives might have been saved, and millions of dollars besides, had our navy been provided with a craft of this type to lead the way into Santiago, Havana, or San Juan, off which ports squadrons were compelled to lie for weeks and months owing to the fear of the mines.[15]

An excellent and unique description[16] of the *Argonaut* below water was given by Ray Stannard Baker, an American guest who was treated more seriously than the unfortunate British Attaché:

Simon Lake planned an excursion on the bottom of the sea for 12 October 1898. His strange amphibian craft, the *Argonaut*, about which we had been hearing so many marvels, lay off the pier at Atlantic Highlands. Before we were near enough to make out her hulk, we saw a great black letter A, framed of heavy gas-pipe, rising forty feet above the water. A flag rippled from its summit. As we drew nearer, we discovered that there really wasn't any hulk to make out – only a small oblong deck shouldering deep in the water and supporting a slightly higher platform, from which rose what seemed to be a squatty funnel. A moment later we saw the funnel was provided with a cap somewhat resembling a tall silk hat, the crown of which was represented by a brass binnacle. This cap was tilted back, and as we ran alongside, a man stuck

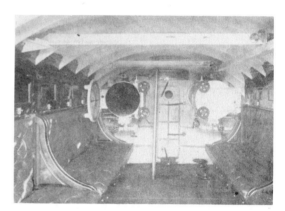

Comfort was the hallmark of *Protector* as can be seen here in the torpedo room forward and the crew's quarters.

his head up over the rim and sang out, 'Ahoy there!'

We scrambled up on the little platform, and peered down through the open conning tower, which we had taken for a funnel, into the depths of the ship below. Wilson (the Engineer) had started his gasoline engine.

Mr Lake had taken his place at the wheel, and we were going ahead slowly, steering straight across the bay toward Sandy Hook and deeper water. The *Argonaut* makes about five knots an hour on the surface, but when she gets deep down on the sea bottom, where she belongs, she can spin along more rapidly.

The *Argonaut* was slowly sinking under the water. We became momentarily more impressed with the extreme smallness of the craft to which we were trusting our lives. The little platform around the conning tower on which we stood – in reality the top of the gasoline tank – was scarcely a half-dozen feet across.

Mr Lake explained that the *Argonaut* was not only a submarine boat, but much besides. She not only swims either on the surface or beneath it, but she adds to this accomplishment the extraordinary power of diving deep and rolling along the bottom of the sea on wheels. No machine ever before did that. Indeed, the *Argonaut* is more properly a 'sea motor-cycle' than a 'boat'.

We found ourselves in a long, narrow compartment, dimly illuminated by yellowish-green light from the little round glass windows. The stern was filled with Wilson's gasoline engine and the electric motor, and in front of us toward the bow we could see through the heavy steel doorways of the diver's compartment into the lookout room, where there was a single round eye of light.

I climbed up the ladder of the conning tower and looked out through one of the glass ports. My eyes were just even with the surface of the water. A wave came driving and foaming entirely over the top of the vessel, and I could see the curiously beautiful sheen of the bright summit of the water above us. It was a most impressive sight. Mr Lake told me that in very clear water it was difficult to tell just where the air left off and the water began; but in the muddy bay where we were going down the surface looked like a peculiarly clear, greenish pane of glass moving straight up and down, not forward, as the waves appear to move when looked at from above.

Now we were entirely under water. The rippling noises that the waves had made in beating against the upper structure of the boat had ceased. As I looked through the thick glass port, the water was only three inches from my eyes, and I could see thousands of dainty semi-translucent jellyfish floating about as lightly as thistledown.

Jim brought the government chart, and Mr Lake announced that we were heading directly for Sandy Hook and the open ocean. But we had not yet reached the bottom, and John was busily opening valves and letting in more water. I went forward to the little steel cuddy-hole in the extreme prow of the boat, and looked out through the watchport. The water had grown denser and yellower, and I could not see much beyond the dim outlines of the ship's spar reaching out forward. Jim said that he had often seen fishes come swimming up wonderingly to gaze into the port. They would remain quite motionless until he stirred his head, and then they vanished instantly. Mr Lake has a remarkable photograph which he took of a visiting fish, and Wilson tells of nurturing a queer flat crab for days in the crevice of one of the view-holes.

At that moment I felt a faint jolt, and Mr Lake said that we were on the bottom of the sea. Here we were running as comfortably along the bottom of Sandy Hook Bay as we would ride in a Broadway car, and with quite as much safety. Wilson, who was of a musical turn, was whistling 'Down Went McGinty', and Mr Lake, with his hands on the pilot-wheel, put in an occasional word about his marvellous invention. On the wall opposite there was a row of dials which told automatically every fact about our condition that the most nervous of men could wish to know. One of them shows the pressure of air in the main compartment of the boat, another registers vacuum, and when both are at zero, Mr Lake knows that the pressure of air is normal, the same as it is on the surface, and he tries to maintain it in this condition. There are also a cyclometer, not unlike those used on bicycles, to show how far the boat travels on the wheels; a depth gauge, which keeps us accurately informed as to the depth of the boat in the water; and a declension indicator. By the long finger of the declension dial we could tell whether we were going up hill or down. Once while we were out, there was a sudden, sharp shock, the pointer leaped back, and then quivered steady again. Mr Lake said that we had probably struck a bit of wreckage or an embankment, but the *Argonaut* was running so lightly that she had leaped up jauntily and slid over the obstruction.

We had been keeping our eyes on the depth dial, the most fascinating and interesting of any of the number. It showed that we were going down, down, down, literally down to the sea in a ship. When we had been submerged far more than an hour, and there was thirty feet of yellowish green ocean over our heads,

Mr Lake suddenly ordered the machinery stopped. The clacking noises of the dynamo ceased, and the electric lights blinked out, leaving us at once in almost absolute darkness and silence. Before this, we had found it hard to realize that we were on the bottom of the ocean; now it came upon us suddenly and not without a touch of awe. This absence of sound and light, this unchanging motionlessness and coolness, this absolute negation – that was the bottom of the sea. It lasted only a moment, but in that moment we realized acutely the meaning and joy of sunshine and moving winds, trees, and the world of men.

A minute light twinkled out like a star, and then another and another, until the boat was bright again, and we knew that among the other wonders of this most astonishing of inventions there was storage electricity which would keep the boat illuminated for hours, without so much as a single turn of the dynamo. With the stopping of the engine, the air supply from above had ceased; but Mr Lake laid his hand on the steel wall above us, where he said there was enough air compressed to last us all for two days, should anything happen. The possibility of 'something happening' had been lurking in our minds ever since we started.

Every imaginable contingency, and some that were not at all imaginable to the uninitiated, had been absolutely provided against by the genius of the inventor. And everything from the gasoline engine to the hand-pump was as compact and ingenious as the mechanism of a watch. Moreover, the boat was not crowded; we had plenty of room to move around and to sleep, if we wished, to say nothing of eating. As for eating, John had brought out the kerosene stove and

USN 'B' class control room. Three boats of this type – *Viper*, *Cuttlefish* and *Tarantula* – were commissioned in 1907. The latter subsequently *B3* (SS12), is seen on the surface, probably in early 1908.

USS *D1* (ex-*Narwhal*) – SS17, commissioned 23 Nov 1909 with Lt J C Townsend in command.

USS *Adder* (SS3) on trials after completion at the Crescent Shipyard, Elizabethport, New Jersey in late 1902. She was commissioned 12 Jan 1903 with Ensign F L Pinney in command.

was making coffee, while Jim cut the pumpkin pie. 'This isn't Delmonico's,' said Jim, 'but we're serving a lunch that Delmonico's couldn't serve – a submarine lunch.'

By this time the novelty was wearing off and we sat there, at the bottom of the sea, drinking our coffee with as much unconcern as though we were in an up-town restaurant. For the first time since we started, Mr Lake sat down, and we had an opportunity of talking with him at leisure. He is a stout-shouldered, powerfully built man, in the prime of life – a man of cool common sense, a practical man, who is also an inventor. And he talks frankly and convincingly, and yet modestly, of his accomplishment.

Having finished our lunch, Mr Lake prepared to show us something about the practical operations of the *Argonaut*. It has been a good deal of mystery to us how workmen penned up in a submarine boat could expect to recover gold from wrecks in the water outside, or to place torpedoes, or to pick up cables. 'We simply open the door, and the diver steps out on the bottom of the sea,' Mr Lake said, quite as if he was conveying the most ordinary information.

At first it seemed incredible, but Mr Lake showed us the heavy, riveted door in the bottom of the diver's compartment. Then he invited us inside with Wilson, who, besides being an engineer, is also an expert diver. The massive steel doors of the little room were closed and barred, and then Mr Lake turned a cock and the air rushed in under high pressure. At once our ears began to throb, and it seemed as if the drums would burst inward. 'Keep swallowing,' said Wilson the diver.

As soon as we applied this remedy, the pain was

relieved, but the general sensation of increased air pressure, while exhilarating, was still most uncomfortable. The finger on the pressure dial kept creeping up and up, until it showed that the air pressure inside the compartment was nearly equal to the water pressure without. Then Wilson opened a cock in the door. Instantly the water gushed in, and for a single instant we expected to be drowned there like rats in a trap. 'This is really very simple,' Mr Lake was saying calmly. 'When the pressure within is the same as that without, no water can enter.'

With that, Wilson dropped the iron door, and there was the water and the muddy bottom of the sea within touch of a man's hand. It was all easy enough to understand, and yet it seemed impossible, even as we saw it with our own eyes. Mr Lake stooped down, and picked up a wooden rod having a sharp hook at the end. This he pulled along the bottom . . .

We were now rising again to the surface, after being submerged for more than three hours. I climbed into the conning tower and watched for the first glimpse of the sunlight. There was a sudden fluff of foam, the ragged edge of a wave, and then I saw, not more than a hundred feet away, a smack bound toward New York under full sail. Her rigging was full of men, gazing curiously in our direction, no doubt wondering what strange monster of the sea was coming forth for a breath of air.

Lake entertained the gentlemen of the Press lavishly and consequently enjoyed a better press than Holland. 'Klondyke is nowhere,' said the *New York Herald* and businessmen were quick to see the merits of a bottom-crawler for commercial operations. 'You mustn't confuse the *Argonaut* with other submarine boats,' said the inventor, 'she is quite different and much safer.'

Much encouraged, Lake went on to build the more powerful, torpedo-armed *Protector* which was launched at Bridgeport, Connecticut on 1 November 1902.

The multi-purpose *Protector* was eventually bought by Russia[17] and it was not until 1911 that Lake started to influence submarine evolution in the United States Navy. Meanwhile John Philip Holland's designs maintained the lead and founded the underwater fleets in practically every navy of the world.

HM Submarine *No 1* on trials at Barrow, Jan 1902.

Chapter Ten
We Know All About Submarines

By 1899 Captain Lowe USN, on behalf of the Navy Department in Washington, was quite convinced that America needed submarines; but in Great Britain the Admiralty were equally sure that neither the Royal Navy nor any other Navy ought to have them. Every possible political obstacle was thrown down in the path of these monstrous vessels advancing implacably first from France and now from America. Reports of their increasingly active demonstrations were the worst possible news for the Royal Navy and the Empire it had won.

Clearly nothing would prevent the ingress of the underwater tide and indignant accusations about striking below the belt were useless. The British Government therefore resorted first to noncommittal statements and then to belittling the threat. In answer to a question in the House of Commons in February 1899 with regard to French progress in the underwater field, Lord Goschen, First Lord of the Admiralty, was 'not at present prepared to make any statement'. A further question by Captain Norton MP on 6 April 1900 drew a lofty answer to the effect that 'submarines were a weapon for Maritime Powers on the defensive' and that, anyway, 'we know all about them.'

Despite these supercilious assurances, which were intended as a sop to anyone who thought that the Government was dragging its feet, My Lords of the Admiralty had, privately and reluctantly, already decided to acquire some submarine boats to find out just how dangerous they were. It was sincerely hoped that they would prove ineffective. 'In habituating our men and officers to them,' said Admiral Hoppins, 'we shall realise more clearly their weakness against us.' Hopeful Hoppins!

HM Submarine *No 1* lying alongside the parent ship HMS *Hazard* c1902. The sailor aft is sitting on the magnetic compass and the one forward is propping himself on the partially opened torpedo-loading hatch. The towing wire running along the port side could be slipped from inside the boat and it was reckoned that a submarine could be taken in tow in any weather.

Britain Orders Holland Boats

The cheapest way of getting some boats was to buy the rights from the Holland Torpedo Boat Company in America where Mr Isaac Rice was most anxious to do business. They could then be built in England at a cost of £35,000 apiece, including delivery to naval ports, so long as they were constructed at the works of Vickers Sons and Maxim Ltd at Barrow-in-Furness. A royalty of £10,000 would have to be paid to Vickers if any boats were manufactured by what were called 'private firms' and £2500 if built in HM Dockyards. Vickers, even at that early date, had something of a special relationship with the Admiralty for submarine construction and the Barrow firm, like the Electric Boat Company in America (which took over the Holland Torpedo Company), has been the lead yard ever since.

Agreement was reached for the construction of five Holland boats, referred to as Type Number VII, by the middle of December 1900. The contract included the provision of a trained American crew 'which will be at the service of the Admiralty for the purpose of instructing a British Navy crew in the working and general operation of the boat under all circumstances of service.'[1] Evidently, the Admiralty, whatever the politicians may have said, did not claim to 'know all about' submarines. Vickers reckoned that they could supply the first boat in nine months and that the subsequent four boats would follow very quickly but the Admiralty wished to test the first boat thoroughly before finally completing the remaining four. After all the arguing that had gone before everybody was now speedily getting down to practicalities.

Vickers were prepared to guarantee that certain conditions would be met at official acceptance trials and were prepared to say that 'because the official guarantees by the Holland Torpedo Boat Company in America were considerably exceeded at the official trials we have every reason to believe that better results than those we have mentioned will be obtained.'[2] In brief, the specifications were:

Number One diving in the Solent *c*1904. As was usual in the early days, the boat was practically stopped. Before commencing operations with other ships, the Admiralty ruled that submarines 'be allowed from 15 to 20 minutes . . . to trim'.

Holland boats lying alongside their parent ship. Although steaming and navigation lights were fitted on the masts, as shown here, night passages, with the attendant risks of being run down, were avoided when possible. Admiralty orders stated clearly that submarines during exercises were 'to surface at one hour before sunset at the latest so that their parent ship may collect them before dark'.

a. Speed and radius of action on the surface: 8 knots in fine weather; 7 knots in ordinary weather. Radius 250 knots at full speed. ['Knots' were frequently used to mean nautical miles and this has led to much confusion amongst naval historians.]

b. Speed submerged and radius of action: 7 knots, radius 25 knots and 'we will guarantee full speed for 25 knots'. [This was absolutely out of the question: somebody at Vickers got their sums wrong for no batteries could possibly have a $3\frac{1}{2}$-hour capacity at the maximum discharge rate; one hour was the utmost that could be expected.]

c. Distance submerged without inconvenience to the crew: 15 knots. Time closed up three hours. [This was over-estimating the oxygen and carbon dioxide problems.]

d. Limits within which course and depth can be maintained: Average depth-keeping within 2 feet, maximum 4 feet.

e. Time required from working on the surface with oil motor to the submerged condition: 2 to 10 minutes according to the skill of the crew.

f. Maximum safe depth: 100 feet. [In fact, the greatest recorded depth for a British Holland boat was 78 feet reached by *No 2*. Nor was that deliberate: 'the downward momentum was caused

114 by too much water ballast being taken in. The air service did not fail as in the case of the USS *Porpoise* and the boat, after experiencing a few leaks from rivets weeping etc, was brought to the surface none the worse for her deep submergence'.[3]]

Meanwhile *Holland VI*, purchased by the US Government for 150,000 dollars, was formally commissioned on 13 October 1900. A fresh contract for the construction of six submarine torpedo boats for the USN was concluded on 25 August 1900. These were given names and called the *Adder* Class. The first of the *Adder* class was launched in July 1901. They were numbered *3–8*[4] and were to a new Holland *No X* design: this, and not *No VII*, is the design to which the British *Holland Boats 1–5* were finally built at Vickers. The Admiralty might, incidentally, have chosen to copy the French *Narval* instead of the *Holland* but *Narval* ran into difficulties and was not sufficiently satisfactory to go on trials until the end of 1900. Such was Britain's trust in the

Holland I 1901

1 vertical rudders
2 aft trim tank
3 air compressor
4 gasoline engine
5 battery fan
6 compass
7 ventilators
8 periscope
9 conning tower
10 steering gear
11 wireless gear
12 spare torpedo

13 batteries
14 main ballast
15 buoyancy tank
16 air bottles
17 torpedo impulse
18 toilet
19 gasoline tank
20 air flask
21 torpedo compensating
22 forward trim tank
23 torpedo tube
24 bow cap

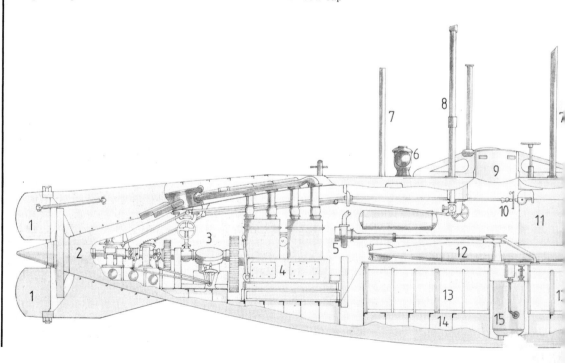

capabilities of American engineers that Isaac Rice negotiated the contract with the Royal Navy without any Admiralty official having inspected a submarine of Holland's design. The trust proved to be justified and, of course, the Admiralty was saved the huge and expensive amount of work which would have been involved with an entirely new kind of vessel.

HM Submarine *No 1* was laid down almost immediately in February 1901 and launched on 2 October 1901 (the official birthday of the Royal Navy's Submarine Service). She started her sea trials in April 1902, some months before the *Adder* went on trials in America. The policy of 'wait and see' had paid dividends. *The Times* newspaper was relieved on behalf of the general public. An editorial pontified: 'slow and sure is a good maxim, but sure and ready is a better. We must not be caught napping, and when a particular weapon has found favour with a nation shrewd as the Americans and as ingenious as the French, it behoves us not to neglect it ourselves.'

Setting up the Submarine Service

Political interests in England were one thing and actualities another. The agreed requirements had been met and by a deeply conservative nation in what was really a remarkably short space of time. But success or lack of it (which was what many surface-bound admirals hoped for) depended entirely on the quality of the crew who were to man the Royal Navy's first submarine. In this the Navy was very fortunate. The cast was headed by an officer who had distinguished himself in torpedo work, Captain Reginald Bacon. Bacon was appointed Inspecting Captain of Submarine Boats and he demanded the services of a support ship for which HMS *Hazard*, an 1894 torpedo-gunboat, was immediately provided and despatched to Barrow-in-Furness. The little 1070-ton ship was less than ideal but a submarine depot ship had not yet been conceived; and at least the little *Hazard* ensured that Captain Bacon received command pay. (The extra money paid to a ship's commanding officer for his responsibility.)

Unlike *No 1* the second Holland boat was given a small but respectable launching party. Capt Bacon is second from the left in this group pictured on 21 Feb 1902 at Vickers.

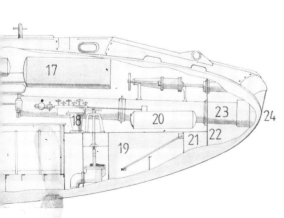

116 Bacon did not have to scratch around for a crew. By chance (and it really does seem to have been by chance) the prospective commanding officer, Lieutenant Forster D Arnold-Forster, who volunteered his services just happened to be the nephew of the Parliamentary and Financial Secretary to the Admiralty of the same name. Uncle Arnold-Forster was the very man who, in the House of Commons on 18 March 1901 during the debate about acquiring submarine boats, confessed he desired that they 'shall never prosper'. He amicably shifted his ground when the admirals shifted theirs and set about pacifying My Lords of the Treasury who sadly regretted that 'it should be considered necessary for experimental purposes to order as many as five boats of a type which may not prove successful'.[6]

The Secretary and Treasurer kept his options open, however, by emphasising that the construction programme was only in the nature of a trial. How glad he was, he said, that Lord Goshen (the First Lord) 'did give this instruction to the Board, which had now borne fruit in the determination to put this experiment in execution . . .'

Anyway, apparently without nepotism or influence of the sort that Jackie Fisher favoured, Lieutenant Arnold-Forster, a young and capable torpedo officer, was formally appointed in command of the boat now building. As things turned out, however, he was kept on a tight rein: Captain Bacon himself took practically all command decisions.

Arnold-Forster came, like practically all British naval officers of the period, from a good upper middle-class family, fully integrated into Edwardian society. He was highly thought of professionally and had done well in his torpedo course so that he could look forward to a successful career in the Royal Navy while enjoying all that society had to offer on board and ashore. He was thus more than a little hesitant about joining the brand-new submarine service which would all too obviously not provide the sparkle of overseas cruises and might offer only a stony road towards promotion. There were plenty of people anxious to point out that submarining was no occupation for a gentleman.

Fortunately Arnold-Forster kept a full and frank diary which has only just come to light through the generosity of his daughter.[7] Arnold-Forster's own words reveal an intimate picture of those early days and also put right a number of muddled assumptions in the history books as the following annotated extracts show.

Saturday 12 January 1901. Uncle Oakley likes his new berth [in the Government]. He is apparently up to his eyes in work.

Sunday 13 January. . . . Yarn with Uncle Oakley. He is apparently anxious that we should start building submarine boats as a reply to the French. Perhaps we ought. It seems to be a matter of policy more than anything else. No doubt if we start they will build all the more. At present they have a few of doubtful value . . .

Saturday 23 February. Read about submarine boats . . .

Sunday 24 February. Wrote service letter to the Captain [of the cruiser in which Forster was then serving] asking for three Lyddite fuses for shell as I have an idea of fitting them to fire with small charges from six-inch guns at submarine boats, Phosphide of Calcium to light fuse after it has sunk a certain depth and so attempt to countermine submarine boat. [This may well have been the first practical proposal for something equivalent to the depth charges which followed.] Practised banjo.

Sunday 24 March. Wrote to Uncle Oakley volunteering for submarine boats duty if any chance. I don't believe in them but I suppose somebody will be wanted to do preliminary experiments and it might be a useful experience. Anyhow no harm in asking . . .

Friday 3 May. [Gave] First lecture in this ship on submarine boats.

Thursday 9 May. Wrote letter to Captain applying for submarine boat. Have no idea what will come of it, probably nothing.

Monday 17 June. Wrote to Allen asking him if he would exchange and let me go to *Implacable* for Mediterranean.

Wednesday 26 June. Skipper sent for me and told me some rather important news, confidentially, that he was forwarding my application for submarine boats. I thought it had fallen through . . . In some ways I would rather go to sea [sic] but if I get in all right I think the job ought to be good for me from the Service point of view.

Number 5 at about 7 knots, close to maximum speed, in normal surface trim.

Learning about the all-important battery – supplying the life-blood of any submarine – at Fort Blockhouse in 1905. The plates have been lifted out of their (then) lead-lined wooden box.

On 20 August 1901 Arnold-Forster was formally appointed to HMS *Hazard* 'For Special Service' (the word submarine being studiously omitted because of secrecy) together with Lieutenant Stephen B Evans, a navigation specialist, and two engineers, Robert Spence and Ernest J Mowlam. He went straight to Barrow where the boat was supposed to be nearing completion but nobody in the yard had heard of any submarine at all. Eventually he discovered her in a shed labelled 'Yacht Shed' where she was being built in utmost secrecy. Only selected, trustworthy men were allowed inside. All frames and other parts made in the yard were marked for 'Pontoon No 1' so she had aroused no special interest in the busy workshops:[8]

What surprised me most when I did find the boat was her small size. She was only 63 feet long and was shaped like a very fat and stubby cigar. She had fins and a tail with a single propeller and two rudders, one for steering and one for diving. There was a small conning-tower on top, just big enough to put one's head and shoulders in. Her speed turned out afterwards to be seven knots on the surface and never more than four or five underwater.

118 (Vickers had submitted in their contract, to a penalty of £1000 for every knot below seven knots not attained when submerged; but there is no record of the firm being obliged to pay the two or three thousand pounds implied.)

The new commanding officer was daunted by what he found inside the craft:

> ... the ingenious designer in New York evidently did not realise that the average naval officer has only two eyes and two hands; the little conning tower was simply plastered with wheels, levers and gauges with which some superman was to fire the torpedoes, dive and steer, and do everything else at the same time, and the inside of the boat was stuffed with wonderful automatic devices ...

The drawings to which Vickers worked were not, in fact, the same in detail as those for the USS *Adder*; but for the fanatical Fenian John Devoy to impute that Holland, out of loyalty to Ireland, altered these and later drawings – and was somehow responsible for disasters in the British 'A' class which followed – was patently absurd. However, there was undoubtedly much that was wrong and Captain Bacon told the Controller of the Navy that it was 'simply courting murder to carry out trials with the boat in her then condition and with no-one on board who had any real knowledge of submarine work.'[9] That fairly brought matters to a head and Vickers called on the Holland Boat Company to send over the trained crew that had been promised.

Working up HM Submarine No. 1

The American team duly arrived with Captain Cable in command. He wasted no time and was astonished to find the boat full of 'jimcrack' fittings to which Bacon had rightly taken objection. In fact, he was astonished to find that such impossible drawings had been sent from America and quickly won the confidence of Bacon, Arnold-Forster and the British crew who described him as 'a thoroughly sound and careful captain'.[10] Cable's favourite remark was that he 'did not go

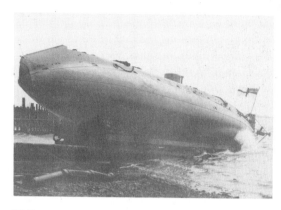

HMS *A-1* being launched at Vickers 9 July 1902. The first four boats of the 'A' class were only a slight improvement on the Hollands although they were 40ft longer and were fitted with a higher conning tower and a short periscope. Weight and reserve of buoyancy were serious problems in both classes.

down in submarines for the benefit of his health' and he took no unnecessary risks. Amongst other major changes he separated the diving-rudder control from the steering wheel and put each in charge of a separate operator leaving the captain free to navigate. He also installed a large depth gauge and a spirit level for 'depth steering'.

Bacon claimed to have hit on the idea of a periscope and it was certainly due to him that one was fitted – a considerable advance on the contemporary American boats which lacked such a device and were dependent upon porpoising up and down to glimpse the surface through glass scuttles in the conning tower. But the idea was by no means new: periscopes had successfully been tried in France and Simon Lake had designed an excellent instrument in America. Indeed, the first periscope used in the United States Navy was fitted to the ironclad monitor *Osage*; it was used during the Civil War to discover a Confederate cavalry unit taking cover behind the high banks of the Red River in Arkansas. Bacon's 'optical tube' had to be erected and secured by stays before diving and it was not until about 1910 that

A-boat coming alongside at Fort Blockhouse *c*1904.

image was rectified.

On 3 October 1901 the *Naval and Military Record* published the following brief paragraphs:

> It is understood that no ceremony will take place at the forthcoming launch of the first British submarine at Barrow-in-Furness.
>
> The Admiralty regard these boats as wholly in the nature of an experiment and, like all other experiments conducted from time to time, this one will be carried out with every privacy.

Privacy was certainly achieved for HM Submarine *No 1* for she had been launched the day before on 2 October. It was a non-event. Arnold-Forster did not even trouble to record it in his diary. His next entry of note concerned the first of the series of 'fug trials' on 21 October in HMS *Hazard*'s tiny breadroom where four men were incarcerated for two and a half hours without any ill effects from carbon dioxide which rose to 9.5 parts per thousand. Bacon thought that, as Inspecting Captain, he ought to take part in later trials himself. Tests in the breadroom were uneventful: the subjects passed the time with cards and music; and, every hour, the doctor took everyone's pulse and temperature including his own. Something serious was expected to happen and the medical experts were disappointed when nobody collapsed. Even when two complete crews were shut down in the submarine itself for a whole night there were no breathing difficulties but the incarcerated submariners were called upon to endure something worse than suffocation. An elderly representative from the Holland Boat Company brought his flute with him to beguile the company and played it all through the long, long night. It was a trial by ordeal that the ship's companies were never able to forget. As Captain Bacon feelingly recalled: '... they all looked upon flutes thereafter with a personal measure of animosity.'

The hard-lying money recently awarded to submariners was generous – six shillings a day for officers and two shillings for able seamen – but it was not sufficient to compensate for that degree of

retractable periscopes were fitted (in the 'D' class). Bacon later complained that he was unable to patent his device because there was already a surgical instrument of a similar nature for examining a patient's bladder.

The optical tube was duly fitted at Vickers and provoked much interest. Captain Cable took the idea back to America with him for inclusion in the *Adder* class. One (British) enthusiast, in light of heated debate about a periscope being too easily seen by the enemy, proposed painting the upper part of the tube in spiral stripes of all the primary colours 'so that when whizzed round by a small electric motor it ought to have been invisible' but sense prevailed and 'the periscope-painting craze gradually died out'.[11] The optics were not good and the lenses required frequent dessication, but the apparent disadvantage of targets appearing upside down when the periscope was trained astern and standing on their ends when abeam was welcomed by the early captains who were able to judge relative bearings without taking their eye from the eye-piece. The oldsters complained bitterly when, in more complex instruments, the

hardship. (In the USN a submarine sailor was paid five dollars a month extra and also received one dollar for each day on which his boat dived up to a maximum total of twenty dollars per month of submarine pay.)

The first surface run on the gasoline engine was made up the Ramsden Dock on 15 January 1902. The little boat was awkward to steer. On one occasion she alarmed the inmates of the sick bay in the *Hazard* by poking her blunt bows right through the ship's side into their berths. On another day she was caught in the wash of a *Majestic* class battleship slowly turning her outboard propeller alongside the dockyard wall: sent careering off course, she crashed into the iron bridge that still spans the channel. She collided with a crash that shook the bridge and the gasping spectators alike; but no damage was done and the Vickers ship-builders were able to boast, in the local public houses that night, that when they built a submarine they built it strong – stronger than the Barrow bridge. There was continual trouble with the hull valves, blank-flanges and the main motor armature during February and March and Arnold-Forster's enthusiasm waned. On 18 March he decided to accept the post of Torpedo Lieutenant in HMS *Ariadne*, Flagship of the North American Squadron. However, that would not be until June.

Meanwhile, on Good Friday 20 March 1902 the first dive was made, as it still is today, in an enclosed shipyard basin. Chains were prudently passed beneath the hull to pull the boat up in case she got stuck on the bottom like *Nautilus* in 1887[12]. The trim was adjusted and Arnold-Forster went down in the boat for the second trim-dive, again on chains, the next day. He was upset when on the following Monday morning, *No 1* went out into the dock for her first free dive and 'the Captain [Bacon] said we could not both go down together the first time . . . so I had to come out and follow in the steam boat in charge of the rescue party.' Afterwards 'the Captain dined in the wardroom . . . he stood champagne to celebrate the first dip.' However, the commanding officer was permitted to go down himself on the afternoon of 3 April 'after waiting seven months and seeing apparently endless difficulties. Captain Bacon tried steering the boat by a new wheel close to the optical tube with successful results. Morrell[13] worked diving wheel. Av depth three to four feet. Hit the bottom twice but quite soft.'

All was now ready for submerged sea-trials. The diary continues:

Sunday 6 April. A fine day . . . left ship and went out to Morecambe Bay for our first deep submarine run. We all went in *Furness* tug, very comfortable, the submarine was towed by steam launch. Laid four buoys two miles apart on a course parallel to Walney Island, Av depth nine fathoms. Captain Cable in charge, Morrell and three other Yankees, Captain Bacon, myself, Spence, TI [Petty Officer torpedoman] and Chief ERA and Williams the Yard Foreman. The first run I did understudy for diving wheel. Did a straight two mile run with optical tube and came up alongside fourth buoy. Depth eight feet. On the run back I worked the diving wheel. Rather tricky at first but shall soon get into it. Kept her fairly steady at eight feet. Lunch in target at 2.30. Everyone was very pleased about the runs. Went back in steam launch. Went to church and wrote letters.
Monday 7 April. Yankees working at *No 1* oil engine all day. Did a trial with *No 2* surface run with motor in the dock. Got 6.3 knots, better than *No 1* owing to new propeller.

No 2 had been launched with traditional celebrations and even some modest publicity: the shipyard Managing Director's little daughter performed the ceremony and a photograph was taken to mark the occasion.

Tuesday 8 April. Decided to go out again to Morecambe Bay. Mrs Bacon came with us in the tug . . . had lunch before going down . . . Captain Cable went back to America this morning, leaving Morrell and one electrician so Morrell took charge. I worked the diving wheel, Captain Bacon steered with periscope. Rather hazy and difficult to see buoys; we steered mostly by standard compass. We had three long dives about six minutes. I am getting more steady on the diving wheel and kept her about ten feet deep. Said goodbye to Morrell as he is off tonight. He is a good sort but some of his yarns are rather too doubtful.

One of the 'A' class referred to in 1904 as 'our
new large submarine'.   *Public Record Office*

The diary, outside these extracts, is devoted to
the less plush pursuits of an Edwardian gentleman
on a very modest income: rabbit-poaching, occasional visits to the Opera and his London Club,
dinners, bicycle journeys and so on; but it studiously omits any mention of what must have been
some hair-raising moments in the submarine.
These are left to Bacon's Memoirs and it is clear
that the most important man on board, apart from
the Inspecting Captain, Bacon and Cable himself
during these American-directed trials, was the
Boss Diver as the Americans called him. Whether
the boat sank or swam depended on him. He was to
become the Diving Coxswain in the Royal Navy
and then simply the Coxswain. Diving Coxswains,
who controlled the hydroplanes, were in the
future to be carefully selected from suitable
Senior Ratings. The first was a most redoubtable
Petty Officer First Class – William R Waller: it was
he who laid the foundations for the Coxswain
being the rightful 'Boss' of a British submarine,

responsible for discipline and administration as
well as taking over the planes in tricky situations.
The later designation of Chief of the Boat in the
United States Navy did not usually imply hydroplane control. The French gave by far the best
name to their key rating – *Le Patron*.

For the critical initial dive in *No 2* (which had
overhauled *No 1*) the boat was carefully trimmed
right down on the surface with the Boss Diver
stationed at the handwheel controlling the diving
rudders. Everybody else on board was ordered to
remain seated on the canvas stool which each man
carried on board with him. Cable cautioned the
crew not to move about in case they upset the trim
and caused a nose dive. When nearly submerged
the rudders were put to dive and the motor to
ahead. With a steepish bow-down angle, green
water could be seen through the conning tower
scuttles and the manometer (depth gauge) showed
that *No 2* was running submerged for the first
time. Even when correctly trimmed for diving the
boat had to maintain a bow-down angle in order to
overcome the small positive buoyancy that Holland thought necessary to ensure that the craft

122 | would return to the surface in the event of any failure.

The British crew watched the Boss Diver and his American team with wide-eyed apprehension. When a bucket got loose and clattered down the engine-room deck-plates 'it sent hearts into mouths'. Otherwise there was no noise except for the hum of the motor and 'the queer sounding American orders' given by the temporary captain. The British crew quickly became accustomed to the business and it took only a few dives before Cable declared them adequately trained.

However, surface handling was an unexpectedly difficult art to master. The force of the planes was unexpectedly illustrated during one of *No 1*'s maiden trips. The boat buried her bows when gathering speed for a speed trial and water crept up to the torpedo hatch while the stern kicked skywards. To the inexperienced it looked as if *No 1* was going to the bottom nose first. The chief draughtsman of Messrs Vickers Sons and Maxim, standing on the casing forward and busily engaged in looking for shore marks so as to take the time over a measured distance for calculating the speed, became more than a little alarmed, shouting 'For God's sake, man, stop her! Look at my new breeks!' The water was by then up to his knees with the deck rapidly inclining downwards and away from him. Arnold-Forster, a little further aft and quite dry by the conning tower, was not in the least perturbed. 'She can't possibly sink,' he blithely called out; but he ordered two degrees up-helm on the diving rudders all the same. The boat felt this at once and a little more angle was added to bring the bows right up. After that, care was always taken to keep a little up-helm on the diving rudders when speeding-up and trimmed low.

A few days later, Captain Bacon who was thoroughly enjoying himself and prone to take direct command 'absentmindedly ran under a low bridge with periscope up on the surface and carried it away. No damage otherwise.'[14] Being the only senior officer for miles around he felt there was no need to report the incident; after all the periscope was his own invention. Arnold-

Forster was left to make the repairs. On 16 April something much more serious occurred: 'four gallons of rum adrift somehow. Beastly nuisance.'[15] That was a gentlemanly understatement. Many a British submarine officer for years to come was to learn the painful extent of that particular kind of beastly nuisance and refer to it in considerably stronger terms.

When Cable returned to the United States he gave evidence before the Committee of US Naval Affairs. He was not very flattering about the British boats: 'their special requirements are less than ours. They do not require the same speed that the United States Government does, and they are not as accurate about the firing of the torpedo. All the British Government wanted was to see the boat underwater, to see that she could dive and manoeuvre . . . the first boat that was accepted did not fire any torpedoes at all.'[16] Bacon now set out to remedy that deficiency.

The Royal Navy's First Submarine Flotilla

In the summer of 1902, a small convoy consisting of HMS *Hazard*, Submarines *No 2* and *No 3* with torpedo-boat *No 42* as escort left Barrow for Portsmouth where *Nos 1, 4* and *5* joined them a few months later.

Submarines were dangerous and discreditable so they were banished to the upper reaches of Portsmouth Harbour along with powder barges, prison hulks and quarantine vessels. The small flotilla was lodged there, well out of the way, alongside the *Severn* class cruiser, HMS *Thames*, until eventually being admitted to the more salubrious Haslar Creek at the mouth of the harbour. In the eighteenth century Oyster Creek (as it was known) on the Gosport side was a genteel resort for sailors who tired of Portsmouth's brazen attractions. Appropriately Fort Blockhouse, on its southern marge, became the Alma Mater of the Royal Navy's select submariners in 1905 with the old hulks of HMS *Dolphin* and HMS *Mercury* lying in support.

The three white bands around this A-boat's conning tower mark her as *A-3*. The method of numbering and designating submarines changed constantly in the early days and old photographs can be most misleading. The rules during exercises were that a torpedo attack failed if the markings were read.

Bacon was glad to get his five *Holland*s away from the artificial protection of Barrow and start serious sea-training in the Solent. There was a lot to be learned. With the Service rapidly expanding and boats of the new 'A' class building, lessons had to be passed from mouth to mouth and hand to hand. Bacon knew that they were all groping in the dark and preached care. He had a brass plate engraved with the words 'No one of us is infallible, even the youngest' and gave the plaque in turn to the boat whose captain had most recently offended.

The Otto engines were far from reliable and did not make training any easier. One of Bacon's first

planned operations was to circumnavigate the Isle of Wight with all five boats – not a very ambitious cruise but more than enough for the day. Three broke down before they passed Spit Fort four miles from the start and only one reached Cowes. At times the game seemed hopeless but patience and dogged hard work gradually eliminated the causes of failure and the captains steadily brought their boats into an efficient state. Once, when Bacon was on deck with a submarine's captain, and the boat was being steered from below, a Ryde ferryboat swept by. To prevent the wash going below they dropped down the lid of the conning tower. Unfortunately the ventilators were not open and the petrol engine rapidly exhausted the boat of air to the point where the hatch could not be opened again. Meanwhile, the boat was steering straight for Spit Fort. There was no way of telling the helmsman to alter course and it was only by good luck that the engine slowed up for want of air in time to alert the crew inside the boat; they managed to open the ventilators and conning tower hatch just in time to prevent a head-on collision with the solid stone fort.

Careful drill was needed to supply air to the engine without flooding the submarine. At Harbour Stations, the long horizontal door-like torpedo loading hatch was firmly screwed down and, while the petrol engine was being started, tests were carried out to ensure that the steering and diving rudders were working correctly. The Coxswain, if the boat was going as far as the open sea, enveloped himself in an enormous Admiralty-pattern oilskin and sat down squarely on the little conning tower with a small, dismountable steering wheel in front of him. The rudder controls were, of course, hand-draulic and required considerable strength to operate. Two ventilating tubes supplied air to the inside of the boat and a third was supposed to carry away the engine fumes. If it did not, three white mice, suspended in a little cage from the engine room deckhead, gave warning 'being extremely sensitive'; a picture postcard of the period declared 'they notify the slightest escape of gasoline by squeaking.' There were prolonged arguments about whether the mice, first by 'notifying' and then by turning their little feet up, indicated the presence of carbon monoxide from the exhaust gases or petrol leaking from the injectors. It was the sort of thing that submariners have always enjoyed debating furiously.

The 160hp petrol engine was started by turning the main electric motor with the propeller clutched in. The starting process was thereby violent and jerky; while the Otto was coughing and spluttering the submarine itself was helpless. The engine was greedy for air but once clear of harbour water soon started washing over the conning tower hatch so that it had to be shut, leaving only the thin ventilating tubes to cope with its needs. If the sea was rough the Coxswain and the Captain retired below to join the remainder of the seasick ship's company and the Captain navigated through the periscope. This imperfect instrument had 'an annoying habit'[17] of clouding over at critical moments and the Captain had then, as Arnold-Forster remarked, 'to trust entirely to Providence and a compass'. Submariners today well understand how 'annoying' this must have been.

When and if the boat reached her assigned diving area the Coxswain unshipped the wheel, took off his oilskin (it was difficult to squeeze through the hatch with it on) climbed down the tower, ordering 'Diving Stations Below'. The ventilators were lowered, the hull valves shut, the engine stopped and the main motor was tested by the Petty Officer TI in charge of the switchboard. The Second Captain, a Lieutenant or Sub-Lieutenant, reported 'All Correct' to the Captain who climbed down the conning tower last, shutting the hatch above him and then ordering 'Flood the Main Ballast Tank'. At this point camp stools were unfolded and the crew took their places while the craft settled into the water until the sea lapped around the conning tower. It was now possible to judge the fore-and-aft trim which was adjusted as required by instructing a suitably portly member of the crew to shift his stool a little further aft or forward as necessary. The auxiliary

tanks were then slowly filled. When it was obvious that only a small amount of positive buoyancy remained, the motor was put ahead and the Coxswain took the boat down steadily on the diving rudders to the ordered depth.

That was what was supposed to happen. It was not always like that. Bearing in mind that 100 feet was the ultimate depth permitted, very hasty action had to be taken to blow main ballast and reverse the planes if it looked as though the descent was getting out of control. An alarming series of ups and downs, often accompanied by steep angles and electrical failure, usually followed. The greatest danger was that on one of the 'ups' a small surface vessel, or even a buoy, would be in the way. There was also a sporting chance of electrolyte spilling from the batteries and a lot of water from the internal tanks finding its way into the bilges to mix with acid and oil.

Printed instructions[19] to submarine officers emphasised the necessity of mopping up spilt battery acid and keeping bilges dry to avoid the generation of marsh gas – yet another hazard for the white mice. They would probably not have noticed anyway, however, because they were reliably reputed to be stuffed so full of food by the sailors – notorious pet-lovers at the best of times – that they were virtually insensible throughout their service careers.

The Second Captain steered the boat submerged with one eye glued to the eye-piece of the tube where he could see the illuminated reflection of the compass card. The compass itself was in a watertight container outside the hull where it was less liable to built-in magnetic influences and distractions than it would have been inside. It was far from reliable.

As always, the most dangerous time for a submarine was on coming to periscope depth from a period deliberately spent deep. The periscope broke surface at a depth of about 15 feet and optimum periscope depth was about 10 feet, measured not from the keel to the surface as it is today but from where the waterline would be if the craft was fully surfaced. Thus, at ten feet the top of

TOP **Postcard of about 1904.**

ABOVE **The unofficial submarine flag in 1904.**

A typical case of collision in the vertical plane occurred in the Solent when HM Submarine *No 2* was demonstrating the art of 'playing porpoises' to the Princess Royal watching from a nearby dockyard tug. The boat had just come up to 10 feet when there was 'a curious scraping noise' overhead, a tremor and a slight roll. An irrepressible able seaman on his stool right forward helpfully sang out 'What Ho! She bumps!' as a hollow series of thuds sounded along the pressure hull. The instinct nowadays, unless water was flooding in, would be to go deep again as quickly as possible and wait until any shipping overhead had drawn clear; but in those days the Captain was strongly in favour of regaining the surface without delay so he ordered 'Hard-a-Rise' while blowing main ballast and stopping the motor.

The consequence was that *No 2* hit an anchored brigantine of vintage years but the surface vessel's captain, despite aggrieved gesticulations by his crew, kindly reassured his underwater opposite number by saying that although some damage must have been caused it was 'nothing to hurt'.[20] The trouble, as on so many occasions to come, had been too little allowance for the tidal stream which had swept the submarine crabwise through a crowded channel. The periscope was bent into a bow but the tough Vickers hull was undamaged. If the brigantine had been underway she would almost certainly have sliced the little boat in half and sunk her.

The incident foreshadowed real disasters ahead; and soon they came. But, for the moment, the new Submarine Service was struggling successfully to its feet, paddling and splashing enjoyably in shallow waters. Upper-deck seamen became engineers almost before they knew it. The glamour and comfort of the surface fleet were soon forgotten by those early volunteers who persisted, boring their contemporaries to rigidity in the Keppel's Head and other well-known hostelries around Portsmouth, with their endless talk of 'Shop'. 'The Trade', as somebody christened it (probably the poet Rudyard Kipling), was in business.

the pressure hull was only a fathom or so down; and at that depth there was no chance of avoiding collision, very possibly fatal, with any ship that happened to be passing overhead. There was no underwater listening gear although the beat of propellers close by could sometimes be heard through the hull. What direction they were coming from was anybody's guess.

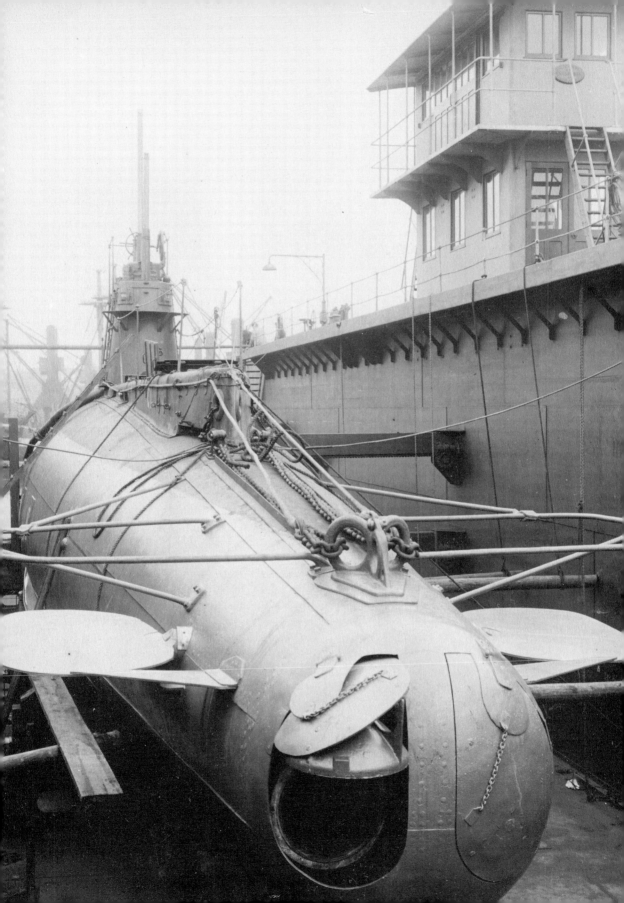

Chapter Eleven
The Weapons

Ratings, obviously from a training class ashore, being instructed on torpedoes in a 'C' class submarine c1910.

LEFT **HMS** *C-1* in floating dock, 1908. Note the conning tower hatch opening to port, the deadlights in the conning tower itself, the forward hydroplane plane-guards (very necessary when coming alongside) and the upward-opening bow-shutter and bow-cap.

'The only use of the *Holland*,' said Admiral O'Neil USN in 1900, 'is to discharge torpedoes and no weapon is more erratic!' There are plenty of submariners even today who would gloomily agree with the tenor of his remark. Underwater weapons, until the advent of ballistic missiles, always lagged well astern of the vehicles that carried them simply because designers consistently devised submarines and then decided what torpedoes they could carry rather than selecting a complete weapon-system and building the best type of underwater vehicle to accommodate it. Nor, even from the start, was anything like as much effort devoted to weapons as to submarine hulls and propulsion. Some impressive-looking submarines resulted but their value as fighting units – at least until the outbreak of war in 1914 – was very dubious. It was not so much the torpedo mechanisms that justified Admiral O'Neil's pessimism, although they were far from reliable: it was more a lack of adequate fire-control and discharge arrangements. The latter, although they compensated admirably for the submarine's trim on firing from a *Holland* and other early boats, were apt to upset a torpedo's depth-keeping device as well as pushing it off course when it left the tube. Add to these a submarine captain's own errors in estimating a target's course and speed, and torpedo-fire was indeed erratic.

By the time that Holland's boats were showing their paces at sea the word torpedo, taken from the cramp-fish or electric ray, implied an independently powered weapon – a miniature submarine in itself. The description no longer applied to mines as it did in Bushnell's and Fulton's inventions, but spar-torpedoes were fitted to some torpedo-boats; so free-running weapons were often called locomotive, automobile or fish torpedoes to distinguish them. In British and American navies they became 'fish' or 'tin-fish' and, on the Royal Navy's lower deck, 'kippers' or 'mouldies' so that, at the beginning of World War I a young submariner would display his trade ashore by nonchalantly telling a wondering audience that he had just 'squirted a mouldie'.

128 The idea goes back at least to 1626 for in that year the dramatist Ben Jonson wrote the following dialogue in *The Staple of Newes*[1]:

Thos:	They write here one Cornelius Son hath made the Hollanders an invisible eel to swim the Haven at Dunkirk, and sink all the shipping there.
Pennyboy:	But how is't done?
Cymbal:	I'll show you, Sir, it is an automata, runs under water, with a snug nose, and has a nimble tail made like an auger, with which tail she wriggles betwixt the costs of a ship and sinks it straight.
Pennyboy:	A most brave device to murder their flat bottoms.

Whitehead's Secret

Despite Ben Jonson's predictions invisible eels made little headway until 1866 when Robert Whitehead built the first of many torpedoes which made him famous. Whitehead was born at Bolton in 1823, apprenticed to an engineer at the age of fourteen and for several years travelled throughout Europe showing the way to improve silk-weaving machinery. In 1866 he became the manager of an Austrian company engaged in providing engines for the Austrian Navy which was at war with Italy. Approached by Captain Giovanni Luppis with plans for remotely controlling a spar-torpedo boat, Whitehead had a better idea.

He built the first automobile torpedo with the help of his twelve-year-old son and a trusted workman. Nobody else was 'allowed to have the slightest glimpse of the mysterious machine during the time that it was under construction, and consequently the surprise of the outside world was all the greater when at last it emerged from its hiding-place in a completed form.'[2] Compressed air drove the prototype at a speed of six knots but sometimes it ran 'skimming on the surface whilst at others it dived down to the depths and exploded on the bottom'[3] where at least the detonator for its eighteen pounds of dynamite proved efficient.

It took less than two years for Whitehead to perfect a depth-keeping mechanism based upon a hydrostatic valve opposed by a spring which could be regulated according to the depth desired. The balance chamber, as it came to be known, housed this device which Whitehead called 'The Secret'; and he succeeded in keeping it secret until about 1891.

It has to be said that the navies who bought and developed Whitehead's torpedoes did not always understand the secret very well. Until half way through World War II, in 1943, the American and German submarine services were unable to ensure that their torpedoes maintained the correct depth and a very large number of targets were missed on this account. The depth-keeping apparatus in modern torpedoes is, at last, reliable. Albeit damped against oscillations and overridden by an acoustic homing device when close to a target it would be readily recognisable to the Victorian engineer.

Following a visit by a Royal Navy representative to his Fiume works in the autumn of 1869 Whitehead was invited to England to demonstrate his weapons. Over 100 tests were made at Sheerness during September and October 1870, most of them from a submerged tube let into the bows of HMS *Oberon*, an old paddle-wheel sloop from which the torpedoes were ejected by an impulse rod driven forward by compressed air. Ranges and speeds were not great: 8.5 knots over 200 yards and 7.5 knots over 600 yards were performances that were gladly accepted.

The final trials were conducted with live warheads (67lb of gun cotton) against the old wooden corvette *Aigle* protected by thick nets, 80 feet long and 12 feet deep, suspended 15 feet from the ship's side. The first destructive firing demonstrated that extraordinary capacity of any torpedo, so familiar to submariners, for doing the unexpected. Craftily slithering off course, it slid outside the after edge of the net and blew a hole 20 feet long by 10 feet deep in the target's quarter. The next shot was far more satisfactory from the Admiralty's point of view because it struck the net with 'the ship not

Holland VI coming alongside, probably just before taking on observers from the USN Board of Inspection in late March 1898. The muzzle door of the forward pneumatic gun can be seen on the bows and the torpedo-tube bow-cap is just below.

Lt Harry H Caldwell and his crew on board USTB *Holland* in June 1901. Acting Gunner Owen Hill, in charge of the trim, is second from right at the top. Caldwell, besides being an outstandingly capable young officer, possessed moral fortitude to a high degree and was the first of many American COs to press the case for the submarine in the face of strong opposition.

being hurt in any way whatever'[1]. The investigating committee duly reported that 'any maritime nation failing to provide itself with submarine locomotive torpedoes would be neglecting a great source of power both for offence and defense.'[5] The old school of gunnery officers protested vigorously but the government thereupon purchased The Secret and the right to manufacture Whitehead torpedoes for £15,000. France, Italy and Germany secured similar deals soon afterwards but the United States Navy was in no hurry to acquire the weapon, presumably because the Navy Department was so addicted to Mahanian gunnery and big ships. It was not until 1897 that Holland's fifth boat, the *Plunger*, incorporated a torpedo tube; before that he had put his entire trust in pneumatic and dynamite guns and still incorporated them in the design that was finally accepted by the Navy. Perhaps, as usual, he was right.

Admiral Jackie Fisher was of an entirely different mind to Admiral O'Neil and a number of senior British officers who did not like torpedoes:

> It is an historical fact that the British Navy stubbornly resists change.
> A First Sea Lord told me on one occasion that there were no torpedoes when he came to sea, and he didn't see why the devil there should be any of the beastly things now!
> This was *à propos* of my attracting the attention of his serene and contented mind to the fact that we hadn't got any torpedoes at that time in the British Navy, and that a certain Mr Whitehead (with whom I was acquainted) had devised an automobile torpedo, costing only £500, that would make a hole as big as his Lordship's carriage (then standing at the door) in the bottom of the strongest and biggest ship in the world, and she would go to the bottom in about five minutes.
> Thirty-five years after this last interview, on 4 September 1903 at 11am, the ironclad *Belleisle*, having had several extra bottoms put on her and strengthened in every conceivable manner that science could suggest or money accomplish, was sent to the bottom of Portsmouth Harbour by this very Whitehead torpedo in seven minutes.
> This Whitehead torpedo can be carried with facility in Submarine Boats, and it has now attained such a range and such accuracy (due to the marvellous adaptation of the gyroscope), that even at two miles

range it possesses a greater ratio of power of vitally injuring a ship in the line of battle than does the most accurate gun. This is capable of easy demonstration (if anyone doubts it).

There is this immense fundamental difference between the automobile torpedo and the gun – the torpedo has no trajectory: it travels horizontally and hits below the water, so all its hits are vital hits; but not so the gun – only in a few places are gun hits vital, and those places are armoured. It is not feasible to armour the bottoms of ships even if it were effectual – which it is not.[6]

Contra-rotating propellers, introduced in about 1875, were intended to keep torpedoes on a straight course but it was not until gyroscopes were introduced in 1895 that torpedoes became reasonably dependable in azimuth, supposedly (and over-optimistically) to an accuracy of half a degree. Hitherto, it had scarcely been worthwhile improving range or speed but now, with a gyro and 'The Secret' combined, a theoretical hitting range of 7000 yards against a beam target was possible so an alternative had to be found to cold compressed air. Various power sources were proposed, particularly in the United States where there was never any lack of inventors, but it was not until 1907 that the right answer was found. This was to spray fuel oil into a combustion chamber with compressed air at a reduced pressure and ignite the mixture for a three or four cylinder radial 'heater' engine. Alternatively, water could be injected to control the operating temperature and generate steam to drive a turbine – the method eventually adopted for American torpedoes.

The first submarine torpedoes, depending upon compressed air alone, had a maximum range no better than 800 yards at 30 knots. They were not the complicated weapons that they are today but, in the Royal Navy, the stores associated with them were accounted for with an unrivalled degree of bureaucratic exactitude. Every tool, bolt, pin, screw, spanner, wheel, cog, socket or plate had its own separate locker in the store room and every item was carefully numbered. When only 4997 tiny brass screws of a particular type were counted instead of the 5000 showing on the ledger,

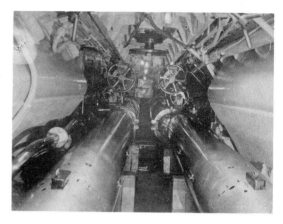

The torpedo compartment of HMS *B-6*, completed in 1906. Although considered, at this time, useful only for harbour defence, the B-boats came to be used effectively in World War I. In the harbour defence role, *B-6* was allocated an exercise area between Plymouth Breakwater and Cawsand Bay and provided with a box of carrier-pigeons for communication with the shore.

voluminous foolscap letters were exchanged with the Admiralty before grudging approval was given to write off the missing three screws which were valued at two-pence-halfpenny a gross.[7] As for losing an entire torpedo (not an uncommon event) submariners soon learned that it could be the most costly mistake of their entire careers, even worse than mislaying a jar of rum. In retrospect the numerous misfires and erratic runs make entertaining reading today but they seemed all too serious, at the time, to the unfortunate officers concerned.

The British Admiralty was not generous in its allowance of practice weapons. The one and only 18-inch torpedo provided for the five *Holland* boats building at Barrow had a charmed life and somehow managed to survive the attentions of the trials parties. It caused many anxious moments. Arnold-Forster recalls:

On one occasion the torpedo was fired as usual, the

The Gunner (T) dourly regarding racked 18in Whitehead torpedoes at Fort Blockhouse c1910.

boat was brought to the surface, and a little water blown out of the ballast tanks, and the conning tower hatch opened. The launch in attendance was hailed.

'Where is the torpedo? Why aren't you after it?'

'Haven't seen a sign of it, sir.'

After looking about, for some time, more water was blown out of the tanks, the bow came up a little, and there, through the dirty, muddy water was our friend, sticking in the tube three-quarters of the way out. When rising to the surface we had noticed that the boat took rather longer than usual, but this was attributed to the suction at the bottom, as in the Dock running we had to go very close to the mud and run a narrow gut. On returning to the Berthing Jetty the submarine was secured, the torpedo hoisted in, and everything got ready for more dives in the afternoon. The crew were then sent to dinner and the Foreman undertook to put the leaky [firing] valve right as soon as possible.

Shortly afterwards messengers were seen running all over the Barrow dockside. One rather breathless person greeted the Lieutenant in Charge of the Boats:

'Will you come and see yon torpedo; he is stuck in yon wall with his screws awhurring and awhurring.'

The messenger was right; and there was the seventeen-foot fish sticking half way into the top part of the shelter that *No 5* was lying in with the propellers rotating at 2000 revolutions per minute and the gathering crowd of onlookers afraid to touch it.

The foreman, bent on putting the leaky valve right in quick time, forgot there was a torpedo in the tube and, in trying the valve, fired the Whitehead straight into the wooden berthing eight feet from the bow of

the submarine. The poor man was rather alarmed at the result and, when informed that the Admiralty would make him pay for a new torpedo, had a vision of a few snug little cottages on the shores of Lake Windermere coming under the hammer to satisfy the claims of My Lords; fortunately for him the wood was rotten and the 18-inch was little the worse for wear after being placed in such an unusual predicament![8]

The weapon-systems, like the submarines themselves, were no more than experimental but the things that went wrong with them were archetypal examples of what was to happen, more and more expensively on each successive occasion, down the years to the present day. The first French and Russian boats carried their torpedoes externally in Drzewiecki Drop-Collars which allowed the torpedoes to be crudely angled and were a good deal cheaper than built-in torpedo tubes. But drop-collars were liable to release fish inadvertently with embarrassing results and the torpedoes themselves were vulnerable to damage on the surface. Despite their relatively complex discharge and compensating arrangements, internal tubes (the *Holland*s had only one apiece) were preferable and, of course, they could be reloaded.

Torpedoes were not expendable in peacetime. Every possible effort was made to recover them and many were the long days and nights spent by unhappy submariners looking for lost fish. It was seldom that torpedoes could be fired in realistic circumstances and, before the days of light dummy warheads (collision heads) which allowed a spent

132 torpedo to surface after striking its target, actual hits were not encouraged. Even without any explosive in the nose a torpedo could make a sizeable hole in a target vessel but that was not the principal objection; holes were easily patched. It was the risk of losing a torpedo in the process that was totally unacceptable.

Tactical Developments

Fortunately the French were not too concerned about economies. That was just as well for the submarine services of the world. It was an incident in December 1898, when the *Gustave Zédé* torpedoed the *Magenta*, that persuaded England and America (amidst profound diplomatic secrecy) that submarine free-running torpedoes were truly effective. However, the historian Herbert C Fyfe took care to warn his readers that from 1898 onwards French underwater vessels had often engaged in mimic warfare and many of the papers had published glowing accounts of their wonderful performances 'but one has to accept such statements with marked caution'[9].

Monsieur Lockroy, the French Minister of Marine at the time, was an ardent submarine supporter and gleefully recorded the attack on the *Magenta*:

Three cruisers were involved – *Magenta*, *Neptune* and *Marceau* and they apparently knew the exact moment when the attack would take place and precisely where the *Gustave Zédé* would be. The manoeuvre commenced at 3.17 in the afternoon and the torpedo was fired at 3.28. The *Gustave Zédé* plunged at 3.20 for the first time; she emerged five times and the longest appearance was one minute thirty seconds, the shortest thirty seconds . . . if the boat had carried her optical arrangements she would not have needed to come to the surface.

The eyes of all on board were fixed on the sea; officers and men stood watching the crest of the waves and every minute there were exclamations, or someone fancied he had seen the submarine. We imagined we saw it everywhere, and it was nowhere.

In point of fact it was proceeding quietly and invisibly towards its mark.

Suddenly a precise and exact observation was made. The cupola of the *Gustave Zédé* had just

HMS *D-4*, completed in 1911 without forward plane-guards and with a dual bow-cap for the two bow-tubes. A third tube was fitted in the stern, a first for D-boats as was the fitting of radio.

appeared 400 yards away, still abreast of us, notwithstanding the distance which we had covered.

Immediately orders were issued. The guns were brought to bear upon her and the quick-firers depressed in her direction. The submarine was no longer there. She was hidden from our fire and from our view. A minute elapsed. Though orders were given to the engineers to put on steam, and the *Magenta* had gone some considerable distance in the sixty seconds, the Admiral and I, leaning over the railing of the bridge, saw approaching us with lightning speed an elon-

Loading torpedoes on board C-boats at the Humberside port of Immingham (which was to become a wartime E. Coast base) in June 1913.

gated body shining like gold.

It was the torpedo of the *Gustave Zédé*! It struck the ship about four yards below the water-line, and was smashed on the iron armour, but if it had been charged the *Magenta* would have been sunk.[10]

The *Gustave Zédé* repeated her feat by torpedoing the battleship *Jauréguiberry* in Ajaccio Harbour in July 1901 acording to the Paris correspondent of the *Daily Express*; but in fact it was the *Charles Martel* which had received the submarine's torpedo and *Gustave Zédé* had very nearly been rammed by the *Jauréguiberry* who had to take violent avoiding action when the little boat crossed her bows at close range. Furthermore, it turned out that the attack had taken place on Wednesday morning although the manoeuvres did not officially commence until Wednesday night. That was cheating but the French newspapers made the most of the 'splendid accomplishment' and boldly imagined that the British Admiralty would be terror-stricken at the notion of what French submarines would be able to accomplish in war. The British *Times* newspaper joined in the general acclamation and added its considerable weight to the general impression of French power underwater. It is difficult to say now whether these complimentary reviews were justi-fied; cynical submariners today would probably feel that they were not.

Submariners on the other side of the Atlantic found it a good deal more difficult to persuade the public to take their efforts seriously. Lieutenant Harry H Caldwell, commanding the USS, or more properly the US Torpedo Boat, *Holland* during Fleet Manoeuvres during September 1900, was sternly denied a success that was almost certainly his by right although he only simulated torpedo-fire and did not discharge a weapon.

The setting for the exercise was a blockade of Newport, Rhode Island by ships of the US North Atlantic Squadron. USTB *Holland* rumbled away from the Naval Torpedo Station at sunset on the second night and headed for open waters where Caldwell instructed Acting Gunner Owen Hill to trim the boat right down so that just the tiny conning tower and a few inches of hull remained above the surface. Captain Cable had only declared the crew sufficiently trained some four weeks earlier. They had no operational experience whatever but it was thought enough that they could dive and surface without undue excitement.

The blockading vessels, three battleships supported by two gun boats, were fully darkened and the only light came from a scatter of stars in the clear September sky. Manoeuvring awash with no navigation lights and unable to submerge fully in less than five minutes, the little submarine was in a very dangerous position. No submariner nowadays would, in peacetime anyway, allow himself to be put in a position where the risk of being rammed tended distinctly towards the probable rather than the possible. However, Caldwell was undismayed: there had, as yet, been no serious collisions in any navy. When the boat was seven miles out to sea a vast black shape suddenly appeared ahead. It was the battleship *Kearsarge*, Flagship of the Squadron and commanded by Captain William M Folger. The huge bulk was either stopped or drifting slowly when, at point-blank range half-a-cable off, Caldwell pointed straight at the centre of his target, waved a lamp

134

and shouted across the flat calm water: 'Hullo *Kearsarge*! You are blown to atoms. This is the submarine boat *Holland*.'[11]

The umpire meanly refused to allow Caldwell the sinking of the *Kearsarge* because *Kearsarge* had already been torpedoed by the torpedo-boat *Dahlgren* and gunned by the defending surface ships. Caldwell insisted, rightly, that he had not been seen by any vessel of the blockading fleet or by its escorts and that the dummy attack was wholly successful. Furthermore, he could have gone on to torpedo the other two blockading battleships had he chosen to do so. Folger in *Kearsarge* acknowledged that *Holland* was undetected but he went on to remark that the submarine in the middle of the fleet stood a good chance of being run down. How right he was!

Admiral O'Neil, who was becoming more and more critical about submarines and their weapons, made a particularly flattening comment on Caldwell's achievement, opening with remarks to the effect that 'The *Holland* on a very fine evening and under exceptionally favourable circumstances steamed seven miles as a surface boat only . . .'

The only player who won the battle in that particular encounter was the umpire, a circumstance not unknown in future exercise engagements. It took a long while to realise that in a real shooting war it is impossible to cheat: the umpire then is Davy Jones and his locker is large. So many false conclusions were drawn in later years from the heavily biased results claimed on the surface and below during peacetime exercises that submarines and surface ships were to find themselves grossly unprepared for war in 1914 and again in 1939.

There is one surviving example, in manuscript[13], of submarine and anti-submarine exercise rules devised by Captain Bacon after manoeuvres in the summer of 1904.[14] Reading between the lines they tell a good deal about the abilities and inabilities of submarine boats and their opponents on the surface:

Rules for putting out of action, by submarines, vessels other than those against which they can fire torpedoes.
(1) Such a vessel is to be considered out of action if an 'A' class sm, having two loaded torpedo tubes, can rise at any distance between 150 and 450 yards, on any bearing between four points before the beam and the beam.
(2) If a *Holland* type boat, having one loaded torpedo tube, can arrive in a similar position, the vessel is to be claimed, but half the total number of such claims will be allowed.

If a submarine wishes to claim a vessel she must rise to the surface as a sign of having done so. She is not to be considered free from subsequent attack. Before, however, she can take part in any further hostile operations she must have remained for at least an hour at some depôt where she could have obtained Whitehead torpedoes.

The above rule is based on the experience obtained in the late manoeuvres, viz, a sm has a 50% chance of hitting a destroyer target from above named position. For purposes of identification both submarines and destroyers should in daytime carry identification marks distinctly visible to naked eye at 800 yards. Bands on lower part of optical tube, and on one or more funnels are suggested as most convenient.

Rules for putting a submarine out of action.
(1) For a submarine boat to be put out of action by any vessel: She must have been under fire with her conning tower above water for at least one uninterrupted minute within a range of 300 yards, or
(2) she is to be considered out of action if the number on her optical tube can be read.

Rule (1) is based on the extreme smallness of the target exposed normally and the practical impossibility of inflicting damage on a sm unless she is forced to remain on the surface.
Rule (2) is merely to enforce proper tactics on the submarine boats when escaping from or avoiding destroyers: it forces them to dive reasonably when near to such craft.

The numbers on the optical tubes should be painted on the fore and on the after side of the tube just below the prism box. They should be of such a size as to be read with a service telescope 150 yards off.
(Signed)
Inspecting Captain Submarine Boats.

The problem for surface ships, of course, was to find the submarines before they could attack. The

The torpedo tube arrangements in one of the eight US 'K' class submarines commissioned in 1914.

Church, still much interested in underwater warfare, had an answer[15] in 1904:

When the Rev. J M Bacon, MA, the well-known scientist and aeronaut, made his trip in the Irish Channel last year he announced that he was able to see objects many fathoms down in the sea from his balloon, and other balloonists have noticed the same thing. Even in the muddy waters at the mouth of the Thames objects were seen with the utmost clearness at a depth of five fathoms. Would it not be a wise step to equip a few of our battleships with a small captive balloon and staff for experimental purposes? If from a certain height above the surface the balloonists could see objects five fathoms or more below the surface the danger in daylight to a blockading fleet of attack by submarines would be lessened if the lookout promptly notified the approach of a hostile boat.

In the same year netting showed promise of physical protection:

In connection with the exercises carried out by submarines and destroyers in the neighbourhood of Portsmouth, it is understood that the torpedo-boats were successful in every way. The nets, above 200 feet long and 7 feet deep, made of steel wire, were spread on booms, which were worked from three steam pinnaces, and so arranged that the nets could be lowered to any depth in the water. Three submarines were told off to try to attack the pinnaces by avoiding or getting through the nets. The submarines tried to dive below the obstruction, but the netting was so nearly invisible in the water, the submarines being also handi-

capped by the dullness of the sky making the water dead grey, that they could not calculate the depth, and in every instance, it is said, were netted. The submarines also tried to force their way through the netting but failed. It remains to be seen whether a live torpedo fired by a submarine against the encircling net would explode on striking it or pass clean through. One of the methods tried to enable a submarine to get within striking distance of a ship unseen was very ingenious. A canvas conning tower was so constructed that it could be fitted over the submarine's tower. On approaching an enemy the submarine dives, leaving the covering floating on the water. While attention is thus being devoted to the false submarine, the real one is stealthily approaching its victim from another direction.[16]

Submariners, even in infancy, were cunning.

It has often been assumed that the *Holland* boats had no real fighting potential;[17] but by 1904 the Inspecting Captain of Submarine Boats had assessed the results of a sufficient number of exercises at sea to justify the rules. There was an even chance of hitting a destroyer from a range of 300 to 400 yards with the torpedo running depth set at 6 feet. Furthermore, the balance of favour was on the side of the submarine in action against a destroyer using guns.

These statistics were excellent for the day and would be quite acceptable now; but no account was taken of a target's probable avoiding action, alterations of course (developing into zig-zags) or speed changes. Realistic problems like these were not faced fairly and squarely until 1910, four years before the outbreak of World War I. Nonetheless it was essential for the young submariners to build up their morale whether or not their confidence was justified; and, of course, money had to be extracted from Government treasuries to construct boats whose true value was very difficult to prove for many years.

Thus men like Jackie Fisher, Percy Scott, Reginald Bacon and John Philip Holland himself were prone to exaggerate achievements and claim unwarranted capabilities which can be admired in retrospect so long as they are taken with a fairish pinch of sea-salt.

Captain Reginald Bacon, first Inspecting Captain of Submarines with Executive and Engineer Officers (the latter without curls on their stripes) on board HMS *Hazard* at Barrow in 1902. Most photographs of this kind include a dog.

HMS *A-3* en route from Barrow to Portsmouth in 1907 escorted by HMS *Hazard* and now being taken under tow. An Admiralty official memorandum remarked wryly that the principle defect of the 'A' class was 'their want of buoyancy'.

Chapter Twelve
The Trade Looks Up

HMS *Thames*, the first in a long line of inadequate and unsuitable submarine mother or depot ships (*Hazard* having been no more than an attendant tender) lying in the upper reaches of Portsmouth Harbour in 1904. A Holland boat is lying alongside and an A-boat is shaping up for the port forward berth. The designation painted on the latter's conning tower is yet another of the idiosyncratic variations which are so confusing in old photographs.

Even before HM Submarine *No 1* (*Holland I*) had undergone her diving trials, the first of thirteen new 'A' boats was laid down. Vickers were responsible for the design broadly based upon an expanded version of the *Holland* and American *Adder* classes with the important difference that no royalty was due to the Holland Torpedo Boat Company. The cost was £41,000 per boat and the 'B' and 'C' classes quickly followed in 1903 and 1905 at £47,000 apiece. The United States Navy, which enjoyed little encouragement from the politicians, had to be satisfied with its first seven *Adder* boats until 1906 when three boats were built to a marginally improved design: the principal characteristics differed only in their being slightly larger with a raised bridge and two periscopes.

It was in the *Holland* class that the traditions of the Trade – the Royal Navy's Submarine Service – were firmly founded. Fortunately several officers put pen to paper and left an intimate record of life below water in the Edwardian Navy. There are disappointingly few surviving accounts by American submariners at this time but it can be assumed that the discomforts, privations, hardships and, overriding all those, the full-blooded enjoyment of a new and exciting challenge were very similar to the experiences of the Royal Navy. Class distinction between officers and men was almost equally inflexible in Britain and America, but the team spirit amongst the crew in both navies was so strong, and indeed so necessary, that no trace of bitterness was evident. A popular hymn for children at the time, 'All things bright and beautiful', included the verse:

> The rich man in his castle
> The poor man at his gate,
> God made them high and lowly
> And ordered their estate.

This was the accepted position, high and low, until World War I brought social revolution in its wake. But there was no castle or gate in a submarine, no quarterdeck for the officers and no forecastle for the ratings. In fact there was scar-

138 cely any division in most early boats and none at all in the *Holland*s. However, in the 'B' and 'C' classes a bunk was provided for the Captain which the Second Captain occupied when not on watch, for there were often only two officers in the crew. Even in the 'E' class which served throughout World War I the wardroom was only a curtained-off space leading out of the Control Room. Nor was there room for hammocks; so the crew slept on the decks as best they could and the Artificers counted themselves lucky to have their tool-boxes for pillows. There was continual reference in contemporary diaries to the officers having a sailor servant but wardroom officers enjoyed practically none of the other privileges and comforts afforded to their contemporaries in the surface fleet. In submarines all the crew were literally and metaphorically in the same boat. Nonetheless, from the moment the officers stepped ashore or into the Depot Ship it was certainly plain that God, or the Admiralty on his behalf, had indeed ordered their estate in a way that set them far apart from the ratings.

Not that the early Depot Ships were comfortable – far from it. 'Seagee' Brodie's story[2] of his joining the Submarine Service in 1904 makes that clear enough.

Life Aboard a Depot Ship

Sub-Lieutenants Brodie and Max Horton, the latter to become arguably the most famous and successful submariner of all time, arranged to join each other over a drink at the Keppel's Head ('The Nut'), that most renowned of Portsmouth meeting places for officers of all ranks. The hostelry was conveniently close to the Hard. Striding into the inner bar, Brodie and Horton butted unknowingly into a nest of fully qualified submariners. Horton's typically brash statement to the effect that he was off to submarines for 'six bob a day and the seven-bell boat ashore' was icily received.

Unabashed and in fair spirits with the prospect of extra pay which would just about double, with 'hard-liers', their normal pittance, the two young officers had only to stroll a couple of hundred

yards down to the boat waiting to take them to HMS *Thames* moored high up Fareham Creek.

HMS *Thames* was the first parent ship for submarines, *Hazard* strictly speaking being but a tender. The aging 2nd Class cruiser was now bereft of the guns intended in 1886 to outmatch those of the Russian *Uraleto* class. There were six other sub-lieutenants in the new Training Class and all had been told to join with their sea-chests, an ominous instruction implying that accommodation in the depot ship would be down to gunroom standards. The small and ancient steamboat which ferried the officers to their new home gave added warning that the Admiralty was not giving high priority to amenities for the three-year-old Submarine Service. The few senior officers of the Trade – Reginald Bacon, the forceful Inspecting Captain and his scholarly successor Edgar Lees – were either in the sea-going *Hazard* or scurrying between Vickers and the Admiralty planning for the future. They had no time to oversee domestic matters and they were scarcely ever glimpsed by the embryo submariners.

Horton and Brodie found nobody on board the *Thames* who showed the slightest interest in them. They were anxious to get started and earn their submarine pay so, by sheer persistence on the following morning, they eventually unearthed a reluctant Engineer Commander purported to be in charge of training. He was a bearded, bewildered old gentleman, left over from the *Thames'* last spell in the Reserve Fleet. He knew absolutely nothing about submarines or internal combustion engines. He was not even aware that a couple of young and supposedly qualified engineers had been appointed for submarine service and that these specialists might conceivably be able to impart something of use to the newcomers. However, the so-called training officer's bleary old eyes still recognised manly muscles when he saw them and there was a good stock of hammers and chisels in his store. The Sub-Lieutenants *en masse* were thereupon set to demolish a steel bulkhead impeding their future smoking room. The subject of submarines was not mentioned and the pros-

Stand-easy on 'A' class submarines at Fort Blockhouse in 1904. The refuelling berth, Petrol Pier (as it is still known) is in the background.

stand nuts and bolts and now, as Second Captains, they found themselves responsible for maintaining engines and motors as well as looking after torpedoes and auxiliary electrics which, if they were torpedo specialists, they had already been taught at HMS *Vernon*. In the United States Deck Officers were much better grounded in engineering and they still are today; but, against that, a natural aptitude in mechanical matters tended to draw them away from using their submarines to the best operational advantage. That tendency, too, was to be long-lasting.

In short, submariners went to sea with very little supervision and scant knowledge of their craft. Some navies were worse off than others and the sad results will be seen in Chapter 14.

Hazards of the Service

Periscopes were a particular mystery. The generally accepted type was patented by Sir Howard Grubb, but Bacon and Lees had a fascination for the various types on offer and were forever trying out Hydroscopes, Cleptoscopios, Omniscopes and Storoscopes. The junior submariners steered well clear of such esoteric technicalities.

Fuelling was unexpectedly dangerous. Submarines took in petrol at moorings abreast of *Thames*, from 50-gallon drums loaded in lighters. The drums were manhandled onto the hatch covers over the vacant holds and emptied by hand-pumps through hoses to the submarines. The fumes from leaking pumps were mildly intoxicating and the evolution generated even more of a holiday spirit, with much less work, than coaling ship.

Brodie was Officer of the Day in *Thames* when the hazards became fully apparent. A loud crash and much shouting from the lighter signalled a disaster of some kind and he called away the lifeboat, an evolution wisely practised at least once a day with 'Fire Stations'. A motley cutter's crew scrambled into the sea-boat and 'smartly if not dressily'[3] pulled for the lighter where too many full drums and men on the hatch cover had been too much for a beam: a dozen men and drums

pects of going down in one looked dim.

Meanwhile their mentor submerged himself in gin which was plentiful and duty-free in His Majesty's Ships at two pence a glass. The hammer and chisel brigade soon proved too noisy for him and he took to spending longer and longer periods ashore imbibing his favourite beverage. Max Horton, already the leader, shipped his second stripe during this frustrating time of inactivity and decided he now had enough authority to take action. Donning a frock-coat and sword he rounded up an escort of seamen, commandeered the antique steamboat and stormed through the public houses which he accurately judged would be the Engineer Commander's favourite haunts. The old man was brought back for just long enough to pack his bags. Then, in that mysterious way that the Navy has in ridding itself of a troublesome character when sufficient evidence for a court-martial is lacking, the gin-sodden old Engineer Commander simply faded away.

There was still no formal instruction. New men, officers and ratings alike, picked up what they could from existing crews who had learned their trade in the building yard at Vickers and by trial and error when commissioning their boats. It was especially difficult for officers. They had to under-

140

had fallen into the hold. The petrol spilt from the capsized containers had done its work well. The injured men were feeling no pain at all and, as the Edwardian expression had it, the rescuers were soon 'very nicely thankyou' as well. In a few minutes an uproarious double-banked cutter was steering an erratic course back to the ship where the blood-stained, bandaged mob affectionately helped each other up the gangway and down to the sick bay.

When the walking-wounded had dispersed the Officer-in-Charge of the operation, Lieutenant Crowther, equably asked the doctor to have a look at his foot. It was badly crushed but fully anaesthetised. Two toes had to be amputated. Brodie made no mention of his friend Crowther's return to duty in his diary but thankfully remarked that he was dancing as well as ever within a month. That was important. It would not be entirely right to say that social obligations took priority over service duties but they were vital to the career of an officer in the Royal Navy. Submariners, up the Creek at the far end of Portsmouth Harbour, were far-removed from feminine frivolities. It was a little unfair to reflect that this jeopardised promotion. Sport on the playing field, too, was at the back of every right-thinking Englishman's mind during King Edward's reign. Thus the length of HM Submarine *No 1*, was not reported by the Press to be 63 feet 10 inches but as 'a yard shorter than a cricket pitch'.

Petrol was a very real menace to health and safety. Petrol Pier, where submarines were fuelled when the Flotilla moved to Fort Blockhouse, was a notorious scene of inebriated hilarity. In fact, there was muted grumbling amongst crews when diesel engines were introduced in submarines some half-a-dozen years before World War I: partial inebriation at the King's expense was for long a recognised perquisite at Petrol Pier. Captain Bacon was of the school who protested that white mice did not squeak when affected by petrol fumes on board; they were there only to give warning of carbon monoxide. It was the crew who first showed the symptoms when petrol leaked into the engine space which was not shut off from the rest of the boat.

A 'sensational explosion' on board HM Submarine *No 1* in Portsmouth Harbour on 3 March 1903 was typical of the petrol-fuelled accidents that occurred. The *Evening News* reported:

Five of the vessels had been out practising a series of manoeuvres and were returning to the dockyard just before three o'clock. Four of the boats had reached their stations but as the last, *No 1*, was between the North Corner and the *Hannibal*, a sudden explosion was observed. Those on board the ships in the vicinity who were watching the curious little craft pass along were astonished to see the man at the wheel suddenly reel while a hat which had been worn by someone on deck was carried high into the air, evidently by the force of the explosion.

It was at once seen that something serious had happened and a pinnace from the *Hannibal* was at once despatched to the rescue. The tug *Seahorse* also lowered a boat and two others from the *Hannibal* were also sent.

In the meantime the Commander of the Submarine had divested himself of his coat and pluckily descended the hatchway to ascertain the effect and extent of the explosion. When he got below he found four men who had been much injured by the explosion and these he carried, one by one, to the deck above. The Engine Room Artificer appeared to be more seriously injured, the upper part of his body, his face and arms being terribly burnt by the flames of the gasolene. The Torpedo Instructor, an Able Seaman and a Stoker were also badly injured. Their injuries were similar to those sustained by the Artificer and all were in more or less a serious condition. . . .

Lieutenant Lutton Bertram Evans RN who performed such a plucky act after the explosion on the submarine at Portsmouth on Wednesday afternoon by plunging into the engine-room and bringing out the men who were injured has seen active service of an exciting character in Africa. While on HMS *Raleigh* he took part in a Niger river expedition sent to punish Fordi Saleh, a rebellious slave raider, and also was one of a punitive expedition against King Koko of Nimby. He was one of the force which captured M'Weli, the stronghold of a rebellious Arab chief.

Legitimate intoxicating liquors were even more of a menace than gasoline in the Royal Navy of those days. Looking back, it is evident that there was a fair proportion of what would now be called problem drinkers amongst both officers and men. Drunkenness was, of course, rife ashore in Edwardian England and alcohol, of a sort, could be bought cheaply. Two young submariners, returning to the Royal Naval College at Greenwich in a cumbersome old motor-car one night, saw nothing particularly odd in discovering that an old man that they ran down (happily without much injury) was finding the way home by running his thumb along inside the tramline.[4]

The United States Navy declared itself dry but the Admiralty knew that British sailors could not be deprived of their gratuitous one-eighth of a pint

The German *U-1* commissioned at Kiel under *Kapitänleutnant* (Lt) von Boehm-Bezing on 14 Dec 1906. Germany and France were the only significant naval powers that did not adopt Holland boats at the beginning. *U-1*, designed by d'Equevilley, was an advanced 238-ton double-hull boat.

of full-proof rum each day without the risk of full-scale mutiny; nor would the wardrooms have willingly given up their wine-cupboards and the world-famous hospitality that they offered. However, unlike their brothers on the surface, it was very seldom indeed that submarine officers had a drink at sea.

If sailors found the rum ration inadequate for their needs it was not unknown for them to drain off the compass fluid and drink that; but a grounded compass jeopardised the Captain's

already limited facilities (and abilities) and even the thirstiest submariners were not inclined to add unnecessarily to the risks of their calling. It was better to strain boot-blacking or metal polish through thick slices of stale bread.

There was another serious liquid hazard in the storage batteries' sulphuric acid electrolyte. Besides recommending plenty of soda being kept handy in case any acid was spilled, the Instructional Notes for Officers blandly advised, 'If you get covered with strong acid, it is a good thing to jump overboard and stay there till the doctor is ready.'[5]

Navigation was tricky at the best of times. Its very low speed submerged put a submarine at the mercy of tidal streams and currents, and fixing with relative bearings through a dim periscope related to the magnetic compass, which deviated wildly when machinery was started and stopped, was often a haphazard business. Submariners admitted, amongst themselves, that their navigation was by Guess and by God[6]. It was no easier on the surface because there was no bridge chart-table and the Officer-of-the-Watch had to sing down bearings to the Control Room where they might or might not be accurately plotted on a frequently sodden chart. Turning the 160 degrees into Haslar Creek was especially difficult for single-screw boats in a roaring tideway. The little spit of land at the entrance to the creek, where malefactors were once hanged in chains,[7] was the scene of many a grounding. It earned an evil reputation until submarine captains learned that running onto 'the putty' in such obviously difficult circumstances was an event that by no means necessarily hazarded their careers. There were only three ways of achieving promotion if an officer was not clearly outstanding: favouritism (as advocated by Jackie Fisher), a wartime exploit (but there was no war) or a respectable court-martial. Going aground when turning into the creek led to many highly respectable courts-martial and the shallow strand soon became known as Promotion Point.

142

Changing Attitudes to the Trade

There seems to have been a rather disappointing absence of laughs and eccentricity in the United States submarine service. Simon Lake, who was not, of course, a naval officer, was the only man in America to leave his mark as a submersible humorist. The officers and men in the Royal Navy affected a different attitude towards the Trade. They lived their squalid life below with less than sombre solemnity, or at least that is the impression they endeavoured to create when recounting experiences which must have been revolting, worrying or frankly hair-raising. On the other hand, some British statements were so pompous and ingenuous that it is hard to believe that they were originally delivered with a straight face. For example, a spokesman from the Constructive Department pontified about hull work in submarines: '. . . it requires', he announced, 'more expert workmanship than in surface ships, which is not generally recognised. The riveting is practically boiler-maker's work.'[8] This masterpiece of understatement must have raised a few eyebrows amongst submariners who hoped to reach the advertised depth of 100 feet safely in all the early

BELOW The Dutch *O-2* pictured on completion in 1909. The hinged and faired torpedo bow-caps (shown open) were unique: like so many excellent Netherlands submarines since then, the design and construction were probably entirely Dutch. The Royal Netherlands Navy has never hesitated to go it alone.

John L Bowers

Cleaning and painting the stern section of a British C-boat in floating dock c1908.

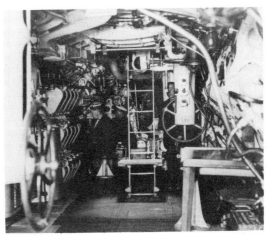

ing. There is evinced on the part of officers and men of His Majesty's Navy a marked desire to serve on these vessels, and the volunteers for that purpose are far in excess of the requirements.

Some of the first submariners were thought a little strange even at the time but that it is not surprising. They had, after all, sacrificed a far more secure career in the surface fleet and a proportion of them were bound to be refugees from the glitter, gunnery and gaiters in the resplendent battleships and cruisers above them. The rewards were not only financial. Responsibility and risk were counted far more highly and they attracted some unusual and colourful personalities to the Trade. A few, said Brodie, were as mad as hatters.

Submarine boats or 'submergibles' (a rather more genteel Edwardian word) were utterly beyond the comprehension of men with old-fashioned ideas like Captain Anstruther, Captain of the battleship *Cornwallis*. This 'Masts and Yards' officer tried to persuade one future submariner that a new-fangled order such as 'Starboard 10' was wholly unacceptable: it had to be 'Starboard one turn, two spokes'[9]. When Brodie was eventually allowed down to a *Holland* boat in October 1904, specifically to see a battery on charge he was, not surprisingly, unprepared for the spectacle that confronted him of a very dif-

classes. It would be wrong, however, to think that writers in magazines and newspapers were all being sarcastic, however oddly their articles may read today. Ignorance and misunderstanding were widespread and the introspective submariners scorned what would now be called a public relations policy.

The Naval and Military Record for 17 November 1904 was genuinely exalting the new submarine branch when it reported that:

. . . a few Lieutenants and Sub-Lieutenants have crossed from Spithead to Cowes and back in a submarine, doing the distance of about 12 knots [sea-miles] each way in excellent time. To have navigated a vessel of this type safely across the Solent, with its currents and peculiar set of tides and its sand-banks, is regarded as extraordinary in modern naval practice, and that it should have been performed by these young officers makes the event additionally interest-

ferent sort of captain, Lieutenant G B Lewis, only a few months senior to himself. The boat was being charged through rubber-covered cables from the *Thames*. The battery boards had been lifted, the cells were gassing furiously and there was nowhere to stand:

> . . . we were peering for a foothold, our eyes smarting, when a tubby little figure in a boiler suit, carrying a red hot soldering iron, shouted 'Out of the way' and rushed back to his task. Later, official warnings about the danger of sparks near gassing cells kept this vision green. At the time my attitude was open-mouthed admiration for a captain of a boat who was expert with an iron . . .[10]

A Captain was titled 'Lieutenant and Commander'. Whatever he might do, his status was unquestioned, his relative seniority was unimportant and his word was law. If he was a technical expert as well deification would follow in the usual way.

Some commanding officers stood more upon their dignity; others adopted a pose to hide their natural modesty; and others were plainly stupid and incompetent. One cheery and popular *Holland* boat captain was a good seaman but petrol-engines, batteries and tank-systems defeated him:

> His battery's failing power led him to consult the newly appointed Torpedo Lieutenant, who told him that white spots on the positive plates were a bad sign. The cells needed longer charging; but the Captain hopefully attacked the symptoms more directly. Wire scrubbers and a drop of 'strongers' had served him well in the past, so he hoisted up the positives and scrubbed them with a wire brush and caustic. He was not unique in lack of experience of large storage cells.

When Brodie joined *A–11* at Barrow as Second Captain (First Lieutenant and Executive Officer) he found his captain

> . . . was tall and lean with a lugubrious face masking a kindly humorous disposition. Mild and diffident, devoid of pomposity, he was known to his contemporaries as 'Unlucky Jim' . . . I fancy he invited the role, posing as the simpleton always meeting trouble;

but he was no fool and one could see that the Chief Engine Room Artificer and the Coxswain, who had been with him before, trusted him. The CERA was David Drummond, perhaps the best of the splendid 'Chiefs' of the period – a magnificent engineer and a fine character. He was some years older than the rest of us and was already famed for his wise and witty sayings, and for hitting odd nails on the head. He and the Coxswain, another forceful personality, sparing of words, set the tone for the community and were pleasant gentlemen to live with . . .[11]

Brodie's description of these splendid men as gentlemen was significant for the time. It suggests a positive break away from social snobbery in the Submarine Service which was nonetheless criticised itself for being snobbish, in an entirely different way, by surface sailors. Perhaps 'clannish' would have been a better word. Certainly, by 1904, it was becoming a private navy and this was to prejudice the interests of submarines and submariners in years to come.

The appalling conditions of life in small, steel tubes required everybody to behave like a gentleman in the true sense of the word. Punishments were almost unheard of: it was enough to know that misdemeanours would result in a defaulter being sent back to General Service.

An enquiry into the health of submariners immediately after World War I implied that, on the whole, the men were tougher than the officers. They had to be; for while the officers lived amidships in a relatively stable atmosphere, apart from a howling gale down the conning tower, the men messed forward and aft with little to protect them against changing temperatures and high humidity. In some boats they were perpetually chilled while in others they were constantly overheated. In the 'C' class it was a struggle to keep warm while in the 'G' class, ten years later, the ship's company were largely accommodated in the Motor Room area where temperatures frequently exceeded 100 degrees. From these unhealthy nests men were expected to emerge for two hours in every six and stand their watch, inadequately clothed, in a draughty Control Room or on a freezing bridge with the seas breaking over them in moderate weather and no chance whatever of drying their soaking garments. 'However,' remarked one commanding officer, 'the only bad effects were a lack of alertness, an unhealthy colour and a tendency to drowsiness . . .'

This Captain was evidently one of the few still burdened by class consciousness for he went on to say that although the general health of the ship's company was not permanently affected, 'the health of an officer in these circumstances would certainly have suffered.' To be fair, he may have been referring to the more arduous duties which officers were undoubtedly called upon to perform at the periscope, on the bridge and at the chart table. Officers had little sleep since they were, at best, watch and watch about. Surface watch-keeping was hazardous, especially in the gale-swept North Sea where the Germans operated for much of the time, practising their trade for the war with England that was regarded as inevitable: the entire crew of a U-boat was counted every two hours and, in bad weather, every half-hour.

Lieutenant and Commander Charles W Craven and the ship's company of *B-10* in 1909.

Conditions were a trifle better in the United States Navy where American ingenuity contrived to make the best of things. Predictably, their submarines were better equipped and the social differentials on board were not quite so wide as in King Edward's Navy. This was one reason why the 'H' class of 1915, predominantly an American design, was to become so popular in the British Navy throughout both World Wars. It is true that American submarines earned the name of 'Pig-Boats' in their own navy but that was because, like all early submarines without retractable periscopes, they had to glimpse their targets by breaking surface momentarily like porpoises or 'sea-pigs'. The American underwater fleet was rather more sensitive than its British counterpart and grew to resent the gibes that were common in all navies. Eventually, the crews came to insist that they were not subm*a*riners, with the accent on the second syllable implying they were less than real mariners, but submar*i*ners in a marine class of their own.

The clothing provided for American submar*i*ners was good, far better than in the Royal Navy where officers could be seen leaving harbour in wing collars, monkey jackets and seaboots – an extraordinary combination of formal attire and fishing rig. Below decks it had to be admitted that accusations by senior officers to the effect that they were oily, foul-smelling and looked like chauffeurs[13] was fully justified.

Despite unfavourable comments about their domestic habits, submariners were made very welcome in surface ships when they went to them for a year's break between submarine appointments. They were appointed to the best ships 'where their technical knowledge and unbounded enthusiasm made them, in short time, first-class big-ship officers . . . they proved wonderful ambassadors . . .'[14]

The choice of food was, according to the system usual in most ships of the time, left to the men themselves and it was often unsuitable. Despite a diet which would have horrified modern dieticians, the crew thrived. On a long and in-

146 | trepid passage from England to Hong Kong by three 'C' class boats from February to April 1911

> ... the men were each given ninepence ha'penny a day and, before quitting each port, purchased what was required for the passage. Every three or four days the parent ship would stop and send along those articles previously asked for by signal: it was a novel way of deep-sea shopping. For the officers, each boat began with six boxes containing everything to mess three persons during a week, apart from eggs, vegetables and fruit. Very few instances of sickness occurred during those weeks of varied temperatures, and notwithstanding all the dampness. Each evening the submarine's captain mustered all his men, serving out pills, castor oil or quinine as required . . .[15]

The mention of castor oil inevitably raises the subject of underwater sanitation. The Holland Torpedo Boat Company included a single pump-action toilet close to the torpedo tube forward but British designs, for many years, omitted any kind of convenience; and when eventually they included internal heads (WCs) from 1910 onwards they could in no way be called 'comfort stations' to use American terminology.

Constipation was the principal health-hazard amongst British crews and, even when proper heads were installed, the crews were sometimes loathe to use them because of the dangers of the system going into reverse if sea pressure overcome blowing pressure – an occurrence descriptively known as 'getting your own back'. As late as 1915, in the middle of the war, one commanding officer of a new 'E' class boat flatly refused to use the apparatus provided although by then it was reasonably civilised. He insisted on coming to the surface daily where he perched on the bridge rail like an overgrown seagull. One day he was literally caught with his pants down by a German Zeppelin which bombed the submarine accurately and severely; but the Captain was unrepentant and refused to alter the manner of his daily habits.

In the British 'A', 'B' and 'C' classes the only concessions to nature were buckets partially filled with oil and placed in each compartment. Submarines seldom remained dived for more than eight or nine hours at a time and a typical First Lieutenant's Standing Order in a 'C' boat read, in the prudish language of the day, 'The crew should keep the boat's original air as pure as possible.'[16]

Max Horton, commanding *E–9* in September 1914 was neither inhibited nor fastidious but his agreement with the 'pure air' theory resulted in *E–9* sinking the first German warship of the war. After nearly a week on patrol one of his officers was suffering severely from the submariner's common complaint and, before he turned in one night, he demolished 'half a guinea's worth' of Beechams Pills from a box he had purchased from a most expensive chemist. While the submarine was quietly resting on the bottom off Heligoland, during an otherwise uneventful night, the pills

C-boats on a 'jolly' to Torquay, probably in the summer of 1912. Submariners were always made welcome ashore on visits like this despite the stench of fuel and compressed humanity which clung even to their shore-going clothes.

Stephen Johnson

suddenly worked exactly as the chemist's advertisement claimed and more. Horton felt compelled to surface immediately into the fresh early morning air. As the submarine rose to periscope depth, Horton was about to take a quick look all round when he found himself staring straight at the enemy cruiser *Hela* steaming slowly past. In less than two minutes one of *E–9*'s torpedoes exploded in the victim's vitals and she was a sinking wreck. For Max Kennedy Horton – officially reported in 1907 as '*good* at his boat and *bad* socially' – the worst situations invariably, somehow or other, turned out for the best.

It was a rough and ready, rude and ruthless school which prepared submariners for war. The slow work-up in the Royal Navy shifted sharply from comedy to tragedy and back again. The poet and author Rudyard Kipling wrote about the Submarine Service, so different from anything that Britain's Sea Kings had known before

... it is a close corporation; yet it recruits its men and officers from every class that uses the sea and engines, as well as from many classes that never expected to deal with either . . . what else could you call it? The trade's 'The Trade', of course.

And trade, as the First World War loomed darkly on the horizon ahead, was definitely looking up.

With regard to that 'close corporation', its all-important tightly knit relationships, in comparison with the much more glamorous surface fleet, were well summed up in the plainest of plain English by a much respected Chief Engine Room Artificer, Bill Sadlier:

If you want to know the difference between ratings and officers in a submarine and ratings and officers in a surface ship, I'll tell you. When I was in boats and the Skipper called me a bloody fool, I knew I was one. If the Captain of a destroyer said something of the same sort – well, I would wonder if he wasn't wrong.

An unkind cartoon.
'By the way, I suppose you've got some sort of Sergeant Johnny who understands all about these thing'umies, what!'

BELOW *Drzewiecki* submarine built 1880 and
pictured at Vladivostok during the Russo-
Japanese War. It was normal to hoist these boats
on standard davits – hence the hull eyebolts.

ABOVE The Russian submarine *Pyotr Koshka* c1903
showing the two drop-collar 18in torpedoes
carried externally. Tsarist submarine officers
were more prone to wear frock-coats.

Chapter Thirteen
The Slower Moving Muscovite

One of the Soviet Union's major contributions towards worry in the West today is her massive submarine fleet. Leaving aside her ballistic-missile boats which, with the Western nuclear-deterrent forces, come under the quite separate and surrealistic heading of Mutually Assured Destruction, Moscow is seen to pose a terrible threat to shipping of all kinds with the huge Soviet nuclear and diesel-electric underwater torpedo fleet.

The supposed threat is of such magnitude that the West's defensive mechanism has constantly to be maintained on an even vaster scale because effective anti-submarine efforts are, by their nature, necessarily far greater than the submarines they are designed to counter. Thus the Soviet Union is, in effect, employing a version of the old 'Fleet in Being' concept at extreme cost to the West while dividing Western forces to such an extent that the Eastern bloc feels that a concentrated attack cannot be launched against it.

It is not the purpose of this book to discuss modern maritime strategy but it is significant that Russian submarine policy was defensive at the start and is arguably still defensive today. Before looking back to the curious beginnings it is also worth noting that the much later performance of Soviet submarines during World War II (known as The Great Patriotic War in the USSR) was abysmally bad and had virtually no effect on the course of the struggle.[1] Very little progress indeed was evident in the real fighting capabilities of Soviet boats from the beginning of the century, through World War I and right up to the summer of 1941 during World War II when Soviet officers in the Northern theatre started to take grudging note of British advice and example. Even then *confirmed* Soviet successes in all theatres were rare. The Soviet Navy has at no time demonstrated a significant underwater capability despite its numerical strength. If history has any meaning there is a good case for questioning the potential wartime capability of the present Soviet submarine force however imposing it may appear in peace.

The characteristics of Russian submarines and

Delfin, probably in early 1904, before her accidental sinking cost 21 lives. A Panhard petrol engine gave a maximum speed of 11 knots on the surface.

150 | submariners before the 1917 Revolution bear a marked resemblance, in sheer ineffectiveness, to their successors between 1941 and 1945 which, incidentally, was the last year in which torpedoes were fired in anger by any navy until the Falklands War in 1982 when the nuclear submarine HMS *Conquerer* sank the Argentine cruiser *General Belgrano* with two out of three Mark 8[xx] torpedoes fired, celebrating that weapon's half century in service.

Tsarist Submarines

The shroud of secrecy which surrounded the Tsarist Navy was almost as impenetrable as the Soviet Iron Curtain. Nor are Russian historians, old or contemporary, reliable in their accounts of submarine development or usage. They lack conviction while politics, misinformation or possibly sheer ignorance all too clearly override objectivity. The only way of peering through the fog is through the eyes of foreign observers such as submarine designers, naval attachés and officers working closely with the Russian submarine service. The bulk of their reports are dated shortly before or during World War I so that they do not all cover the whole period under review. But, unlike earlier newspaper reports, they can be checked, one against the other, and they have the ring of truth about them. They are therefore used, even when not strictly contemporary, in the compilation of this chapter which includes detailed footnotes of the sources.

It is difficult to avoid the impression that the Tsar favoured submarines initially as toys, expensive playthings, comparable to the elegant Fabergé baubles so popular at court. A submarine conferred a certain status. Although its use was rightly seen as an excellent defensive weapon no great thought was put to its tactical employment.

One of the first vessels built at Kronstadt and launched in 1902 was christened *Pyotr Koshka* (wrongly *Kochka* in some Western books). It was an endearing name meaning 'Peter Kitten' or 'Peterkin' and was called after the 1855 hero of Sevastopol. The cost was 50,000 roubles (£7500).

One of the world's principal authorities remarked about this 20-ton, 50-foot boat, with its two external torpedoes, that it 'proved very successful, but owing to its small radius (nine miles at full speed) and erratic motion when submerged, she is of no fighting value. The torpedo launching apparata (drop collars) at the submarine manoeuvres in 1903 twice failed to work'.[2] It was the first of a long series of torpedo failures and mishandling that were to attend the Russian and Soviet submarine services throughout their history. On 10 June 1904 the *Newcastle Chronicle*, commenting on a vigorous discussion about submarines at the Royal United Services Institution, remarked that 'there has been hitherto no opportunity of testing the value of such vessels in the actual conditions of a hostile struggle. The Russo-Japanese conflict might have furnished some splendid object lessons but, curiously enough, neither the go-ahead Japanese nor the slower moving Muscovite had taken the precaution of adding submarines to his Fleet.'[3]

Admiral Jackie Fisher was saying much the same; but the Muscovite, or rather the Tsar at St

The Lake-type *Paltus* in 1905. Five Lake boats were despatched in sections to Vladivostok. When eventually assembled 'the officers had not the faintest idea of how to handle these boats', and breakdowns were rife. One boat was lost and another had a severe explosion.

Petersburg, was not moving so slowly as the British thought. Between the years 1876 and 1896 Drzewiecki had been hard at work designing small defensive submersibles which, in the event, proved impracticable and were eventually used as buoys and supports for the ends of pontoons. Drzewiecki did, however, invent the 'drop-collar' mechanism for torpedoes which came to be widely used, especially in France on the *Narval* and several subsequent boats.

A much more realistic petrol-electric craft *Delfin* (No 150), built by the engineer Dubnoff was launched in 1903 and might have been quite successful had not twenty-two untrained men, in addition to the complement of ten, been let loose in her in the Neva at the Baltic Shipbuilding Yard on 29 June 1904. The intention was to make a practice dive alongside and the Captain did not bother to attend because, as he said, he trusted his three officers. The extra weight of the men under instruction – more than one-and-a-half tons – brought the hatch down to a point perilously close to river level. Just as the ballast tanks were being flooded a passing tug washed water down the hatch which had, very imprudently, not yet been fully shut and secured. The novices immediately panicked and some of them tried to scramble out while the older hands were still screwing the hatch down firmly. Water poured in and the submarine was totally swamped. She sank like a

stone. Lieutenant Cherkasoff and twenty men lost their lives: the remainder were saved by being blown up in the escaping bubble of air. When *Delfin* was raised four days later four men were injured by an unexplained explosion when she reached the surface.

There is little doubt that the accident was caused primarily by bad drill and lack of discipline which a writer at the time correctly noted was 'the one great essential in submarine work and without which the most perfect underwater boat is valueless . . .'[4] Discipline – of the right sort – was sadly absent from the Russian fleet and the solicitous attentions of the ubiquitous Okhrana secret police – no less powerful than the KGB today – were a poor substitute for leadership.

Orders for American Submarines

Meanwhile, the Russian Minister of Marine was looking, still disregarded by the British Admir-

Three Holland boats in a St Petersburg railroad siding c1905. These submarines apparently survived World War I without having seen active service. Transferred to the Black Sea, two of these boats, *Losos* and *Sudak*, were sunk by the British when the Bolsheviks approached Sevastopol in 1919. *Losos* was raised in 1938.

alty, to America and Germany for *podvodnii lodki* – underwater boats. On 14 October 1904 *The Morning Post*'s correspondent reported from New York that a Russian order for 30 submarines of Lake's *Protector* type had been followed by an order from Japan for 50 submarines of the *Holland* class. Holland's experimental *Fulton* was bought specifically for use against the Japanese, and although there is no record of her employment there seems little doubt that the Russian Navy had firmly grasped the submarine's potential. It is tempting to think that, if action had been taken a little earlier to procure submarine boats, they might have influenced the outcome of the war; but contemporary evidence strongly suggests that training was so poor that no boat, however well designed, would have been able to fight successfully. The Tsarist Navy was rapidly heading for disaster, not only in the Far East but at home in the major naval ports where discontent was rife amongst the poorly paid and badly treated sailors.

Unaware or unappreciative of the seething lower decks within his fleets, the Tsar ordered negotiations to be started for Holland's *Fulton* and Simon Lake's *Protector*. Lake had built the *Protector* with wheels for running on the bottom, as a natural successor to his *Argonaut*. She was a multi-purpose vessel which could be used for salvage and other work on the bottom as well as for war. She had three internal torpedo tubes, two bow and one astern, and was the first submarine to offer any degree of comfort to the crew of seven with padded bunks and a galley. Lake, an excellent salesman, was justly proud of the *Protector*, and her flexibility appealed to the Russians who probably saw in it the possibility of minelaying – an occupation to which they were much addicted.

The *Protector* was shipped to Kronstadt where she arrived on 15 June 1904 to be met by Captain Second Rank Beklemishev. Captain Third Rank A O Gadd was appointed in command of the boat renamed *Osetr* ('Sturgeon'). The *Fulton*, renamed *Som* ('Sheathfish', a variety of freshwater fish common in the Danube) was delivered at about the same time.

On 31 August the *Osetr* was undocked after having had a layer of cork added to the deck to increase her buoyancy in the fresher waters of the Baltic. She commenced trials with the *Som* (whose ballasting arrangements catered for a wide range of water densities) in September while Admiral Rozhdestvenski was outfitting his Battle Squadron before sailing for the Far East. None of the Admiral's officers had ever seen a submarine in operation so Lake was requested to conduct some of the trials close to the anchored fleet. The Russians were astounded. One of the senior officers told Lake afterwards at the Officers Club at Kronstadt: 'Mr Lake, I do not like your submarine boat. One can never tell where it is going to bob up. I think if you were my enemy I should slip my anchor and run.'[5]

The admiral's opinion was reinforced soon afterwards when the *Osetr* was nearly run down. The periscope had fogged due to a leaking joint – a common occurrence – so a worried Gadd had to resort to bobbing up and down to see through the glass sighting ports in the tower. This was not as easy as in the *Som* which was designed, like all *Holland* boats, for porpoising and diving at an angle: the Lake submarines were built to operate on a level keel which Lake contended was much safer. After a brief run submerged the *Osetr* was brought up until the glass scuttles broke surface. At this point Gadd became very excited and shouted in German (which Lake could understand) that a big ship was coming towards them. Lake pulled the Russian out of the way to find the bows of a very large white steamer pointing straight at him.

Lake had very unwisely agreed to carrying out the trials in water that was too shallow to go deep in safety: there was no time to alter course so he did the only possible thing and blew main ballast. Both vessels went full astern and collision was averted by a very narrow margin. Learning the lesson, Lake now instructed the helmsman to steer out of the main channel where the chart showed deeper water but Gadd, not understanding English, failed to grasp the significance of the new

Drakon, a Lake type launched in 1908 and employed in the Baltic. *Drakon* and three sister boats were reported by the British Naval Attaché to have an unusually long range on the surface.

course when the submarine again dived.

When next the *Osetr* came up to take bearings the Russian Captain evinced even more distress because they were now navigating in the middle of an uncharted minefield which had been laid to prevent the possibility of a Japanese attack. Once again the little submarine escaped unharmed but the normally imperturbable Lake was beginning to get nervous. He had even more reason to be worried than he supposed because the next near-fatal incident was provoked by the sheer irresponsibility of a high-ranking Russian officer who had come on board to witness the final acceptance trial.

Running trimmed down on the surface, a condition which Lake believed to be perfectly safe, the inventor stepped out onto the casing for a breath of air leaving the hatch open. Suddenly the craft started to submerge beneath him and he only just succeeded in jumping down the conning tower and slamming the hatch shut before the water lapped over. Looking around to see what had happened he found the Russian observer

'shaking with laughter'[7]. That extraordinary phenomenon which passes for Russian humour (and which few Westerners have ever understood outside a Russian circus) had prompted the officer to put the diving-rudder control hard down to see if he could frighten the American. Lake freely admitted he succeeded. It was a relief when the *Osetr* was finally accepted and commissioned under a new Commanding officer, Captain Third Rank von Lipgart, before being sent by rail to Vladivostok where she and *Som* arrived on 18 April 1905, six weeks before the fateful Battle of Tsushima some four hundred miles to the south.

The Russo-Japanese War

By the middle of October Admiral Rozhdestvenski's force was ready. Leading the fleet in his flagship *Suvoroff* he commenced the long journey around Africa (the Suez Canal being closed to him) which was to culminate in defeat at the hands of the Japanese on 27 May 1905. The crews were jumpy. A Japanese attack was feared from the moment they sailed. Every ship sighted might be hostile. The nerve-ridden group of eight battleships, five cruisers, eight destroyers and a number of auxiliaries successfully avoided their own Baltic minefields and altered course south-west through the North Sea. The ships steamed slowly on their way without undue alarm until the night of 22 October when their searchlights picked up a group of vessels off the Dogger Bank. The inexperienced lookouts took them for enemy torpedo-boats and, racing to action stations in alarm, the Russians opened fire. At very close range their aim was accurate. Successive salvoes exploded with devastating effect and sank or damaged what turned out to be a number of British trawlers who had been quietly minding their own business.

The surviving fishing boats hurried back to port and, a few hours after the incident, the Cabinet in London was informed that the Russian fleet had committed an Act of War against Great Britain.

Admiral Fisher, who had only just assumed the post of First Sea Lord, was in bed with influenza

154 and in his absence urgent orders were issued that would lead inevitably to a full-scale war with Russia. The Second Sea Lord, Sir Charles Drury who was deputising for Fisher, hurried round to his house to give him the news whereupon he jumped out of his sick-bed and hastened to the Cabinet Room. Fortunately, he succeeded in calming the agitated politicians and putting a stop to their inflammable and quite unnecessary activities for, as Fisher realised, the whole affair was no more than a stupid, albeit tragic, mistake.

However, before the First Sea Lord was able to grasp the situation the submariners at Portsmouth scented blood. For the first time in history submarines with Whitehead torpedoes set out for war. Three out of the five *Holland* boats and three new 'A' boats embarked a full load of torpedoes at breakneck speed and, on the morning of 24 October, joyfully sailed out of Portsmouth Harbour to meet the Russian fleet.[8] The commanding officers and crews must have been bitterly disappointed when they they were told to turn back. At least they had the satisfaction of knowing that they were considered war-worthy although the incident has seemingly escaped the notice of historians. Subsequently the boats were towed round to Chatham to meet any new threat that might appear.

In June 1905 the crew of the battleship *Potemkin* mutinied at Sevastopol. There were subsequent mutinies in the Baltic Fleet in October 1905 and during the summer of 1906 on board the old cruiser *Pamiat Azova*. The Black Sea sailors again mutinied on board the *Oushakoff* in November 1905. Following the *débâcle* in the East and these mutinies at home the Russian surface ships were impotent and the Tsar demanded that greater efforts should be made to build up a submarine force primarily to defend the Baltic and the capital city of St Petersburg.

By 1908 there were seventeen supposedly operational boats based on Kronstadt. Six were an improved *Holland* type (usually known as *Biriliff* but sometimes *Golland* in Russia); eight were designed by Lake; two were from the Germania

Works; and one was a Russian *Bubnov*.[9] There were probably four *Holland* and *Germania* boats in the Black Sea but the fate of *Osetr* and *Som* at Vladivostok is uncertain.[10]

The Russian economy during this period was, as usual, far from sound and it was reported that about one half of the submarines had been paid for by public subscription.[11] A major contributor was Field Marshal Count Sheremetlieff, presumably under pressure to make recompense for some political misdemeanour; a boat was said to be named after him but she does not figure in any of the lists. Significantly, it was generally agreed in Europe that the German boats, notably *Karp*, *Karas* and *Kambala*, were the best.[12] They certainly had an advanced and warlike appearance and were better suited than the Holland or Lake boats to excursions into rough waters. Furthermore, they were powered by paraffin which was far safer than petrol even if the exhaust left a smokey trail along the surface. Germany herself came late into the submarine business and *U–1* did not leave the slipway at the Germania Shipyard, Kiel until 30 August 1905; but German designers benefitted fully from the experience and failures elsewhere and, indeed, from the boats they built for foreign powers, especially Russia, which gave them all the information they needed at no cost to Germany.

Public opinion in England was strongly anti-Russian at this time. When King Edward visited the Tsar at Reval in 1908 he was accused by the Labour Party in the House of Commons of 'hob-nobbing with bloodstained monsters'. Invitations for the forthcoming Royal Garden Party at Buckingham Palace were refused by Keir Hardie and other Labour members. The Russian reaction was to withdraw even further from the rest of Europe and there is an almost total lack of information about the Russian Submarine Service from 1908 until the outbreak of World War I in 1914. As the probability of war increased on various fronts, outgoing information was suppressed to conceal the faded fortunes of the fleet which was becoming increasingly anachronistic. But it was the incompetence of the personnel[13] rather than the quality

One of three *Tyulen* class boats launched in 1913 for service in the Black Sea where *Tyulen* herself was to sink by gunfire (calibre unknown) the 1545-ton Turkish steamer *Zonguldak* on 10 Aug 1915. She is seen here at the Tunisian port of Bizerta in 1920 after escaping from the Bolsheviks.

of the fleets that denied any real respect, as naval allies or opponents, for the ships and submarines which flew the blue and white ensign of St Andreas.

It has been said that a few foreign writers[14] tried to balance the scales by pointing out that, when war came, the Russian Navy was adept at minelaying and combined Army-Navy operations. It was also noted[15] that the Revolutionary Year of 1917 had considerably less effect upon the Navy than on the Army and that the fighting spirit of naval crews in the smaller ships, especially in the Bay of Riga, remained high. It may be that some ships did fight bravely against the German forces even during those chaotic days; but there is scant reason why they should have done so and there is

no circumstantial evidence to support the claim. Every now and again a submarine disaster illuminated, for all to see, the sorry state of the Tsar's submarines in the years before the war. The pitiable accidents are described in the following chapter but, so far as the operational value of the boats is concerned, very little is known until the British submarines were despatched to the Baltic in 1915. It can fairly be assumed that the conditions which they found amongst Russian personnel, their colleagues in the battle, were not far different from those that had been suffered for many years of Tsarist rule.[16]

The Imperial Russian Navy

Tsarist submarine ratings were separated from their officers by a vast, unbridgeable gap. The officers were autocratic in their behaviour and aristocratic by birth. The ratings, in their eyes, were no better than peasants from the steppes and it is almost certainly true that, in most cases, their education was so limited that the sailors were unable to accept the training and responsibility that the European and American navies recognised as essential for submarine crews. At the same time the majority of the officers were even

156 | more reluctant to dirty their hands than those in
the disdainful surface wardrooms of Edwardian
England. British naval officers overcame their
fastidiousness; the Tsarist aristocrats did not.

The only common ground between officers and
men in the Russian Navy, outside times of extreme
danger, was religion and, for the peasant sailors,
this was much more a matter of superstition than
reverence. There was more truth than the Church
cared to admit in the declaration by Karl Marx
that 'religion is the sigh of the oppressed creature,
the feelings of a heartless world, just as it is the
spirit of unspiritual conditions. It is the opium of
the people.'[17] As the *Daily Graphic*[18] said in a
caption below a photograph showing the commissioning of one of the Germania boats complete
with a splendidly robed priest:

To the official life of Russia – which is usually
presented to the public in its blackest aspect – there is
an intensely religious side. Hardly any expedition,
great or small, is undertaken without the Blessing of
the Church upon the enterprise and such scenes as
that depicted in our illustration are a frequent
occurrence.

Even at the height of the 1917 Revolution
sailors could be seen crossing themselves and
bowing before ikons at railway stations – a sen-

One of four British 'C' class submarines (seen
here on a barge in the Sukhana river) which,
because of strengthened German defences, were
obliged to reach the Baltic by a tortuous route.
They were carried to Archangel by ship and then
crossed Russia by railroad, river and canal
arriving at their destination in Oct 1916.

Submarine of the *Bars* type, possibly *Volk* or
Gepard, alongside the depot ship *Tosno* at Reval,
Estonia. The date is probably 1916 because the
drop-collar launching equipment for Drzewiecki
torpedoes, originally low down where they
affected submerged handling and were liable to
damage, were re-sited higher up (as shown here
with four torpedoes) from autumn 1915 onwards.

sible precaution in view of the state of Russia's railroads. British submariners, if they bothered at all, touched wood for similar reasons but they did also attend Divine Service, when obliged to do so, with a certain happy-go-lucky belief (carefully denied by casual blasphemy) that the Almighty would protect them when the time came although, of course, the gentry had first claim on His services.

The Russian officers were brave enough, as evidenced by the duels they fought and the risks they took in bedchambers; but, at the same time, they were curiously inhibited and effete. When a Russian officer from the battleship *Poltava* turned out (exceptionally) to play football with his men against the British he was found, on removing his overcoat, to be wearing the longest of long shorts and, under them, pyjama trousers tied with ribbon just below the knee.[19] British football shorts were considered thoroughly indecent under Nicholas II, Tsar of all the Russias where moral attitudes were even more hypocritical than in England under Edward VII, King and Emperor.

The Russian officers were aloof and suspicious of foreign officers in public and touchingly generous and warmhearted in private. They longed to be liked as individuals but when it came to war they were professionally jealous of any successes achieved by their Allies and did their utmost to belittle them. It was a story to be repeated in World War II. In both conflicts mistrust and jealousy were so marked that they grossly inhibited an efficient working relationship with the British submariners operating from Russian ports. In World War I the Russian submarine force did not really become active until 1916 and then it was apparent that the officers were poor seamen and worse submariners. They were not able to bring their boats in and out of harbour under their own power; they were invariably towed out to sea and towed back again on return.

Alcohol for the Russian Navy was banned and there was, for some time, an effort to enforce prohibition throughout the Motherland. That, however, was quite impracticable. 'Food for the

The Red Flag being hoisted, probably for the first time afloat in 1917, on the depot ship *Dvina*.

sailors,' said a British submariner, 'consisted of only the barest necessities – tea, black bread and a sort of combination soup-stew in which floated gobbets of meat and vegetables. On board the Depot Ship at Reval and in the barracks ashore there was no butter or jam, never an egg or a proper meat dish while pay for the average seaman was a miserable five roubles a month'[20] (about ten shillings or two dollars fifty cents in

Lt-Cdr Max Kennedy Horton bringing *E-9* back from patrol to Reval in the winter of 1915.

158

English and American money). Nor did the Russian submariners draw any extra allowances. Furnishings in the depot ship *Dwina*[21] were sparse and cheerless. Even in the wardroom there was only a mess table and a few hardbacked chairs. There were no armchairs or settees on which to relax and read but that hardly mattered because there was scarcely anything to read anyway. Sailors on the mess-decks were still worse off. They lived a life of profound boredom with too little professional activity to enliven it. It is not impossible, in fact, that boredom amongst the masses in dull, cold Mother Russia was a prime cause of mutiny and, ultimately, revolution.

The boats built entirely in Russia at the New Admiralty Dockyard at St Petersburg evidently engendered less confidence than those constructed abroad. The *Morning Post* noted in 1909 that '. . . in order to expedite the work more than one hundred extra skilled hands have been engaged. The crews of the submarines have petitioned that their lives be insured.'[22] Insured or not, sailors at death were subjected to singularly crude post-mortems. When a British submariner died from illness in a Russian hospital one of the senior British Petty Officers asked permission to go to the hospital to 'lay him out properly'. He came back a few hours later looking shaken and sick. His Captain, Lieutenant Ashmore, asked if everything was all right. ''e's all right now, sir', muttered the Petty Officer wryly, 'but you should 'ave seen the post-mortem them Roooshians did! I 'ad to come out quick when they started to cut 'is 'ead off.'[23]

It is not surprising that the fathomless gulf between officers and men placed the sailors of the Russian Fleet in the forefront of any violent revolutionary movement and led them to the savage excesses that occurred in 1905 and 1906 and later in 1917 and 1918. The life for a Russian rating was of a standard that no western nation since the early nineteenth century could conceivably have imposed on its sailors. Relations with their officers denied them all sense of self respect. Speaking to an officer, a Russian rating had to use such obsequious forms of address as 'Excellency' or 'High-born'. Throughout a conversation he had to stand at the salute, a custom hardly conducive to encouraging communication between officers and men or fostering the mutual respect upon which the very special kind of discipline in submarines absolutely depended.

If a sailor ashore on leave saw an officer approaching he was required to step off the pavement into the gutter and remain there, saluting at attention, until the officer had passed by. Smoking was prohibited ashore and on the mess-decks no card-playing was allowed, a particular hardship to a man who could hardly read or write and for whom no organised form of recreation was provided. Punishments were appallingly harsh. Sentences of banishment for years to Siberia or imprisonment in some grim bastion like the Fortress of Saints Peter and Paul at St Petersburg were meted out for offences which would have earned ninety days detention, at most, in the Royal Navy.

The only relaxations that a Russian sailor could enjoy were his music, singing and dancing. At the slightest encouragement the balalaikas or harmonicas were brought out and 'the glorious sound of Russian male voices in perfect harmony and the wild exhilaration of Russian dancing would bring an air of gaiety and sentiment to a community that had been, a moment before, languishing in the depths of deadly depression'.[24]

The singing made the ceremony of divisions on board the *Dwina* a matter of delight to British onlookers. It opened with the arrival on deck of the Captain who would salute and greet his ship's company with some phrase such as 'Good Health, my brave sailors.' In perfect unison the whole ship's company would reply, 'Good Morning Excellency. We are happy to serve under you'. It was an impressive little scene. Morning prayers would follow and, in the absence of a priest, 'an officer would intone the prayers most beautifully'.[25]

All in all, it is difficult to avoid the conclusion that the average Muscovite was indeed slower-moving and, in naval terms, well astern.

Chapter Fourteen

Disaster and Escape

HMS *A-3* was, by bitter irony, rammed and sunk by HMS *Hazard*, the original submarine tender, during exercises off the Isle of Wight on 2 Feb 1912. The entire company of 14 was lost and the bodies were accorded a service funeral, when the boat had been salvaged, on 13 March. The collision occurred at the moment of surfacing (as shown here on an earlier exercise).

No sooner had submariners submerged themselves in steel shells with a reasonable degree of security than the public started asking how they were going to get out again if anything went wrong. Judging by newspaper columns in the early part of the century escape, or, more often, the impossibility of escape was considerably more interesting than the most earnest endeavours to operate safely and efficiently underwater. There was a markedly morbid side to the Edwardian mentality, probably a hangover from the Victorian predilection with death. The thought of sailors in 'iron coffins'[1] was relished by the Press and funereal dirges were composed when tragedies occurred. The public was even more eager to devour stories about men entombed at the bottom of the sea than about miners trapped below the ground – hitherto a most popular subject. Submarine disasters were peculiarly harrowing and thereby a source of particular fascination. When no disaster was currently available for reporting the Press was able to conjecture what would happen when one occurred with headlines like 'For Those in Peril Undersea'[2].

Submariners loathed the sickly sentimentality

KING'S THEATRE.
DUNDEE.

- AMATEUR -
MATINÉE
SAT: FEB: 24
- 1912 -

SUBMARINE DISASTER.

PLEASE HELP THE WIDOWS
AND CHILDREN!

160 which attended tragedies and were at pains to point out that their extra pay was not 'danger money' but a grant for professional skill and some recompense for uncomfortable living conditions. The bulk of submarine pay was technically known as hard-lying money and due allowance for discomfort is still paid today. Some of the published pieces were written in the jocular, muscular Christian style drummed into English public schoolboys of the period. The following offering from the Army, 'Reflections of a Garrison Gunner', appeared, in questionable taste, three months after the loss of HMS *A–1* in 1904. It was dedicated to HM Submarine *No 4* (a *Holland* boat)[3]:

Artists' impressions of *A-1* and her loss. In detail, they are hopelessly wrong: for example, *A-1* is shown as a Holland boat and the periscope as an Omniscope. From the *Daily Telegraph* March 1904. (1) Approximate plan of *A-1*. (1a) Look-out box used while running on the surface. (2) Compartment and tap regulating the water-ballast. (3) Preparing to launch a torpedo. (4) Steering by periscope. (5) Watching the manometers while running submerged. (6) *A-1* moored beside her parent ship.

> Divin' down among the dead,
> Goes the bloomin' submarine,
>   With the sunlight over'ead,
>   An' the ocean in between.
>   An' I couldn't tell ye w'en
>   She's a-comin' up again.
>
> Ye may talk o' British valour wot is never
>   know'd to fail,
>   But 'valour' as a word ain't gettin' near it,
> For men as plays at Jony in the belly o' the
>   w'ale,
>   An' knowin' of the danger – doesn't fear it.
>
> Fer if this divin' man-o'-war should get 'er
>   works askew,
>   Wot ain't a rare occurrence in the Navy,
> There ain't no gettin' out of it fer any of
>   'er crew,
>   The lot 'as got to go to Mr Davy.
>
> I'd prefer to do me dyin' with the sun
>   a'lookin' on,
>   An' a bullet in the 'ead to end me troubles,
> To disappearin' sudden – no one knowin' that
>   I'd gone,
>   Without they chanced to see a lot o' bubbles.
>
> (Chorus) Divin' down among the dead . . . etc.

Diving down among the dead to visit Mr Davy Jones was by no means a submariner's own view of his occupation. There is no evidence whatever, anywhere, that submariners were unduly worried about failing to surface or anxious to escape despite sombre reports by journalists like the one which said that, thirty feet below the waves, there was 'the silence of the tomb and an enshrouding dense-like darkness exceeding that of a thick London fog'[4]. Nor were escape suits, when they eventually arrived, welcome because they took up a great deal of space which could otherwise have been put to better use. Furthermore, expensive escape apparatus had to be added to the long list of naval stores which a hard-pressed crew was obliged to muster and account for.

The First Escape

The first escape from a sunken submarine was made a quarter of a century before Holland set about constructing submersible men-of-war. It deserves to be remembered because it embodied an essential principle: pressure inside and outside a submarine had to be equalised before an escape

hatch could be opened. Corporal Wilhelm Bauer, a Bavarian by birth, built two diving boats in the middle of the nineteenth century. The second, *Le Diable-Marin*, was constructed at St Petersburg and made 134 dives before foundering. The 'Sea-Devil' is mainly remembered for embarking some unusually patriotic Kronstadt musicians to play the Russian National Anthem underwater at the coronation of Tsar Alexander II. The tones, although clearly audible from the surface, were said to be lugubrious in quality. The musicians had good reason to be mournful. Bauer's claim to fame already rested on his being the first to accomplish an escape. This was made from his first submersible *Le Plongeur Marin*, the harmless 'Sea-Diver', when the sheet iron at the stern of the slab-sided boat gave way at the bottom of Kiel Harbour on 1 February 1851. *Das Bayerland*[5] covered the event:

The iron ballast having slipped forward they went down in a vertical position . . . in 18 metres of water. The situation seemed desperate but Bauer . . . ordered the two crewmen to flood the whole interior so that . . . as the water entered it would become equal to the exterior pressure on the hatches which could then be opened. . . .'

Bauer was ahead of his time in escape procedure. Some reports mentioned his qualities of leadership in this hazardous situation; they were compounded of rather un-Bavarian blarney and gestures with a large, serviceable spanner which Bauer's two colleagues duly heeded. It is not a natural reaction to flood yet more water into a sunken submarine; but there is no other way of opening an escape hatch.

The sinking of *A–1* on 18 March 1904[6] heads a long, grim list of accidental peacetime losses. The lives of the crew, said Admiral Fisher in a stirring General Signal to the Fleet, had 'not been thrown

162

away if we consider their splendid example and cheerful and enthusiastic performance of a duty involving all the risks of war'. Jackie Fisher hit the nail squarely on the head. Submariners had to learn, all too often the hard way, that they were always at war with the sea itself: that was the real enemy.

Tragedies are tragedies wherever they occur and for whatever reason. They are remembered with the respect due to the dead, and *de mortuis nil nisi bonum*, but the early disasters suggest a distinct pattern of operational risks being accepted on the one hand and gross negligence being tolerated on the other. On the whole, the Royal Navy was prepared to accept risks in the interests of realistic training and the evaluation of submarine boats as a new weapon of war. Thus, British boats were, in the main, lost through their commanding officers trying to operate realistically, without due regard to the attendant dangers, which were not really appreciated or understood. Thus *A–1*, *C–11* and *A–3* were sunk by ramming being submerged (or partially submerged) while bravely endeavouring to demonstrate the effectiveness of submersibles. Other accidents, with many fatalities, were due to battery and gasoline explosions and to unmerited dependence on inadequate buoyancy on the surface at high speeds. HMS *A–8*, for example, sank on 8 June 1905 in Plymouth Sound when the Captain exceeded the (unknown) critical speed on the surface and dipped before the hatch could be shut. The loss of her sister submarine *A–3* on 2 February 1912 was tinged with bitter irony when she was struck during exercises in the Solent by the Royal Navy's first submarine support-ship HMS *Hazard*.

Between 1901 and the outbreak of war in August 1914 there were no fewer than 68 serious accidents in submarines which caused loss of life or very costly damage in the various navies. Included in the total were 23 collisions, 7 battery (hydrogen gas) explosions and 12 gasoline explosions: no fewer than 13 sinkings were due to hull openings being improperly shut through sheer carelessness which was particularly evident in France and Russia. The United States Navy suffered fewer accidents in the early days than others (although the numbers rapidly caught up later on) but whether this was due to greater professionalism or a rather cautious approach to submarining is unclear.

The lessons learned were the need to ventilate thoroughly when battery charging, change to diesel oil from petrol, take frequent all-round looks through the periscope when shallow and always to station a sentry on hull openings, particularly hatches, when at low buoyancy. The latter precaution was neglected even in modern times. It resulted in HMS *Artemis* sinking alongside at Fort Blockhouse on 1 July 1971 and the nuclear submarine USS *Guitarro* being flooded on 16 May 1969 at Mare Island Naval Shipyard.

A First-Hand Account

It was seldom possible to determine what really happened or what it felt like to be in a stricken submarine. The evidence from shocked survivors was usually fragmentary and contradictory. Nobody wanted to recall their inmost thoughts. But one brave man, the Captain of Japan's Submarine *No 6*, left a careful record when his boat went down in Hiroshima Bay on 15 April 1910. Lieutenant Sakuma spent his last moments in compiling a meticulous, pathetic, selflessly heroic letter. Sakuma, in command, was the last to die – a Captain's unwelcome privilege gained by will-

power alone. The letter, a diary, was stroked with immaculate calligraphy. It was found with his body when the little submarine was salvaged:

I am very sorry that, owing to my carelessness, I have sunk His Majesty's Submarine and killed the Officers and Men under my orders; but I am glad that they all faithfully discharged their duties and in everything acted calmly until death. We have sacrificed our lives for the sake of our country. What I fear, however, is that this mishap may cause public misunderstanding as to the safety of the submarine and thereby a blow may be given to its future development. If you, my dear Sirs, investigate the future development and progress of the Submarine with more zeal and without this misgiving I will be most gratified.

The cause of the accident is as follows.

While cruising with the gasoline engine we dived too deeply and when we tried to close the slide-valve on the ventilator the chain broke. [They were probably running very low in the water, with scarcely any buoyancy, on the Main Engine with the Engine Induction open. It was the chain to this valve which broke.]

Thereupon we endeavoured to shut it with our hands but it was too late, the after part of the boat being flooded, and she sank stern first. The angle was about 25 degrees.

After the boat had settled down her inclination was about 13 degrees. As the switchboard was submerged the electric lights went out and a noxious gas issued making breathing difficult. The boat sank at about 10am on 15th. We tried to pump out the water in the boat with the hand pump. As soon as the boat sank we pumped out the Main Tank and, although we could

not see the gauge owing to the darkness, I believe we succeeded. The electric current failed and, although the solution in the cells overflowed a little, sea water did not get into them which prevented the generation of chlorine. We depend upon the hand pumps entirely.

The foregoing was written in the conning tower at 11.45am. The clothes of the crew are nearly all wet with sea water and they feel very cold.

I have always been of the opinion that the crew of a submarine must be very calm and careful but, unless they behave boldly, the progress of the submarine will never be accomplished; and therefore I have always warned my men not to be too cautious through timidity. Some people may laugh at my failure on this occasion but I am confident that I am right in my opinion.

The depth gauge in the conning tower shows 52 feet and although we have done our best to pump out the water up till noon, the boat is still fixed. I think we must be in about ten fathoms. The crew of a submarine should be composed of specially selected men lest they should suffer a similar experience to this one. I am satisfied that my Officers and Men have all done their duty. Whenever I leave my home to join my boat I feel that I may never return alive and therefore I have made my will and left it in a drawer in my home at Karasaki.

I beg, respectfully, to say to his Majesty that I respectfully request that none of the families left by my subordinates shall suffer. The only matter I am anxious about now is this. Atmospheric pressure is increasing, and I feel as if my ear-drums were breaking. At 12.30 o'clock respiration is extraordinarily difficult. I am breathing gasoline. I am intoxicated with gasoline. It is 12.40 o'clock.

Japanese submarine *No 6*.   *Stephen Johnson*

Means of Escape

Some means of saving lives from sunken submarines had to be found as the tragic records of disasters continued to mount. A few weeks after *A–1* was sunk the United States Navy set about experimenting with methods of escape. The first subjects were two large dogs, of unknown but respectable ancestry, which were ejected unharmed through the 18-inch torpedo tube of USS *Shark*. It was reported that 'they swam around on the surface quite unconcerned'[7] and the *Marine Journal* published an article under the optimistic headline 'Submarine Boats Safe!' Serious trials were started with men instead of animals some five years later.

Opinion in the press that men could not follow dogs through a torpedo tube was disproved on 15 April 1909 by Ensign Kenneth Whiting USN, Captain of USS *Porpoise*. However, the *Daily Telegraph* reported five years earlier that Chief Machinist Harry Schaub USN also carried out a trial in the same boat, immediately following the loss of *A-1*, under the direction of Lt Cdr Fletcher USN, Commandant of the Torpedo Station at Newport, Rhode Island.

On 15 April 1909 Ensign Kenneth Whiting USN, Commanding Officer of the USS *Porpoise*, crawled into a torpedo tube. The boat was on the surface. When the rear door had been shut, the tube was flooded. As the bow cap swung upward and open Whiting pulled himself clear and emerged safely. The *Porpoise*'s log recorded the incident laconically with a single throw-away line: 'Whiting went through torpedo tube...' What seems to have been a more important note followed: 'Machinists working on exhaust heads.'

Whiting's experiment was not much acclaimed. He was immediately rebuked by the hierarchy and by the Chairman of the Electric Boat Company, Mr L Y Spear, who declared flatly that the venture was foolhardy and unnecessary because American submarines were already fitted with means of escape[8] 'effective in all conceivable circumstances'. It was an unwarranted claim.

A belief that submarines were always running aground was not entirely justified: like *B-9* here in March 1907 the old practice of careening was sometimes employed on convenient mud-flats.

Not all accidents were tragic. *Holland 5* was one of the first boats to go aground on Promotion Point off Fort Blockhouse in 1910.

Attention was soon focussed world-wide on escape methods. There is disagreement about who should take credit for the first practicable escape apparatus but it is probable that Mr R H Davis from Siebe, Gorman & Co of London invented a workable set before anybody else. Davis and a young man named Fleuss, with whom he was collaborating at the time, built a self-contained breathing apparatus (primarily designed, like Garrett's Pneumatophore, for use in flooded tunnels and collieries) to obviate the need of dragging, and the probability of snagging, heavy air hoses behind an operator.

Unfortunately, the Fleuss–Davis apparatus was bulky – too large to pass comfortably through a submarine hatch. Davis therefore turned to a principle developed in France by Dr Georges Joubert. Joubert's apparatus contained sodium peroxide which not only absorbed carbon dioxide but, after a disquieting delay for the wearer, gave off oxygen in the process. Captain S S Hall (by then Inspecting Captain of Submarines) and Fleet Surgeon Rees devised between them a new Hall–Rees apparatus. It consisted of a helmet attached to an open diving frock belted at the waist with a canister of sodium peroxide hung

The Hall-Rees escape apparatus, 1907. Capt W O Shelford, doyen of submarine escape experts from 1941, was told it *'might* offer a sporting chance'.

from the chest. It could go through a hatch but its storage took up almost as much room as a man himself. It was not popular amongst submariners, nor was it used: no mention of it was made in the subsequent Board of Enquiry when HMS *C–11* was sunk off Cromer by collision with the cargo steamer *Eddystone* on 14 July 1909 with the loss of thirteen lives.

It was another fifteen years before the smaller (but potentially lethal) Davis Submerged Escape Apparatus (DSEA) with its oxygen breathing bag was generally adopted in the Royal Navy and the similar and equally dangerous Momsen Lung was accepted in the United States Navy; and then it was not until the 1950s that the hazards of breathing pure oxygen under pressure were generally recognised – far too late for a tragically large number of escapees who may have died from oxygen poisoning.

Escape methods were steadily advanced in Germany, America and France during the first few years of the century. Draeger's apparatus for U-boats was particularly promising and remained practically unchanged until after World War II. From a submariner's point of view the German inventor scored a notable success for a perceptive paragraph he wrote in 1911: 'It seems essential that a life-saving apparatus must have excep-

tional qualities if it is not to be superfluous ballast in the restrictive space of a submarine.'

One important conclusion was generally agreed: individual escape was much more likely to save lives than any attempt at salvage. The loss of HMS *A–8* brought the matter to a head and it was decided that '. . . if a naval salvage corps was started it would only be saddling the country with heavy expense for which there would be little or no return.'[1] Nonetheless salvage lifting eyes were fitted to all British submarines in 1905 and in 1912 slings were prepared for salvage purposes. Incidentally, the Admiralty was not unduly generous in rewarding the rescuers of the four survivors from *A–8*: the master of the trawler *Chanticleer* was given £5 for pulling them out of the water and two of his crew had £3 each – not a flattering price to pay for the lives of trained submariners.

In 1908 approval was given to fit five submarines of the 'C' class (HMS *C–12* to *C–16*) with air-locks or 'air-traps' as they were then called. They were built of steel skirting projecting from the pressure hull on the port side, abreast the torpedo hatch, about ten feet long and three feet deep. The enclosed space was divided into the air-locks and a fourth air-lock was fitted on the starboard side. Sixteen escape helmets were stowed in three air-locks, one for each man in the compartment. Similar arrangements were subsequently installed in all 'B' and 'C' class boats.

The escape route was through the torpedo hatch, a flat rectangular plate secured by six clips and pushed open from the inside by an iron-cored wooden bar. Mechanical linkage was substituted in later boats and an after 'conning tower' specifically designed for escape was built into the 'D' class. The Italian Navy went a stage further in 1913 and carried out trials with a detachable conning tower which floated to the surface but the idea was abandoned.

There is little reason to think that any of the escape arrangements installed in early submarines anywhere offered much hope of survival; but at least they seemed to satisfy the public and the Press.

Chapter Fifteen

Unadulterated Devilry

The 'vast revolution in naval warfare'[1] predicted by Admiral Jackie Fisher would never have come about with petrol or steam engines for submarines. The revolution was actually accomplished by compression-ignition engines which were first patented not by Herr Rudolf Diesel but by the English engineer Herbert Akroyd Stuart in 1890. However, the German inventor made such marked improvements that in 1893 his name was given to this type of engine thereafter.

Adoption of the Diesel Engine

Oil fuel, with a high flash-point, could safely be carried in large quantities and diesel engines, although heavy and rather tall, developed more power in less space than a petrol equivalent. The standard reference books on early submarines have led readers to think that 'heavy oil' was the same as diesel fuel and hence that the first German U-boats were diesel-powered. This was not so. Although the Germans very sensibly rejected petrol engines their Korting engines were fuelled by crude paraffin and it was not until *U-19* was launched in 1912 that diesel power was adopted.

View from the wardroom area of HMS *E-31* showing the curtain rails which screened it from the main motor and electrical controls. Note the stacked camp-stools, a feature of British submarines from *Holland 1* onwards.

168

The fore-ends of HMS *D-8*. It is all too obvious that the new diesel D-boats offered no more room or comfort than earlier classes.

The Captain relaxing on patrol in an E-boat *c*1915. The remainder of the crew did not have backs to their folding camp-stools!

The two vertical single-acting 6-cylinder diesels in HMS *D-8* completed in 1912. Compared with petrol engines, they were safer and more reliable besides having a better fuel consumption. They could be started by air or by the electric motors.

CHAPTER FIFTEEN

The first submarine with a diesel plant was the British *A–13* and, with a Vickers fuel-injection system, it was running successfully by 1905. It proved more efficient and more economical than petrol engines of the period but it was three years before the first of the 'D' class, specifically designed with twin screws for diesel propulsion, was launched.

On 19 May 1908 an intriguing paragraph appeared in the *Western Daily Mercury*[2]:

> True to their present policy of rigid secrecy, the Admiralty have just brought forth a new design of submarines concerning which it is scarcely an Irishism to say nobody knows anything.
>
> The new craft was launched from the yard of Messrs Vickers Sons and Maxim. She had been reared in a private and strictly guarded shed and all the men who had been employed upon her are all sworn to secrecy. The ceremony of bringing forth the new submarine was confined to Departmental Heads of the great Barrow Firm and to several of the officers of the cruiser *Mercury* which is moored off the Yard. Immediately on taking the water, the mysterious submarine was hurriedly towed to a wharf, barricaded on land and rendered invisible from the sea by a huge pontoon. Here she will be darkly and furtively brought to completion. All that has leaked out concerning her is that she is substantially larger in every way than her predecessors and in certain features she differs from any other craft of this sort in the world.
>
> It is expected that she will possess a greatly extended radius of action and indeed may be regarded as the first specimen of an ocean-going submarine class.

The mystery boat was the diesel-driven *D–1*. Security was evidently effective because four months later the *Daily Telegraph* was still saying that 'the British official development of the submarine is hindered considerably by the difficulty of getting a paraffin engine to suit the Admiralty

HMS *D-6* and two E-boats alongside their depot ship at Parkestone Quay, Harwich, in 1916 – a typically dismal wartime scene.

...petrol is disliked heartily, and the man who can fashion an engine to burn Admiralty oil ... will be welcome when he comes.'[3] The 'D' class and the 'E' boats which followed, together bearing the brunt of World War I, were very successful and had few teething troubles. External main ballast saddle tanks were fitted for the first time allowing more space inside the submarine and enabling the reserve of buoyancy to be increased from 10 per cent or less in previous boats to a dryer and safer 25 per cent on the surface. The radius of action at $11\frac{1}{2}$ knots was nearly one-third greater than the 'C' class at 9 knots; but the hull diameter was no larger and with only a 20-foot increase in length and a crew of twenty-five – nine more than in a 'C' boat – the accommodation was poor. In fact, endurance was limited more by the ability of the crew to remain alert than by the fuel – a constraint still encountered in nuclear submarines today.

The fourth of the new class *D–4* was the first submarine (apart from the unrealistic nineteenth century boats of Nordenfelt and others) to carry a gun. This was a 12-pounder and in the housed position it rested upside down inside the casing forward of the bridge. Compressed air brought it up very quickly to the firing position. It is extraordinary that when, half a century later, streamlining became so important this simple, workable system was not copied. It would have solved the problems of speed reduction and noise which arose when guns were once again called for to deal with brush-fire situations in the 1960s.

The 'E' class, diesel-driven of course, was arguably the most successful type of submarine ever built until the advent of the German Type VIIC U-boats shortly before World War II. Starting in February 1911, 56 'E' boats were constructed, 20 by Vickers and the remainder by yards which were mostly new to submarine building. The boats ordered before the war took 20 to 30 months to complete but *E–19*, ordered in November 1914, was built, equipped and handed over in the record time of eight months, setting the pace for several later boats from Barrow. Two more boats of the class *AE–1*[4] and *AE–2* were built for the Royal Australian Navy and they sailed to the Antipodes under their own power, one of them accomplishing 30,000 miles before a complete refit of her engines was thought to be desirable. In other words after a slow start and some inspiration from an Irishman, England was fairly provided with the method and means for an exceedingly formidable submarine force by the time that World War I was under way.

Meanwhile the United States submariners had faltered in their stride. It was difficult to justify an American submarine service when the initial euphoria had died down and it was harder still to find the money for new boats. The United States was unostentatiously changing its policy from expansionism to isolationism; men in military uniforms were not highly regarded and European arguments were better left for Europeans to sort out. However, American submarine designers were still exceptionally talented: the British and Italian navies were to have much to thank them for in the dependable and long-lived wartime 'H' class which, by devious means via Canada, found its way to the appreciative European navies. Admiral Jackie Fisher told Mr Schwab of the Bethlehem Steel Works that he had become accustomed to submarines taking fourteen months to build but he would like the 'H' boats in six months: Mr Schwab, working with Vickers (Montreal), delivered the first batch in five months – a clear record.

The 'E' class was 30 feet longer than the 'D' class and some 15 inches broader at the pressure hull amidships. It displaced 667 tons on the surface against 495 tons and the safe diving depth was doubled to 200 feet with a 1.7 safety factor: that is to say the crushing depth was about 350 feet (160lb per square inch). The speed on the surface was 14 knots ($1\frac{1}{4}$ knots less than designed) and $9\frac{1}{2}$ knots submerged on the battery ($\frac{3}{4}$ knot less than hoped for but rather better than most submarines at sea in World War II twenty-five years later). The range submerged on main motors was 10 miles at 9 knots or 65 miles at 5 knots – an excellent performance. With two 18-inch bow tubes, one 18-inch stern tube and two 18-inch beam tubes (with a

CHAPTER FIFTEEN

full load of 10 torpedoes) together with a 12-pounder gun the armament was formidable. Apart from greatly improved habitability, the British submarines of 1939–1945 vintage were frankly not much better. The fact that, throughout the 1914–1918 war, more than half the 'E' boats in commission were lost was due, not to lack of ability, but to their relentless employment against the German and Turkish fleets and the extraordinary heroism of their commanding officers.

The conspicuous success of British submarines during World War I was the result of hard, imaginative and realistic training. Unfortunately for the Allies, this was equalled in the German

The artist Claus Bergen accompanied *U-53* on a lengthy patrol into the Atlantic in June and July 1917. His pictures became a memorial to those who died in U-boats: this painting is of an Allied freighter sent to the bottom with demolition charges after the crew had taken to their boats.

underwater fleet which had less time to prepare itself but flung itself into battle with such vigour that it nearly succeeded in bringing the British Empire to its knees.

The First World War

War was declared on 4 August 1914. Britain's ultimatum to Germany expired at midnight. Three hours later, before dawn, HMS *E–6* and *E–8* sailed from Harwich to carry out a reconnaissance in the Heligoland Bight. The opening move of the war at sea was thereby made by British submarines which were prepared for battle in a peculiarly British and gentlemanly sort of way. In this great game of cricket against the Hun, the British captains carried a straight bat – standfast Max Horton and a few other exceptionally talented and crafty characters who were not too inhibited by expensive English public schools; and the captains, all of them, were supported by those truly magnificent petty officers and men born and bred in the late Victorian Navy for a lifetime of solid,

172 utterly dependable service. Together they made a strong, unbeatable team.

Plenty of boats were available in the Royal Navy: no fewer than 70 were ready or nearly ready for service and 20 more were under construction. Germany was weaker with about 30 U-boats in all, of which 12 were newly built, with a large radius of action and reasonable habitability. However, the Royal Navy was, in the pre-war years, committed to operations far from Home Waters and the large underwater force was too dispersed to bring its full effect to bear against the Kaiser's fleet.

Operational flexibility demanded submarine depot ships. As Commander Hackforth Jones remarked it had

> . . . always been a Service custom that depots were regarded as unfortunate necessities, and that no ship would be used for that purpose unless it was clear that she could fill no alternative role. Thus the early depot ships were furnished from the scrap heaps; they abounded with rats and generally speaking were incapable of movement being moored both fore and aft and aground amidships on beef bones and empty gin bottles.

The Royal Corps of Naval Constructors did not, it was said, know what a depot ship ought to look like so 'they concentrated their designs on a rapidly dying but beautiful ornament – the bowsprit'. Thus His Majesty's Ships *Maidstone*, *Adamant* and *Alecto* 'were frequently mistaken for Khedival yachts when travelling incognito . . . of the interior of these strange packets let us draw a veil, for the imaginations of the constructors had ceased to function once the bowsprits had been incorporated.'[5] That was being a little unfair but the Royal Corps was well used to criticism from its customers.

It was some eighteen months before the Great War that a submarine, the Greek Laubeuf-type *Delphin*, discharged the first 'locomotive' torpedo ever aimed in anger. Based on the Greek-occupied island of Tenedos the little boat had been sent to guard the Dardanelles passage during the Balkan Wars. At 0830 on 9 December 1912 Lieutenant Commander Paparrigopoulos sighted the Turkish cruiser *Medjidieh* leaving the narrows with five escorts. At 0930 he fired one torpedo at a range of 500 metres. It failed to function properly and sank; but *Delphin* achieved immortality, not only for inaugurating submarine torpedo warfare of the modern kind but also for gently ushering in the disappointments and frustrations that (for submarines) attended it.

The first torpedo attack of World War I was made by *U–15* against the battleship HMS *Monarch*. The *Monarch*, slowly working herself up to regal fury four days after war was declared, was only carrying out a battle-practice shoot off Fair Island so the attack by the dastardly Fritz was patently unfair, underhand, damned un-English etc. The torpedo missed but the track put the British ships on their guard. The lookouts started to take a keen interest in affairs. Towards evening a periscope was sighted by both HMS *Dreadnought* and the flagship *Iron Duke*. Both leviathans put the helm hard over and sheered out of line to ram whatever lay beneath the slender glass-tipped tube; but the U-boat slipped down into the depths and easily escaped. The first attack and counter-attack had failed.

At dawn the next morning the cruiser *Birmingham*, part of a screening force ahead of the battle-squadrons, suddenly sighted, amongst wraiths of mist, the hull of a U-boat lying immobile and hove-to. This was *U–15* again and from the sounds of hammering which could be heard across the water, the crew were apparently trying to remedy an engine breakdown. Turning swiftly towards the enemy, the *Birmingham* bore down and opened rapid fire at close range. The U-boat slowly began to move ahead but it was too late: the bows of the light cruiser caught her fair and square, cutting her completely in two. The incident encouraged the Allied politicians, if not the professional naval officers, to believe that submarines were not a serious menace to surface warships after all. The politicians were wrong. On 5 September Kapitänleutnant Otto Hersing, commanding *U–21*, sent the scout cruiser HMS *Pathfinder* to the bottom of the Firth of Forth.

The crew of HMS *B-6* not taking the war very seriously in the Adriatic in 1915. Clearly, there was no threat from the air (and the photographer, evidently clutching the jackstaff, must have been getting his feet wet).

Typical World War I cartoon.

The first sinking of the war was not enough to convince the very strong anti-submarine party in the German Navy that U-boat warfare would be effective. The Imperial Navy had little faith in the new underwater arm: it was up to a handful of dedicated and confident U-boat commanders to prove the value of underwater warfare. They applied themselves to the job with a will.

On 22 September *U–9*, under Kapitänleutnant Otto Weddigen, was patrolling off the Dutch coast. Soon after surfacing to recharge batteries at 0645 German time, 0545 for the British, smoke was sighted on the horizon. Weddigen dived and found himself looking through the periscope at three four-funnelled British cruisers steaming almost straight towards, in line abreast, two miles apart. As targets, unescorted, they were a submariner's dream. In the space of one hour before the British wardroom stewards had served breakfast, successive torpedoes from *U–9* sent the *Aboukir*, *Cressy* and *Hogue* totalling 36,000 ar-

174 moured tons to the bottom of the German Ocean.

The loss of three old cruisers was not in itself important but 1459 officers and men went down with their ships or succumbed to the sea, a loss of life greater than that suffered by the whole of Nelson's fleet at the Battle of Trafalgar.

The British Admiralty was rudely shaken and alarmed. No longer did the expressions 'Allied waters' or 'British waters' have any meaning; no sea areas were henceforth safe from the depredations of prowling undersea marauders. The worst fears of the surface admirals at the turn of the century were fully realised.

On the other side of the North Sea the vociferous U-boat opposition was silenced. And, in case the point had been missed on either side, Weddigen struck once more on 15 October, destroying the 23-year-old cruiser *Hawke* off Aberdeen. The loss of life was again exceptionally heavy and about 400 officers and men were killed. Armour-plating against gunfire was, as Holland had foreseen, wholly ineffective against torpedo attack from below.

Surface ships lacked any kind of defence against the submarine menace except, perhaps, high speed. Only warships had that capability and even they could not steam at full speed all the time. The slower merchant vessels appeared frighteningly vulnerable.

On 20 October the British Steamship *Glitra* became the first non-combatant victim of a U-boat. Oberleutnant Feldkirchner in *U–17* did not have to fire a torpedo. Surfacing alongside he ordered the crew to leave the ship and then sent a party on board to open the sea-cocks. The U-boat then towed the ship's lifeboats towards the Norwegian coast, the sort of gentlemanly action that had soon to be discarded by reason of operational necessity in the regrettably correct German view.

Feldkirchner expected to be censored on return to base because only a month earlier an attack on British shipping had been discussed amongst the German naval staff and had been disapproved, not on the grounds of inhumanity but on the score that the number of submarines available was inadequate to conduct such a campaign. But in November, after the *Glitra* sinking, the policy of a German *guerre de course* by U-boats on British shipping began to be openly and actively advocated. 'As England completely disregards International Law,' said the German Naval Staff[6] (unfairly as it happened),

> . . . there is not the least reason why we should exercise any restraint in our conduct of the war . . . we must make use of this weapon, and to do so in a way most suitable to its peculiarities. Consequently, a U-boat can not spare the crews of steamers but must send them to the bottom with their ships. The shipping world can be warned . . . and all shipping trade with England should cease within a short time.

A few weeks afterwards on 4 February 1915, the Kaiser ratified a decision published by Admiral von Pohl, Chief of the Naval Staff, which included in the first paragraph, the warning that 'every merchant ship met in this War Zone [the waters around Great Britain and Ireland including the whole of the English Channel] will be destroyed, nor will it always be possible to obviate the danger with which the crews and passengers are thereby threatened.'[7]

A U-Boat in Peace and War

Turning from these ominous political pronouncements from on high it is interesting to see how the dreaded U-boat men viewed their task from below. Despite Allied propaganda to the effect that German underwater sailors were cowardly fiends incarnate (as opposed to the heroic, upright British submariners) U-boat crews were entirely human. Johannes Spiess, Weddigen's Watch Officer in *U–9* from 1912–1914, wrote a fascinating account[8] of the underwater war as seen from inside a U-boat. His story starts on 1 October 1912 when he boarded *U–9* as Watch Officer and it concludes with the dramatic action against *Aboukir*, *Cressy* and *Hogue*:

> Submarines did not count for much then [1912]. Nothing much was expected of them because they had

The outstandingly successful *U-9*, commanded by *Kapitänleutnant* (Lt) Otto Weddigen, emitting white exhaust-fumes for which the paraffin engines were notorious. She may be completing a lap of honour round the High Seas Fleet.

not been tried out and developed, while in some of the foreign navies many accidents had occurred . . . further there were the poor living conditions on board . . .

The boat lay at the dock and awoke in me quite indescribable feelings. The officer whom I was relieving initiated me into the multifarious duties of a submarine Watch Officer. These included the supervision of the torpedo armament with the numerous tanks and valves, general knowledge of the boat, depth-keeping, assistance to the Commanding Officer in the conning tower, caterer for the Officers' Mess, Watch and Signal duty at sea and in port, keeping records, etc . . .

Far forward, inside the pressure hull which was cylindrical, was the Forward Torpedo Room containing two torpedo tubes and two reserve torpedoes. Further astern was the Warrant Officers' mess, which contained only small bunks for the Warrant Officers (Quartermaster and Machinist) and was particularly wet and cold.

Then came the Commanding Officer's cabin, fitted with only a small bunk and clothes closet, no desk being furnished. Whenever a torpedo had to be loaded forward or the tube prepared for a shot both the Warrant Officers' and Commanding Officer's cabins had to be completely cleared out. Bunks and clothes cupboards then had to be moved into the adjacent wardroom which was no light task owing to the lack of

space in the latter compartment. In order to live at all in the wardroom a certain degree of *finesse* was required. The Watch Officer's bunk was too small to permit him to lie on his back. He was forced to lie on one side and then, being wedged in between the bulkhead to the right and the clothes cupboard to the left, to hold fast against the movements of the boat in a seaway. The occupant of the berth could not sleep with his feet aft as there was an electric fuse box in the way. At times the cover of this box jumped open and it was all too easy to cause an electrical short circuit by touching it with one's feet. Under the sleeping compartments, as well as through the entire forward part of the vessel, were the electric accumulators which supplied current to the electric motors when submerged.

On the port side of the wardroom was the berth of the Chief Engineer, while the centre of the compartment served as a passage-way through the boat. On each side was a small upholstered bench between which a folding table could be inserted. There were also two folding camp-stools.

Further aft was the crew's space which was separated from the Officers' wardroom by a watertight bulkhead with a circular watertight door. There was a small electric range for cooking on one side of the crew's space. The cooking question was not solved at that time since both the electric heating-coil and the oven short-circuited every time an attempt was made to use them so meals were always prepared on deck. For this purpose we had a small gasoline stove such as was common in use on the Norwegian fishing vessels. This had the particular advantage of being serviceable even in a high wind.

The crew's space was equipped with bunks for only a few of the crew – the rest slept in hammocks when

World War I anti-submarine air protection for an Allied convoy complete with semaphore communication system.

not on watch or on board the depot ship in harbour.

None of the living spaces were lined with wood. Since the temperature of the interior of the boat was considerably greater than the sea water outside, the moisture in the air condensed on the steel plates and formed drops which had a very disconcerting way of dripping on the face of a sleeper . . . efforts were made to prevent this by covering one's face with foul-weather clothing or rubber sheets. It was really like living in a damp cellar.

From a hygienic point of view the sleeping arrangements left much to be desired; one awoke in the morning with considerable mucus in the nose and frequently a so-called 'oil-head'.

The control room was abaft the crew's space, shut off by bulkheads forward and aft. Here was the gyro compass and also the depth-keeping hand-operated gear with which the boat was kept at the required depth or angle similar to a Zeppelin. Bilge pumps and blowers for emptying the ballast tanks – all electrically driven – as well as air compressors were also located here. A WC stood in one corner of the control room. It was screened by a curtain and, after seeing this arrangement, I understood why the officer I relieved had recommended the use of opium before all trips which were to last more than twelve hours.

There were four Korting paraffin engines in the engine room. They could be coupled in tandem, two on each propeller shaft. The air required to feed them was drawn in through the conning tower hatch while the exhaust led overboard through a long demountable exhaust pipe. Astern of the engines were the two electric motors for use submerged.

At the stern of the boat, right aft, was the after torpedo room with two stern torpedo tubes. There were no re-load torpedoes in this compartment.

The conning tower . . . was the battle station for the Commanding Officer and Watch Officer. Here were the two periscopes, the platform for the helmsman and the diving 'piano' which consisted of 24 levers on each side for controlling the main-vent valves. Indicators, a depth gauge and test-cocks were nearby together with voice-pipes and the electrical firing device.

Above the conning tower was a small bridge which was used when cruising under conditions which did not require the boat to be at constant readiness for diving. A rubber cover was stretched along a series of stanchions screwed into the deck: it reached chest-level. When patrolling and ready to dive there was no protection against the seas or from the danger of being washed overboard. The Officer of the Watch then sat on the hatch coaming, the Petty Officer near him, with his feet dangling through the hatch through which the air for the engines was being drawn. I still wonder why I was not afflicted with rheumatism in spite of the leather trousers. The third man of the watch, a seaman, stood on a small three-cornered platform in the rear of the conning tower, and was lashed to his station in heavy seas.

This was the general arrangement for all sea-going boats at that time of the type U–5 to U–18 with a few exceptions. All but two of these boats are now lying at the bottom of the sea . . .

At that time [1912] diving was somewhat of an event, since the boat was not quite technically reliable and the manoeuvre was very troublesome, taking over five minutes.

CHAPTER FIFTEEN

It is an exciting moment when one stands for the first time in the conning tower and notes through the thick glass of the small ports how the deck becomes gradually covered with water and the boat slowly sinks. Have all openings been properly shut and is the pressure hull tight? In the clear sea water when the sun is shining air-bubbles sparkle all over the boat's hull and rise as in an aquarium . . .

To bottom a submarine without undue shock requires a certain amount of expert handling by the Commanding Officer. The boat is brought down by the horizontal rudders until contact with the bottom is slowly made and then, after stopping the motors, the regulating tanks are flooded until the boat is heavy by several tons and remains anchored by its own weight, that is, provided that there is no strong tidal stream.

Serious tactical development was only commenced in January 1913 . . . up to that time the submarine had been principally the subject of technical developments. From now on service on board became more strenuous, and more useful work was accomplished . . .

Most of our exercises at the time were extremely simple: depth-keeping, signal drill and cruising in formation. . . . Once we fired torpedoes at the *Friedrich Karl*. At night we slept ashore at a hotel. The predisposition against sleeping on board lasted some time . . .

Manoeuvres at sea were mainly concerned with establishing submarine patrol lines . . . the submarines steamed behind a leader – an old torpedo-boat – and by flag signal one submarine after another was stopped, each one putting a buoy over the side and remaining stationary until the enemy came in sight whereupon it dived to attack.

Safety zones were established between the boats which lay at regular intervals. These were to prevent boats ramming each other as a result of uncertain navigation underwater. At that time the consequences of a submerged collision, as well as many other hazards, were much overrated. When such events actually occurred during the war, the boats escaped with bent diving rudders or periscopes and, at times, bent guns . . .

During tactical exercises in the North Sea *U–9* achieved considerable success. On 21 May 1913 with a salvo of four torpedoes fired one right after the other (two bow shots and two stern shots) we put three battleships out of action. The torpedo which struck the third ship, however, had an error of 15 degrees in the course angle. Originally, the two ships should each have been hit by two torpedoes. This first attempt at salvo firing – Weddigen's speciality – attracted considerable attention at the time . . .

When a torpedo is set for a shot at an angle it does not run straight ahead after leaving the tube but turns through as many degrees to one side as the angle is off set . . .

. . . there was in those days a strong prejudice against deep diving. For a while it was absolutely forbidden and later we hesitated to dive deeper than 15 metres . . . there was also a prejudice against the use of alcohol, and no one was permitted to take a drink for one hour before diving.

On 23 June 1914 the saluting guns of a visiting English squadron boomed out in salute to the German flag over the waters of Kiel Bay . . . although we younger officers preferred to avoid these guests, we could not avoid attending the Reception held aboard the English flagship (HMS *King George V*) . . . the quarterdeck, where dancing was in progress, looked quite different from the decks of our own ships. An orchestra, composed of Marines in their historical red coats, played with a foreign orchestration which was something novel . . .

We exercised diligently . . . our latest exercise was the reloading of torpedoes at sea both on the surface and submerged . . . it is a remarkable coincidence that *U–9* was the only German boat that had practised this manoeuvre in time of peace and was two months later to make use of this experience in real earnest against three English armoured cruisers. No one thought at the time of such a distant possibility . . .

On 28 July we screwed the warhead on one torpedo and removed the practice heads from the others . . . the situation seemed to be critical.

. . . on 6 August we sighted the first smoke clouds and made haste to get under water . . . the order to dive had to be given by word of mouth . . . an electric diving alarm had been disapproved on several occasions on grounds of its 'high cost'. When the Chief Engineer reported from the control room 'Crew at Diving Stations, diving tanks are open', the Commanding Officer ordered, 'Set vents for flooding, open vents; vent cocks in the tower are open.'

After I had operated the diving 'piano' I squatted down on the deck of the conning tower and, armed with a pocket flashlight, waited for the moment when only water was visible flowing through the glass-indicator tubes of the 24 main-vent ducts. . . . When no more air bubbles were seen in the tubes I sang out 'All tanks full' and Weddigen would give the order, 'Go to periscope depth' whereupon we would try to hold to 9 metres by using the regulating tanks and opening the reserve vents in the conning tower. *U–9* had no less than twelve ballast tanks of which the majority were further subdivided in two . . .

On coming to the surface on the morning of the memorable 22 September . . . 22 miles north-west of Scheveningen . . . the damned white paraffin fumes made *U–9* visible and obscured the view . . . but through my prismatic glasses I glimpsed a masthead coming over the horizon . . . could this be the first sight of the enemy? Weddigen gave the order to dive.

U–9 answered the diving rudders very well in spite of the heavy swell . . . I stood in the tower behind the Commanding Officer and from time to time raised the periscope for him . . . 'Spiess,' said he, 'they are three English cruisers . . .' I said, 'Revenge for the *U–15*'. From now on we worked with the greatest nervous energy . . . the periscope was only raised for a few seconds while in the vicinity of the English . . . Weddigen lined up on the centre ship and ordered 'Number One Tube, bow shot'. I unscrewed the safety cover over the electric firing button of number one tube and with my left hand operated the periscope hoist lever.

At 0720 came the order 'Up periscope . . . Stand by Number One Tube', then 'Fire. Down periscope.' . . . it was a short shot at 500 metres so that the detonation followed 31 seconds after the command to fire . . . the cruiser [she was HMS *Aboukir*] turned slowly over to one side and disappeared beneath the waves. Meanwhile I had gone below to the Torpedo Room to reload the first tube, an operation which was effected with trained alacrity . . . between times a part of the crew were running back and forth under orders of the Petty Officer in charge of the trim to keep the boat horizontal with the weight of their bodies . . .

At 0755 I fired both bow torpedo tubes on the Captain's order . . . we heard 2 detonations . . . the range was 300 metres. By going astern on one screw we were just able to clear the stricken *Hogue* but with our very large turning circle, the periscope almost rubbed the side-armour.

Now the third one came on . . . Weddigen held on [*despite the battery being almost flat*] and manoeuvred to approach the third cruiser. We in the conning tower sought by cursing the English, who had incited the Japanese and all Europe against us, to dispel the humane and gruesome impression made on us by the drowning and struggling men who were in the midst of the mass of floating wreckage and clinging to over-turned lifeboats.

At 0820, exactly one hour after the first shot, the two after torpedoes left the stern tube. A long interval passed . . . then sounded the first dull noise of a hit. . . . It was a long shot at 1000 metres and the victim did not sink. Weddigen then decided to fire our last torpedo at the damaged ship. At 0855 it left the tube and struck

the *Cressy* abeam. . . . The giant with four funnels fell slowly but surely over to port and, like ants, the crew crawled first over the side and then on to the broad flat keel until they disappeared under the water. A tragic sight for a seaman.

This vivid and uniquely detailed story of operations in a U-boat on peacetime exercises and then during the early days of the first underwater war is especially revealing in that there was practically no opposition. It might be as well to look at what the surface fleets on both sides were endeavouring to do. It was not much.

Anti-Submarine Warfare

No anti-submarine weapons existed in 1914 and a submarine could only be attacked by ramming or by gunfire if surprised on the surface. Nor were there any reliable methods of detection. When hydrophones first came into use the hunting vessel had to stop her own engines in order to listen and this was dangerous when U-boats were around. The first anti-submarine success, using a hydrophone, was not achieved until 1916 when a U-boat was attacked and destroyed by depth-charges.

It was very difficult to distinguish the sound made by a submarine from the multitude of noises in the sea. However, one dedicated experimenter had his own method. To determine propeller frequencies, Sir Richard Roget (who had a very keen sense of pitch) was held suspended by his legs over the side of a boat whilst a submarine circled around. He was hauled up humming the notes he had heard and relating them to the standard G Sharp which he got by tapping his head.

Deep-laid minefields and nets were the principal barriers; but many of the British mines had defective firing mechanisms and frequently failed to explode on contact. Nets extended downwards for only 60 feet so that, even in the relatively shallow waters of the English Channel, U-boats generally managed to dive below them. Three years of war passed before depth charges were available, with suitable throwers, in the huge quantities required by the anti-submarine vessels of all kinds who were waiting to use them.

Many kinds of imaginative devices were suggested as a counter to the U-boat threat and the Admiralty listened politely to all of them. The psychic powers of mediums were employed (unhappily without results) and, later in the war, the Board of Invention and Research conducted a serious and expensive investigation into the *Behaviour of Sea-Lions towards Subaqueous Sounds*[9]. Experiments with various anti-submarine devices had, however, been started as early as 1904 and were described in the *Naval and Military Record*. They included 'explosive charges towed by fast craft; small torpedoes adjusted to explode over a submarine if bubbles are seen; miles of fishing nets fitted at intervals with small gun-cotton charges; spans of grass hawser intended to upset the longitudinal stability of submarines; offensive mines dropped off submarine bases; and smoke-balls to cloud periscopes.'[10]

The smoke-balls were a French invention and French submariners had the answer to that. It was reported[11] that during manoeuvres off Cherbourg a number of bottles were left to float in the track of the coming enemy. The necks were shaped to resemble the periscope of a submarine and, from the deck of a ship, were easily mistaken for the real thing. The men-of-war were caught by the trick, opening fire on the bottles while the submarine was at work on the opposite bow. As a leading historian remarked, 'On the other side of the Channel, they were never idle.'[12]

British submariners employed a similar ruse during Fleet exercises. One boat towed an empty cylinder shaped 'to imitate exactly the back of a submarine. When well in sight of the enemy vessel, with the certainty of being discovered, the submarine plunged, leaving the dummy to occupy the attention of the gunners while it made its way to the opposite side of the vessel to be attacked and succeeded in successfully delivering its torpedo.'[13]

Submarine and anti-submarine warfare was a splendid field for inventive ideas on all sides; but

Final victory over the U-boats after more than four years of war. *UB-98* at Fort Blockhouse after the surrender in 1918.

the hard facts of war and the cold relentless waters of the grey North Sea soon quashed the more light-hearted and extravagant proposals. A glimmer of dry, sardonic humour emerges from time to time amongst the surviving records of British submariners in the early days of the war but there was, frankly, nothing funny about submarines anywhere as their new giant diesels drove them further and further afield to ravage shipping that had no answer to their depredations.

A newspaper correspondent, at the time when Jackie Fisher was exercising his most persuasive powers on King Edward, hit upon a splendid description of submarine warfare: 'As a concentration of unadulterated devilry the submersible beats the ordinary torpedo-craft hollow.'[14]

John Philip Holland, who died at the age of 73 just eight days after war was declared, would have smiled wryly.

Chapter Sixteen

The Prophecies come true

There are now more than one thousand submarines in the navies of the world. At any one time about 250 are at sea; and of these a large proportion are submerged, armed and ready for action. Many are nuclear-powered and are entirely independent of the atmosphere. These are the true submarines which John Philip Holland envisaged a century ago and although they are fifty times larger than HM Submarine *No 1* they have a marked family resemblance to the classical Holland designs adopted in the early 1900s by most navies.

Nuclear hunter-killers (SSNs) are the most powerful warships that have ever roamed the seas. They are like gigantic steel sharks, ever watchful for their prey. Their even larger cousins, the nuclear missile-launching submarines (SSBNs), mount the nuclear deterrent but these are not the vessels Holland dreamed of. It is the deep-diving attackers, faster than the fastest ocean liners, which the Irish-American inventor would lay claim to as his own; and these, just as he predicted, actually prevent war by the threat they pose to any nation which puts to sea bent upon aggression. The nuclear hunter-killers and, indeed, the less powerful but extremely effective diesel-electric boats are just as much a deterrent, at a lower but arguably more realistic level, as the ballistic-missile monsters.

Admiral Sir Percy Scott wrote, prematurely, before World War I: 'as the motor has driven the horse from the road, so has a submarine driven the battleship from the sea.'[1] That is substantially true today: submarines dominate the oceans from below. Admiral Jackie Fisher's revolution has been accomplished. The hardships, frustrations and losses suffered by the early submariners were not in vain. Seapower, as they foresaw, lies hidden underwater. Fisher was the most forceful and

John Philip Holland in late middle-age. Failing to form a new company of his own from 1904–6 in the face of the reorganised Electric Boat Company, the prophet may have been consoled by Japan's Order of the Rising Sun in 1910.

clear-sighted prophet of those distant Edwardian days, but he made one false prophecy. It was so far in error that it has to be recorded: 'My beloved submarines', he said, 'are not only going to make it damned hot for the enemy . . . but they are going to bring the income tax down to threepence in the pound!'[2]

If only Jackie had been right!

USS *Skipjack* (SSN 585) commissioned 15 April 1959, the direct descendant in shape and purpose, albeit nuclear-propelled and some thirty times larger, of Holland's first designs towards the end of the last century.

Technical Appendix

Representative Types

Name and launch date	Length overall	Hull diameter	Surface displacement	Surface/ Submerged propulsion	Crew officers + ratings	Armament	Remarks
CSS *Hunley* (1864)	40ft (approx)	3ft 6in (5ft vertically)	Not known	Hand-cranked 3–5kts	1 + 8	Spar torpedo	First semi-submersible to sink an enemy vessel
Holland's first design (1878)	14½ft	3ft (Ht not known)	2.25 tons	4hp Brayton petroleum	1	None	Experimental
Resurgam II (1879)	45ft	7ft	30 tons	Lamm Locomotive steam 3kts	1 + 2	None	Latent heat submerged
Holland's *Fenian Ram* (1881)	31ft	6ft (Ht 7⅓ft)	19 tons	15–17hp Brayton petroleum 9kts	1 + 2	1 underwater pneumatic gun	
Holland's *Fenian Model* (1883)	16ft	2ft (Ht not known)	1 ton	'Explosive', probably Brayton petroleum	1	None	Experimental
Holland's *Zalinski Boat* (1885)	50ft	8ft (Ht 10½ft)	Not known	Brayton petroleum	1	Zalinski dynamite gun	Wood on iron frames
Swedish *Nordenfelt I* (1885)	64ft	9ft	60 tons	Lamm locomotive steam 9/4kts	1 + 2	1 14in external torpedo tube; 1 1in gun	Latent heat submerged
Turkish *Nordenfelts* (1887)	100ft	12ft	160 tons	250hp Lamm locomotive steam 10/5kts	1 + 4?	2 14in torpedo tubes; 2 1in guns	Excessively unstable submerged
Spanish *Peral* (1887)	70ft	8½ft	80 tons	2 × 30hp electric motors 5/3kts	1 + 5?	1 torpedo tube	First successful electric propulsion

Name and launch date	Length overall	Hull diameter	Surface displacement	Surface/ Submerged propulsion	Crew officers + ratings	Armament	Remarks
French *Gymnote* (1888)	59ft 10in	5ft 10in	31 tons	55hp electric motor 6/3kts	1 + 3	1 14in torpedo tube	Rebuilt 1898 with 2 drop-collar torpedo-fittings; internal tube removed. Gyro compass
French *Gustave Zédé* (1893)	160ft	10ft 8in (Ht 12ft)	270 tons	220hp electric motor 10/5kts	2 + 8	1 14in torpedo tube	Periscope
Holland's *Plunger* (1897)	85ft	11½ft	154 tons (168 tons submerged)	1625hp 3 propellers. Steam triple expansion; 70hp electric motor 14/8kts (doubtful)	1 + 6?	2 14in torpedo tubes	Abandoned in favour of *Holland VI*
Holland VI (1897) later **USS Holland** (1900)	53ft 10in	10¼ft	63.3 tons (74 tons submerged)	45hp Otto gasoline engine; 75hp electric motor 8/5kts	1 + 8	2 underwater pneumatic guns; 1 18in torpedo tube	First USN submarine (SS-1)
HM Submarine Torpedo Boat No 1 (Holland I) (1901)	63ft 10in	11ft 10in	113 tons (122 tons submerged)	160hp petrol; 70hp motor 7.4/5kts	2 + 6 (variable)	1 18in torpedo tube	Similar to Holland *Adder* class. Max design diving depth 100ft
HMS *A-1* (1902)	100ft	11½ft	190 tons (270 tons submerged)	600hp petrol 126hp motor 9.5/6kts	2 + 10 (variable)	2 18in torpedo tubes	British development of Holland design
Russian *Ostr* (1904) **ex-Lake's** *Protector* (1902)	67½ft	14ft 2in (extreme over guards)	136 tons (174 tons submerged)	2 propellers; 2 × 120hp gasoline engines; 2 × 55hp motors 10/6kts	2 + 5 (variable)	2 bow, 1 stern 18in torpedo tubes	Omniscope. Wheels for running on bottom. Prospective minelayer and, with divers, mine-clearance vessel

Name and launch date	Length overall	Hull diameter	Surface displacement	Surface/ Submerged propulsion	Crew officers + ratings	Armament	Remarks
Japanese *Holland* (1905)	63ft 10in	11ft 10in	115 tons approx (124 tons submerged)	160hp petrol; 70hp electric motor 7/5kts	2 + 6?	1 18in torpedo tube	Reinforced to dive to 125ft but otherwise similar to British *Hollands*
Swedish *Hajen* (1905)	76ft 5in	11ft 10in	111 tons (120 tons submerged)	200hp petrol engine; 70hp electric motor 9/5kts	2 + 6	1 18in torpedo tube	Holland type
German *U-1* (1906)	139ft	12⅓ft (max)	238 tons (283 tons submerged)	2 × 200hp Korting paraffin engines; electric motor 10.8/8.7kts	2 + 10 later 3 + 19	1 18in (45cm) torpedo tube	Similar to *Karp, Karas* and *Kambala* exported to Russia
Dutch *O-1* (1906)	67ft	13ft 5in	105 tons (124 tons submerged)	160hp Otto petrol engine; 65hp electric motor 8.5/8kts design; probably 7.5/5kts actual	2 + 8	1 18in torpedo tube	Holland type
HMS *D-1* (1908)	164ft 7in	13ft 11in	495 tons (620 tons submerged)	2 × 1200hp diesels; 2 × 550hp electric motors 14.5/9kts	2 + 23	2 18in bow tubes; 1 18in stern tube	First successful diesel
USS *Skipjack* (SSN 585) (1959)	251⅔ft	31½ft	3075 tons (3500 tons submerged)	15,000hp S5W nuclear reactor. 30kts +	10 + 102	6 21in bow tubes	Reversion to Holland shape following trials with USS *Albacore* (AGSS 569) (1953)

Notes

Chapter two   pages 14–31
1 Frederick Ponsonby, *Memoirs*
2 *Ibid*
3 Variations on this unattractive but typical expression included 'not quite one of us!' and – by a big ship officer about his destroyer brethren at Malta – 'decent enough chaps but socially quite impossible'. The officers of that particular destroyer thereafter gloried in being known as the SQIs.
4 Adm Sir Percy Scott referring to an 1880–82 world cruise by the corvette HMS *Bacchante* with the Princes Albert Victor and George on board.
5 An acid comment by J P Holland quoted in Richard K Morris *John P Holland* (USNI, Annapolis 1966)
6 Fisher subsequently wrote this in the log at the Royal Naval College, Dartmouth.
7 Private letter from Fisher 1903 (*Records*)
8 Lady Fisher, letter to her son 25 Feb 1904
9 Lord Esher was heading the War Office Reconstitution Committee on which Fisher served believing that the Army should be subordinate to the Navy and provide a reserve of men to supplement naval crews in war.
10 Wilson to Selborne, First Lord, March 1901
11 Wilson to Adm Noel 22 May 1904
12 No fewer than 101 boats were to be sunk due to peacetime disasters (up to the present day) with Great Britain losing the most (24) followed by the United States (19) and France (18); the total of 5 losses admitted by the Tsarist and, in modern times, the Soviet navies is likely to have been considerably greater in reality. See also Chapter 13
13 *Jane's Fighting Ships* 1905–06, Appendix
14 *Ibid*
15 See Chapter 8

Chapter three   pages 32–44
1 George Washington's description, 11 years after the event, of Bushnell's *Turtle* in a letter dated 26 Sept 1787 to Thomas Jefferson in Paris. Jefferson had written more than a year earlier enquiring about Bushnell's invention.
2 HMS *Eagle*'s log (available at the Public Records Office, London) includes no reference to the *Turtle* and *Eagle* affair and there is good reason to doubt much of the story that has grown up around it.
3 Copies of relevant letters and books in the RN Submarine Archives and Library
4 *Blackwood's Magazine*, article by Hobart Pasha, June 1885

5 Letter from Navy Department 14 Jan 1864
6 A prototype, built in 1861 and preserved at New Orleans, was unfortunately sold for scrap in 1901.
7 Admiral David Porter USN *Naval History of the Civil War* (1887)
8 *Philadelphia Evening Bulletin* 17 May 1861
9 *Le Navigateur* quoted in Pearce's *La Navigation Sous-Marins*
10 Original in Office of Navy Records
11 Letter to *Philadelphia Public Ledger* 26 March 1862
12 T O Selfridge Memoirs, quoted in USNIP June 1938
13 *The Engineer* of 17 July 1896 said only one crew (of 13) was drowned.
14 *Cassius Magazine* Marine Number 1897

Chapter four   pages 45–53
1 *Questions Théologiques, Physiques, Morales et Mathématiques* Mersenne et Fournier (1634)
2 Letter from James O'Kelly to John Devoy 11 Oct 1878 *Devoy's Post Bag* Vol I
3 *Manchester Courier* 7 May 1880
4 By William Bourne, a gunner in the navy of Queen Elizabeth I.
5 *Manchester Courier* 6 Dec 1879
6 *Ibid*

Chapter five   pages 54–62
1 *Devoy's Post Bag* Vol I
2 Quoted in Simon Lake *The Submarine in War and Peace* (J P Lippincott Co, Philadelphia and London, 1918) from which a number of other quotations attributed to Holland are used in this chapter. Lake's sources are not known but his quotes suggest that he had to hand one of the lengthy and rather journalistic accounts of his work which Holland was prone to write.
3 Holland's 'Notes on the *Fenian Ram*' held, in part, in the RN Submarine Museum and also quoted in the excellent book *John P Holland* by Richard K Morris.
4 *Ibid*
5 A device for running the engines submerged was patented by Scotts of Greenock in 1915 but true schnorchels were only introduced in the Italian and Dutch navies in the 1930s and the device was only put to use when German U-boats were fitted with a schnorchel mast from 1942 onwards.
6 Frank T Cable *The Birth and Development of the American Submarine* (1924).
7 Rear-Admiral Sir Sydney M Eardley-Wilmot *An Admiral's Memories: Sixty-Five Years Afloat and Ashore* (Low, London 1927)
8 Letter from J W Garrett to J T Arm 27 Nov 1933 (in RN Submarine Museum Archives)

186

Chapter six — pages 63–71

1 Nordenfelt lecture to the Royal United Services Institution (RUSI) 1886
2 *The Times* 1 and 9 Oct 1885 summed up in his article in *The Naval Review* 1933
3 Eardley-Wilmot *op cit* (Ch 5)
4 Questions on Nordenfelt lecture to RUSI 1886
5 *Newcastle Daily Chronicle* 24 July 1909
6 Letter from J W Garrett to M J J Arm 27 Nov 1933 (RN Submarine Museum Archives)
7 The family recovered their fortunes and produced some notable engineers.

Chapter seven — pages 72–79

1 See Chapter 3
2 Lt-Col Alan H Burgoyne MP *Submarine Navigation Past and Present* (Grant Richards, London, and E P Dutton, NY 1903)
3 *Espagne Contemporaire* (1862)
4 *Ibid*
5 *Invention* (1895)
6 *Ibid*
7 Burgoyne *op cit*
8 Details of Boucher's design are given by Burgoyne *op cit*
9 See Chapter 8
10 From a press-release by Campbell (1888)
11 Cdr (later Rear-Adm Sir) Sydney M Eardley-Wilmot and Mr Bennett Burleigh.
12 Admiral Sir Reginald H S Bacon *From 1900 Onwards* (Hutchinson, London 1940)
13 Eardley-Wilmot *op cit* (Ch 5)
14 *Western Electrician* May 1892 quoted by Burgoyne *op cit*
15 *Truth* 29 Sept 1904

Chapter eight — pages 80–91

1 *Naval Chronicle* Volume XXI
2 Quoted by Henri le Masson *Du Nautilus (1880) au Redoutable (1969)* (Presses de la Cité, Paris 1969)
3 Adm Sir Percy Scott writing to Lord Sydenham of Combe: original source not known.
4 Lord Sydenham of Combe to Adm Sir Percy Scott, quoted in *The Naval Review* 1933
5 *Temps* 5 Sept 1888
6 Willis J Abbot Quoted in *Aircraft and Submarines* (1918)
7 *Le Figaro* 1899
8 Laubeuf figured widely in the European Press from 1905–9. This typical quotation is from the *Hampshire Telegraph* 30 May 1908.
9 Admiral of the Fleet Sir Roger Keyes *Naval Memoirs* (Thornton Butterworth, London 1934)

10 *Naval and Military Record* 18 June 1908
11 From collected MS reports on foreign navies in RN Submarine archives
12 Evidenced not only by historians but also in the French Press from 1905 onwards
13 Report (amongst others) from the Captain of the battleship HMS *Hercules* visiting Cherbourg in March 1914
14 See Chapter 13

Chapter nine — pages 92–109

1 J P Holland quoted in Lake *op cit* (Ch 5)
2 *Ibid* It is not known where the original article was published.
3 See Chapters 4, 6 and 7
4 Senate records
5 Burgoyne *op cit* (Ch 7) lists *Holland VI* as No 9
6 *Ibid*
7 Cable *op cit* (Ch 5)
8 *Ibid*
9 *Ibid*
10 Morris *op cit* (Ch 2)
11 Burgoyne *op cit* (Ch 7)
12 The quotations which follow are taken from Lake *op cit* (Ch 5), Burgoyne *op cit* (Ch 7) and archival papers in the RN Submarine Museum.
13 *Argonaut First* is how Simon Lake called his first full-size bottom-crawler because he actually conceived it before the experimental *Argonaut Jr*. Some books refer to it, however, as *Argonaut No 2*.
14 Lake *op cit* (Ch 5) and fragments in the RN Submarine Museum and Library
15 'The splendid little war' with Spain, as Secretary of State John Hay called it, over Cuba in 1898
16 From the article 'Voyaging under the Sea' in *McClure's Magazine* Jan 1899
17 See Chapter 13

Chapter ten — pages 110–125

1 Vickers to the Secretary of the Admiralty 27 Oct 1900
2 *Ibid*
3 Commander Murray F Sueter *The Evolution of the Submarine Boat* (J Griffin, Portsmouth 1907)
4 The Holland boat first accepted into the US Navy (see Chapter 9) was initially listed as *No 9*; *Plunger* and *Fulton*, the ill-starred prototype for the *Adder*-class, being listed as *Nos 7 and 8*.
5 *The Times* 11 Jan 1901
6 Treasury minute
7 Mrs Margaret Barnett
8 The following extracts are taken from Rear-Admiral Forster D Arnold-Forster *The Ways of the Navy* (Ward Lock, London 1931)

9 Bacon *op cit* (Ch 7)
10 *Ibid*
11 *Arnold-Forster op cit*
12 See Chapter 7
13 A Holland Company man
14 Arnold-Forster diary
15 *Ibid*
16 Quoted by Sueter *op cit*
17 Bacon *op cit*
18 Diary *op cit*
19 RN Submarine Museum Archives
20 *Ibid*

Chapter eleven   **pages 126–135**

1 Ben Jonson *The Staple of Newes* Act III, Scene i.
2 Lieutenant G E Armstrong (late RN) *Torpedoes and Torpedo-Vessels* (G Bell, London 1896)
3 *Ibid*
4 *Ibid*
5 Admiralty report Nov 1870
6 Admiral of the Fleet Lord Fisher *Memories* (Hodder, London 1919)
7 Armstrong *op cit*
8 Arnold-Forster *op cit* (Ch 10) and Sueter *op cit* (Ch 10)
9 Herbert C Fyfe *Submarine Warfare* (Grant Richards, London 1902)
10 Edouard Lockroy *La Défense Navale*
11 Quoted from Morris *op cit* (Ch 2)
12 *Ibid*
13 Capt Bacon's hand-written orders (RN Submarine Museum Archives)
14 Compare with Jane's *War Game* quoted in Chapter 2
15 *The Marine Engineer* 1 March 1904
16 *Ibid* 1 July 1904
17 *Ibid* Feb 1903 said flatly that 'at present they have little or none'.

Chapter twelve   **pages 136–147**

1 'All things Bright and Beautiful' by Mrs C F Alexander (1823–95) The verse quoted was omitted in the new Church Hymnal (1933)
2 'Seagee' (Rear-Adm C G Brodie) writing in *The Naval Review* Oct 1962
3 *Ibid*
4 Reminiscences (unpublished) of Captain Ronald W Blacklock
5 *Instructional Notes on Submarines for the Use of Officers Under Instruction* (c1905)
6 Foreword and book of that name by William Guy Carr subtitled *The Story of the British Submarines in the War* (Hutchinson, London c1930)
7 The last victim thus displayed was the American Revolutionary James Aitken executed at Portsmouth Dockyard Gate 10 March 1777 for setting fire to the Rope-house.
8 Quoted by the late Warrant Engineer Jan Honeywill (RN Submarine Museum archives)
9 Blacklock *op cit*
10 Brodie *op cit*
11 *Ibid*
12 MS reports to Rear-Admiral (Submarines) (RN Submarine Museum archives)
13 The word 'chauffeur' at that time was still connected with the French usage meaning a Stoker.
14 Keyes *op cit* (Ch 8)
15 From the diary of Lt A A L Fenner, Co of *C-37*
16 MS note by Second Captain of *C-7* (RN Submarine Museum archives)
17 Rudyard Kipling *Sea Warfare* (Macmillan, London 1916)

Chapter thirteen   **pages 148–158**

1 See evidence assembled in Richard Compton-Hall *The Underwater War* (Blandford, Poole 1982) and Vice-Admiral Friedrich Ruge *The Soviets as Naval Opponents* (English edition published by Patrick Stephens, Cambridge 1979)
2 Charles W Domville-Fife *Submarines of the World's Navies* (G Bell, London 1910)
3 Comment on Burgoyne's paper on submarine development read at the Royal United Services Institution on 9 June 1904. The lecturer was 'fairly pulverised' by Capt Bacon and Sir William White but, in the light of modern knowledge, most of what he predicted was correct.
4 Sueter *op cit* (Ch 10). The author was one of the first British submarine COs.
5 Lake *op cit* (Ch 5)
6 *Ibid*
7 *Ibid*
8 RN Submarine Museum archives
9 Reports on Foreign Submarines: MS summary of reports by naval attachés (RN Submarine Museum archives)
10 *Ibid*
11 *Illustrated London News* 14 December 1907
12 Press cuttings and MS reports originating from naval attachés.
13 Reported privately by several sources and remarked openly in publications such as Domville-Fife *op cit*
14 Notably René Greger *The Russian Fleet 1914–1917* (Ian Allan, Shepperton 1972)
15 *Ibid*
16 The following description is taken from the unpublished diaries of (then) Lt L H Ashmore, Acting Capt F N A Cromie and Lt R W Blacklock together

188

with published biographies, notably of Adm Sir Max Horton, and other MS and printed records held in the RN Submarine Museum

17 Karl Marx *Introduction to a Critique of the Hegelian Philosophy of Right* (1844)
18 *Daily Graphic* 26 Oct 1906
19 Lieutenant L H Ashmore *Russian Scrap Book* (unpublished)
20 *Ibid*
21 Ex-*Pamiat Azova*. The name was disgraced by the 1905 revolution and changed to *Dvina* but was changed back again when the revolutionaries took over in 1917.
22 Reuter in *The Morning Post* 29 Jan 1909
23 Ashmore *op cit*
24 *Ibid*
25 *Ibid*

Chapter fourteen   pages 159–166
1 An expression unpleasantly common, especially in Germany. It became the title of a 1969 book by Herbert A Werner about World War II U-boats.
2 *Daily Graphic* 8 April 1908
3 Author not known but his crested writing paper was headed 'Craigendowie, Reigate'.
4 *The Red Letter* 10 September 1904
5 From the report by *Das Bayerland* Feb 1851
6 See Chapter 1
7 *US Naval Institute Proceedings* (1904)
8 Quoted by Captain W O Shelford in *Subsunk – The Story of Submarine Escape* (Harrap, London 1960). Shelford headed the RN Escape Training School
9 *The Marine Engineer* 1 Aug 1905

Chapter fifteen   pages 167–179
1 See Chapter 1
2 First quoted Cdr F W Lipscomb in *The British Submarine* (1954, 2nd edition published by Conway Maritime Press, Greenwich 1975)
3 *Daily Telegraph* 24 Sept 1908
4 *AE-1* was lost by accident, cause unknown, 14 Sept 1914
5 Gilbert Hackforth Jones *A Submariner Remembers*
6 Memorandum addressed by 'the leaders of the Fleet' to Adm Hugo von Pohl, Chief of the Naval Staff, Nov 1914
7 Order by Chief of Naval Staff dated 4 Feb 1915, to be effective from 18 Feb
8 USN Office of Naval Intelligence document 'for official circulation only' dated Feb 1926
9 BIR 2228/17 (RN Submarine Museum archives)
10 *Naval and Military Record* 3 Oct 1905
11 *Christian Globe* 29 Sept 1904

12 Burgoyne op cit (Ch 7)
13 *Christian Globe op cit*
14 *The Morning Post* 8 Aug 1904

Chapter sixteen   pages 180–181
1 Adm Sir Percy Scott, letter to the *Daily Mail* 2 June 1914
2 Adm Sir John Fisher, letter 1904

Index

All vessels are submarines unless otherwise indicated. Their nationality and date of launch are given. Numerals in bold refer to submarine drawings, those in italic to all other illustrations and captions.

INDEX

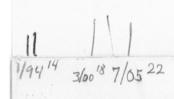